The Anthropology of Europe

EXPLORATIONS IN ANTHROPOLOGY
A University College London Series

Series Editors: Barbara Bender, John Gledhill and Bruce Kapferer

Joan Bestard-Camps, *What's in a Relative? Household and Family in Formentera*

Henk Driessen, *On the Spanish-Moroccan Frontier: A Study in Ritual, Power and Ethnicity*

Alfred Gell, *The Anthropology of Time: Cultural Construction of Temporal Maps and Images*

Time Ingold, David Riches and James Woodburn (eds), *Hunters and Gatherers*

Volume 1. *History, Evolution and Social Change*
Volume 2. *Property, Power and Ideology*

Bruce Kapferer, *A Celebration of Demons* (2nd edn.)

Guy Lanoue, *Brothers: The Politics of Violence among the Sekani of Northern British Columbia*

Jadran Mimica, *Intimations of Infinity: The Mythopoeia of the Iqwaye Counting System and Number*

Barry Morris, *Domesticating Resistance: The Dhan-Gadi Aborigines and the Australian State*

Thomas C. Paterson, *The Inca Empire: The Formation and Disintegration of a Pre-Capitalist State*

Max and Eleanor Rimoldi, *Hahalis and the Labour of Love: A Social Movement on Buka Island*

Pnina Werbner, *The Migration Process: Capital, Gifts and Offerings among Pakistanis in Britain*

Joel S. Kahn, *Constituting the Minangkabau: Peasants, Culture, and Modernity in Colonial Indonesia*

Gisli Pálsson, *Beyond Boundaries: Understanding, Translation and Anthropological Discourse*

Stephen Nugent, *Amazonian Caboclo Society*

Barbara Bender, *Landscape: Politics and Perspectives*

Christopher Tilley (ed.), *Interpretative Archaeology*

Ernest S. Burch, Jr. and Linda J. Ellanna, *Key Issues in Hunter-Gatherer Research*

Daniel Miller, *Modernity – An Ethnographic Approach: Dualism and Mass Consumption in Trinidad*

Robert Pool, *Dialogue and the Interpretation of Illness: Conversations in a Cameroon Village*

Cécile Barraud, Daniel de Coppet, André Iteanu and Raymond Jamous, *Of Relations and the Dead: Four Societies Viewed from the Angle of their Exchanges*

Christopher Tilley, *A Phenomenology of Landscape: Places, Paths and Monuments*

The Anthropology of Europe

Identity and Boundaries in Conflict

Edited by
Victoria A. Goddard, Josep R. Llobera and
Cris Shore

BERG

Oxford • Washington, D.C.

First published in 1994 by
Berg
Editorial offices:
150 Cowley Road, Oxford, OX4 1JJ, UK
22883 Quicksilver Drive, Dulles, VA 20166, USA

Reprinted in 1996.

Berg is the imprint of Oxford International Publishers Ltd.

Library of Congress Cataloging-in-Publication Data

A catalogue record for this book is available from the Library of
Congress.

British Library Cataloguing-in-Publication Data

A catalogue record for this book is available from the British
Library.

Cover Photograph: reproduced with kind permission of NERC
Satellite Receiving Station, University of Dundee.

ISBN 0 85496 901 2 (cloth)
　　　 0 85496 904 7 (paper)

Printed in the United Kingdom by WBC Book Manufacturers,
Bridgend, Mid Glamorgan.

Contents

Acknowledgements

In various ways, the chapters in this book address key issues that have affected, and continue to shape, patterns of social organisation in contemporary European societies: kinship and gender; immigration and racism; ethnicity and nationalism; the resurgent questions of state-formation, national identity, citizenship, multinational corporations, the boundaries of Europe, and the effects of European integration on each of these areas. The present volume grew out of a conference held at Goldsmiths College, London, in June 1992 entitled 'The Anthropology of Europe: *After 1992'*. The primary aim of that conference was to debate issues of current concern for European anthropology, with particular reference to the study of those wider social, political and economic processes that are affecting change and levels of integration within and between European societies. A number of people contributed to those debates, either as participants or as discussants and commentators. We would like to thank in particular the following: Andrew Barry, Pat Caplan, Anthony Cohen, Daniele Conversi, Mary Douglas, John Hargreaves, Olivia Harris, David Lazar, Mike Levin, Carl Levy, Maryon McDonald, John Mitchell, Nici Nelson, Stephen Nugent, Akis Papataxiarchis, Nanneke Redclift, Nükhet Sirman and Sue Steadman-Jones. A particular debt of gratitute is owed to Jean York for organising the conference and for liaising with the participants at the conference. We also wish to express our gratitude to Jenny Gault, Diana Lee-Wolf, Marylin Stead, Tabitha Springhall and Elaine Webb for their help in the preparation of this manuscript during its various stages. Finally, we would like to thank the British Academy for its generous grant which enabled our overseas colleagues to attend the conference.

Notes on Contributors

Annabel Black has a PhD in social anthropology from the University of London. She did research in Malta and has published a number of articles on tourism and gender. She has taught anthropology at the universities of London, Malta and Maynooth. She is currently involved in a research project on the position of diplomatic wives in Brussels.

Jeremy Boissevain is Professor of Social Anthropology at the University of Amsterdam.

Glen Bowman obtained a D.Phil. in anthropology at the University of Oxford. He lectures in the Department of Image Studies at the University of Kent. He has carried out research in Palestine and ex-Yugoslavia. He has published extensively in the areas of ethnicity and nationalism.

Malcolm Chapman obtained a D. Phil. from Oxford University and currently teaches at the Management Centre, University of Bradford. He has published several books and articles on Scotland and Celtic identity. Among his recent work is an edited collection of essays by Edwin Ardener, *The Voice of Prophesy*.

Dolors Comas d'Argemir is Senior Lecturer in Social Anthropology at the University Rovira i Virgili (Tarragona, Spain). She has done fieldwork in the Pyrenees and in urban areas of Catalonia. She is the author of several books on kinship, work and women, including *Vides de dona* ('Women's Lives') and *Trabajo y genero* ('Work and Gender'). She is the co-editor, with J.F. Soulet, of *La familia als Pirineus* 'The Family in the Pyrenees').

Soledad Garcia obtained a Ph.D. at the University of Hull. She is Senior Lecturer in the Department of Sociology of the Universitat Central de Barcelona. She has carried out research in urban sociology and published a number of papers in this area.

Victoria A. Goddard was born in Buenos Aires, Argentina. She lectures in Social Anthropology at Goldsmiths College London.

She carried out fieldwork in Naples, Southern Italy and has published a number of articles on gender, sexuality and outwork.

Josep R. Llobera is a British anthropologist and sociologist of Catalan origin, who teaches at Goldsmiths College. He has done research in Catalonia and Barbados. He has published extensively in the areas of the history of the social sciences and nationalism. His most recent work is *The Development of Nationalism in Western Europe* (Berg Press). He is a Reader at the University of London.

Ruth Mandel received her Ph.D. in Anthropology from the University of Chicago and has carried out field work in Turkey, Germany and Greece on migrant workers and repatriation. She has published on issues of identity, ethnicity, nationalism and gender. Her current research is in Central Asia, in the former Soviet Union.

Oonagh O'Brien is completing a Ph.D. at University College London, based on fieldwork in Northern Catalonia, France. She has lectured in Anthropology at the Universitat Autonoma de Barcelona and at Hammersmith and West London College, London. She is currently working on a research project funded by the European Union on HIV and AIDS in relation to Irish migrants living in Britain and Ireland.

Joseph Ruane lectures in the Department of Sociology at the University of Cork. He has worked on nationalism in Ireland and has published on this topic.

Cris Shore lectures in the Department of Anthropology at Goldsmiths College. He has done research in Italy and Brussels (on the European Commission). He has published a number of papers on European identity and political anthropology, including a book on *Italian Communism* (published by Pluto Press). He is currently editor of the journal *Anthropology in Action*.

Gareth Stanton did fieldwork in Gibraltar in the mid-1980s at the time when the border with Spain was finally fully reopened. His work has appeared in the journals *Third Text* and *Critique of Anthropology*. He is a lecturer in the Media and Communications Department of Goldsmiths College.

Chapter 1

Introduction: The Anthropology of Europe

Victoria A. Goddard, Josep R. Llobera and Cris Shore

It would be impossible, in a short introduction, to do justice to the breadth and complexity of anthropological studies in Europe in the post-war period.[1] What follows is simply an attempt to map out the broad developments that have shaped the scope and character of anthropological work in Western Europe. For heuristic purposes only, a rough periodization is given, setting out the general context within which the main themes of this introduction are explored. In particular, we focus on the category of the 'Mediterranean' as a culture-area and the slow and erratic emergence of `Europe' as a distinctive object of anthropological investigation. As we point out, much of the controversy surrounding these issues is bound up in wider questions of method (particularly the centrality of fieldwork), and the epistemological legacy of small-community studies which anthropologists have struggled to transcend. We ask, what have been the achievements of the past four decades of anthropological forays into Europe? When addressing this question we have focused predominantly on the Anglo–Saxon tradition of anthropology. There is an element of arbitrariness in our selection; but while recognizing that there is no single approach to doing anthropology **in** Europe, we have tried to outline some of the problems associated with an anthropology **of** Europe. We have therefore concentrated on those works which we deem to be significant in defining the area of study.

---

1. We would like to thank Dr Jane Cowan for her helpful comments on an earlier draft of this chapter.

The Early Post-War Context: Cold War and the Modernization Paradigm

The political geography of the post-war world and the changing climate of East–West relations had profound implications for the development of the social sciences in Europe and the USA. These factors not only influenced the context within which social theory developed, but also shaped the agenda for researchers. Political considerations were particularly important. As Almond and Verba (1963) pointed out, the phenomena of Fascism and Communism in Europe had raised a number of questions regarding the character of European societies and cultures, not least the potential of their democratic institutions and values.

The devastation inflicted on European economies by the Second World War brought an urgent need for policies and funding mechanisms to fuel recovery. One response to this was the Bretton Woods Agreement of 1944. This created the International Monetary Foundation (IMF) and the International Bank for Reconstruction and Development (or World Bank), both of which were designed to guide an impoverished Europe towards economic recovery. But United States involvement in promoting European defence and development was not innocent of political interest or doctrine. The popularity of the modernization paradigm can only be understood in relation to the political profile of Europe at the time – a Europe sharply divided between East and West, 'Communism' and 'Free World'. The Cold War division of Europe was significant in itself, but in addition it fuelled policies (particularly US policies) aimed at containing or eradicating the dangers of the spread of Communism (cf. Crockatt 1987; Shore 1990). The uncertainty regarding the democratic character and stability of European institutions expressed by Almond and others favoured the expansion of anthropological studies into Europe, particularly into its vulnerable underbelly, the Southern European countries of Italy, Spain and Greece.

The problems encountered by national governments and international organizations in implementing strategies for development in line with modernization theory presented anthropologists with a challenge. They were uniquely placed to understand the cultural differences that were identified as a crucial obstacle to the smooth operation of change in the direction of a market economy. Traditional societies and peasant values were central concerns of study at this time, particularly in the United States, where anthropologists saw their work as having practical application (Redfield 1971 [1956]; Foster 1973 [1962]; Friedl 1958). The growing interest in peasant societies prompted a number of ethnographic studies, focused initially on Central and South America and on Southern Europe, but rapidly coming to include other areas, and more general discussions and a dialogue between anthropologists and other specialists.[2] It was within this context that Banfield proposed that 'amoral familism', a cognitive orientation prevalent among peasants in Lucania, Southern Italy, was a significant factor in maintaining the persistent backwardness in the region (Banfield 1958).[3] Psychological tests utilized by Banfield were also resorted to by other researchers, such as Anne Parsons (1967) in her study of the urban poor of Naples. The anthropologist was concerned not only with defining cultural institutions and values, but also with the enculturation of individuals. In some instances this was linked to the recognition of wider sets of allegiances and a wider cultural context (Benedict 1946a,b; Friedl 1959; Lowie 1954).

Although the dominant themes at this time were peasant orientations rather than national cultures (but see Lowie 1954) and 'community', meaning small, homogeneous and relatively self-contained groups, there was an increasing awareness of the links between such 'communities' and wider entities and processes. It is in recognition of these connections that, in the Mexican context, Redfield proposed the 'folk–urban continuum' and the distinction between the 'great tradition' and the 'little tradition' (Redfield 1971 [1956]). Redfield recognized the increasing globalization of relations and the growing limitations of the community-as-isolate model. Indeed, he saw anthropologists as instrumental in bringing

2. See in particular Wolf (1966a). The work of specialists in Eastern Europe became central to discussions during the late sixties and seventies, in particular the work of Chayanov.

3. Peasant society and culture were seen as a focus which broke down the distinctiveness of ethnographic areas, in that common problems were identified within peasant societies in different geographical areas. In these early years there was a particularly important cross-fertilization of ideas between Southern Europe and Latin America. Several anthropologists (e.g. Pitt-Rivers, Foster, Redfield) had worked in both areas, and the two regions were seen to converge not only in respect of the significance of peasantries in much of the areas concerned but also in terms of cultural values and traditions. This was probably understood in terms of the historical heritage of the Hispano-Lusitanian empires in the New World.

about these transformations by informing policy decisions (1971 [1956]:9).[4]

There was some convergence at this time between the work of US and British anthropologists, although in Britain, owing to its position within the post-colonial world, most anthropologists were not fired with the same enthusiasm over the applicability of their research as were their North American counterparts. Here the agenda was less clear, and the concern with 'applied anthropology' was less prominent at this point. However, the continuing (though increasingly beleaguered) influence of the structural-functionalist paradigm did result in some interesting parallels between cultural and social anthropology – particularly when the focus of study was European societies. A number of European scholars, heavily influenced by the Oxford brand of social anthropology, set about creating and defining a new area of study. In the course of their discussions, while retaining a strong interest in social structure, and particularly in kinship and marriage, these anthropologists, in liaison with researchers working in North Africa and the Middle East proposed an approach which focused primarily on cultural values.

The 1960s: The Invention of 'The Mediterranean'

In 1959 a conference was held at the European headquarters of the Wenner-Grenn Foundation. Here, a group of anthropologists first discussed the values of Mediterranean honour and shame.[5] This was followed up in 1963 with a number of conferences convened by the Social Sciences Centre in Athens and sponsored by the Greek government and subsidized by UNESCO. The discussions of these conferences revolved around the 'continuity and persistence of Mediterranean modes of thought'. Peristiany (1974 [1966]) clearly

---

4. There were other attempts at analysing the links between the local and the national, such as that of Barnes, trained in the British tradition of structural functionalism, who approached the study of a Norwegian fishing–agricultural village through the concept of 'social fields' (Barnes 1954; Redfield 1973: 26). He was concerned to trace the relationships between the village and the wider context, which was accomplished through the 'country-wide network'. Networks in complex societies were expected to be wider and looser than those characteristic of the isolated community, but in spite of this they offered a solution to the problem of defining a field of study in a complex social context and of tracing the links between the village and the wider framework. In fact, networks were used in various ways and in different contexts, ranging from the study of kinship and marriage in Britain (Bott 1955, 1957) to the study of stratification and of patron–client relations (Wolf 1966; Boissevain 1966; 1974).

5. The proceedings of the 1959 conference were published in Pitt-Rivers (1963).

saw these meetings as the initial steps in the formulation of a problematic that could define and orientate a Mediterranean field of investigation, based on his belief that the cultural parallels encountered within the area made for the possibility of systematic comparisons.[6]

Mediterranean values were deemed to constitute a valid object of study because, although preoccupations with reputation might be universal, in this particular instance we are dealing with a social system based on face-to-face personal relations: small-scale societies. It is the nature of the social system then that differentiates the Mediterranean from other European systems, in that 'social mobility and urbanization have completely altered our outlook' (Peristiany 1974 [1966]:12). Redfield's concerns regarding the community and the erosion of self-reliance and homogeneity by processes of change is echoed here, as change – and modernization in particular – is seen to break down face-to-face communities and their corresponding value systems.

The essays contained in Peristiany's (1974 [1966]) edited volume are enlightening because of their geographic distribution. All of course focus on honour, and the Southern shores of the Mediterranean are represented, as well as the Northern shores (though to a lesser extent than in his later collection on Mediterranean family structures). Despite numerous fieldwork studies which had been carried out throughout Europe, there is a noticeable shift of emphasis away from 'Europe' and towards 'the Mediterranean'. But the relationship with a European entity was not entirely forsaken.

Pitt-Rivers, who in many respects represents a landmark in the development of an anthropology of Europe, in particular maintained a polite and distant dialogue with systems and values which could characterize a more broadly defined European culture. The first part of his essay is intended as a general discussion of the concept of honour, and there is little attempt to discuss the North African or Middle Eastern cases (1966). Instead, Pitt-Rivers tries to discover the general structure of the notion of honour in the literature of Western Europe, stressing the continuities whilst recognizing the variations. 'Honour' is a term which is common in all the languages of Europe, and Pitt-Rivers

---

6. Cowan suggests that Peristiany, being an Oxford-trained Greek Cypriot, might have had a particular interest in the question of cultural continuity. Many Greek intellectuals, particularly folklorists, were concerned with this (Jane Cowan, personal communication).

makes a point of drawing numerous historical examples from Northern Europe and Spain, as well as Andalusia, which is the site of his own fieldwork and the focus of the second half of his essay. In spite of his more general treatment of honour, his discussion reinforces the view, already stated by Peristiany, of honour as a code relevant to a social system which had largely been superseded in North-Western Europe; a value-system associated largely with aristocrats, clergy and poets of former times.[7]

His Andalusian case-study is more convincing. This provides a sophisticated and penetrating analysis of the different meanings honour and shame can have within a single village, pointing out the contradictory nature of value systems in general.[8] Of particular interest are his comments regarding the community. Pitt-Rivers recognizes that 'community' is a complex and shifting fiction. The difficulty, as he sees it, is that values are effective and coercive only in the event of consensus and in a context which permits of control of information and persons. The *pueblo* is seen as a community of equals, within which the system of values operates coercively upon the individual. But the *señoritos*, young unmarried men (as well as the women) of the upper class, escape these constraints. They move and operate *within* the community, but because of their class position they are not *of* the community. They are therefore situated beyond the reach of pueblo public opinion and moral sanctions. Thus, Pitt-Rivers draws attention to another key featue of Mediterranean and European societies: their complex class structure. Pitt-Rivers suggests that the mobility of the upper classes, combined with urban life in Spain to expose individuals to cosmopolitan influences, and these influences are incompatible with the values of honour and shame. This constitutes a way of defining the area of expertise of the anthropologist: the area of study appears to correlate with the relative progress of modernization and of the 'great tradition', restricting research to smaller populations where 'traditional' values might persist.

Peristiany's volume represents a tentative step in the direction

7. The point is echoed by Blok (1981).
8. Pitt-Rivers acknowledges his debt to Caro Baroja. Caro Baroja describes himself as a social historian and ethnologist trained within a very different school from the Oxford group, with whom he nevertheless collaborated extensively in the 1950s. He wrote the introduction to the Spanish translation of Peristiany's collection on honour, and contributed an interesting historical account of the concept of honour to the same volume (J.G. Peristiany, *'El concepto del honor en la sociedad mediterranea'*. Barcelona: Editorial Labor, 1968). Another important influence was G. Brenan's *The Spanish Labyrinth*.

of outlining a none-too-clear field of enquiry. The agenda is not set out explicitly, but a number of propositions suggest themselves:

(a) The focus is on small-scale, face-to-face and relatively bounded social units: the community.

(b) Associated with the social structure of such communities are specific value systems which ultimately create and reproduce consensus and define the community.

(c) It is assumed that modernization and consequent processes of urbanization and population movement result in the breakdown of these communities and the erosion of the value systems that characterize them, which cease to be effective in the new context.

This echoes much of the debate within cultural anthropology in the United States. It also reflects marked continuities with concerns current in the anthropology taught and practised in British institutions at the time. In the Foreword to the first edition of Pitt-Rivers' book on the Andalusian town (Pitt-Rivers 1971 [1954]), Evans-Pritchard confirms Pitt-Rivers' credentials as 'in every sense a son of Oxford and an Oxford anthropologist' (Pitt-Rivers 1971 [1954]: ix). These credentials are owed him because of his personal genealogy and because of his endeavours as a student and researcher. Evans-Pritchard recognized the 'initiative' and 'courage' involved in Pitt-Rivers' decision to 'show that the methods and concepts which have been so successfully employed in studies of primitive societies could equally well be used in the study of the social life of our own civilisation'. Here the anthropologist competes with sociologist and historian. But he defines Pitt-Rivers' work as an anthropological account because it is based primarily on direct observation. 'The people he writes about are real people and not figures taken from the printed page of units in statistical tables' (Pitt-Rivers 1971 [1954]: x). What constitutes an anthropological study is, therefore, the specific object of study (a complex set of interpersonal relations and their value systems) and the method of research employed (participatory observation). Although the anthropologist is concerned with problems which are of a general nature and are relevant to what Evans-Pritchard describes as the 'larger society', the method limits the anthropological contribution to the study of relatively small-scale communities.

Further insights into the connections between the anthropological establishment and these first steps in what was seen as European ethnography are provided by Pitt-Rivers' own Preface to the second edition of his book. He recognized the difficulties encountered by his training, which was specifically focused on East Africa. Finding no lineal principle and no age-sets in Andalusia he was bereft of any guiding concept. Although recognizing that he was 'on his own', he felt he had been able to recover aspects of anthropological theory at a higher level of abstraction, notably in relation to the centrality of the principle of social solidarity. Indeed, there were important continuities with the structural-functionalist paradigm, in terms of focusing on small-scale communities, or interpersonal relations and the (eventual) achievement of consensus and solidarity. But at the same time there was a need to adapt and invent concepts and method to cope with the 'changing relationships dependent upon context' which he sees as characterizing modern complex societies. Individuals in Alcalá could choose their allegiances and their attitudes – unlike the member of a tribe. Again, the fact that the inhabitants of the *pueblo* were simultaneously members of the community and of the state presented a different configuration of relations of authority than that represented by the Nuer leopard-skin chief (ibid.: xix). This meant that, as an anthropologist, he must tackle the 'wider social structure', recognizing the political, ideological and institutional structures, and struggles, of which the village was a part.

The centrality of the 'community', derived from the structural-functionalist paradigm, caused difficulties elsewhere. Although Campbell's work on the Sarakatsani shepherds of Greece (1964) reflects a similar set of concerns and similar continuities and discontinuities in relation to the received anthropological wisdom of his day, and his choice of a transhumant pastoralist group is of course consonant with the anthropological enterprise, Campbell too had to qualify his discussion of 'community'. The Sarakatsani community was problematic: it had no structure of authority and no effective organization. Although here too the focus was on values, reputation and consensus, Campbell argued that there was little cohesion at the level of community, and instead families competed in often destructive rivalries. Community could only be defined in fact in relation to 'a social space within which values are shared and the conduct of men and women is evaluated by other Sarakatsani' (1964: 9). Prestige, reputation and honour are the main ingredients of the struggle between families. Yet while these values provided the munition for competition, they also constituted a field of what we might today call shared discourse, or, from the perspective of structural functionalism, social order. Echoes of Evans-Pritchard's analysis of the Nuer segmentary lineage system, the feud, the processes of fission and fusion, are evident here (see Herzfeld 1981).

Concern with small-scale social units, largely dictated by the requirements and limitations of the anthropological method, while at the same time having to grapple with the difficulties of defining community, is thus a dominant theme in this early literature. The focus on values appeared to provide the means for dealing with the contradictions of an ideal of community (in the minds of anthropologists and informers) and the impossibility of defining community unproblematically on the one hand, and with the ideals of consensus and order and the tensions, rivalries and shifting statuses witnessed by these anthropologists on the other. But 'values' also provided a means of locating the individual within the social system. As Pitt-Rivers stated: 'Honour provides a nexus between the ideals of a society and their reproduction in the individual through his aspiration to personify them' (1966: 22). Furthermore, the values of honour and shame facilitated the discussion, the comparison of ethnographic accounts and the definition of common interests and of a common field. However, this field was by now almost necessarily a Mediterranean and not a European one. In fact, as Peristiany noted ten years later, a new confidence had been gained in that period within the Mediterranean field, expressed in the proliferation of periodicals and publications, and of Mediterranean sections in a number of departments of anthropology.

The limitation of the field to the Mediterranean thus originated from the strategy of focusing primarily on rural communities and on the values of honour and shame. But this can only be understood when taken in conjunction with the assumptions provided by other sets of ideas derived from perspectives current in anthropology and related disciplines at the time, such as Redfield's folk–urban continuum or the theory of modernization. Much of this work on rural populations and cultures ran parallel with Pitt-Rivers' discussion of European and Andalusian social structures and values, although these models were seen as having a much wider application as well.

The shift to the Mediterranean was not supported by theoretical work aimed at clarifying either the concept of Europe or that of the Mediterranean. On the whole these were taken as unproblematical. A more rigorous approach was suggested in 1963, in a special issue of the *Anthropological Quarterly* aimed at promoting an anthropology of Europe. Arensberg saw this issue of the *Quarterly* as a first step in the direction of a comparative and generalizing study of European societies within a 'world ethnography'. This ambitious project was to take account of the contribution of each continent to 'illuminating the nature of culture in general and of man's evolution with it' (Arensberg 1963: 77). In order to understand culture in general, the models developed from studies of simple societies by anthropologists had to be extended to complex societies, including Europe, with their specific challenge of a 'coexistence of high and folk cultures' (1963: 77).

Arensberg pointed to the advantages and the difficulties involved in studying Europe. Europe demanded a broader perspective than the single-society studies which prevailed in the discipline, and required the collaboration of historical sociology and the analysis of urban and 'socially superstratified segments of culture' (ibid.: 79). Europe presented an intimidating variety of cultural and social forms, which nonetheless could be encompassed by a refined and adapted culture-area approach. In this enterprise, the principal commonality identified by Arensberg is that Europe is an Old World Culture with a subsistence culture based on the use of the plough, based on open-field villages and the cultivation and consumption of grain, meat and milk. From this same perspective he suggests significant internal divisions within Europe: the Atlantic Fringe, the European East and North, and Mediterranean Europe, defined according to the particular configurations of subsistence and society dominant in each of these areas (cf. Pitkin 1963).

At the same time, Kenny in the same volume (Kenny 1963) recognized the growing internationalization and interdependence of all economies, and recognized too the dual nature of Mediterranean Europe, which he saw as sharing structural and geographical characteristics with non-European lands surrounding the Mediterranean. Perhaps the most important characteristic of Mediterranean Europe is, for Kenny, its urban character. Ironically, many years later Kenny and Kertzer (1983) were to bemoan the paucity of urban studies in the area.

The 'Old World' framework was also used by Friedl (1962), who tackled at some length the specificities of Mediterranean and European anthropology and attempted to distinguish the subject matter in terms other than a hasty reference to 'complex societies'. The 'primitiveness' of the Incas, West Africans, Mayas and Aztecs was based on their autonomy in relation to the cultural influence of the West. In other words, they were external to the flow of European history and tradition. Eurasia had been subjected to sets of influences emanating from the same origins, in particular the diffusion of specific neolithic techniques, crops and practices. The difference between the European and the 'exotic' societies was thus a difference in cultural tradition and history.

Friedl raised a number of questions in relation to the new field of study of what she calls 'the rural populations of modern nations': the problems of defining and delimiting the unit of study when the village, in Latin America or Europe, was part of a wider system, and the problem of the representativeness of these units. There was also the question of the dangers posed to the fieldworker of what she sees as a superficial familiarity of institutions and practices. In contrast to Evans-Pritchard's concern that in this area the anthropologist was threatened by rivalry from other specialists, Friedl saw the presence of other specialists as an advantage to those studying 'old national cultures'. Thus she argued that an anthropologist could delegate many problems to other experts and concentrate on 'the observation of the behaviour of those he lives with for the purpose of discovering its regularities, its range of variation, its internal interrelationships, and its association or articulation with the culture of the nation of which the village community is a part' (1962: 05). Although Friedl is fairly unique in attempting to locate her village study within a thought-out specialist area, the result was a definition of anthropological enquiry which differed very little from that offered, in earlier decades, by Evans-Pritchard and others.

The 1970s: Expansion and Fragmentation

Changes in the discipline during the 1970s were prompted not only by the limitations and failures of the structural-functionalist paradigm and the modernization perspective, but also by developments in the wider political arena. The late sixties saw a wave of protests and unrest across Europe and the USA as students and workers demanded change in the institutions and values of Western society. At the same time, the Comecon countries also witnessed upheavals and social unrest. Events in Eastern Europe prompted many Western European Communists and their sympathizers to review their positions *vis-à-vis* the Soviet Union. Intellectually, debates and reappraisals of Leninist orthodoxy contributed to dislodge the narrow and economistic version of Marxism which had dominated both political and academic discourse. In particular, the innovations of Gramsci, Lévi-Strauss and Althusser offered new ways of understanding social systems and processes of change and transformation. Meanwhile, from Latin America and elsewhere in the Third World, the dependency perspective challenged the assumptions and conclusions of modernization theory. In its place, some governments and academics turned to a more radical (though to markedly different degrees, as explained by Kay 1989) approach to understanding poverty and uneven development. However, the impact of these new approaches on the work of anthropologists was uneven, and generally they were expressed in exploratory ways alone (but see Schneider and Schneider 1976).[9]

The Cold War division of Europe into Soviet and Nato camps was again showing signs of strain. According to Cole (1977: 356) these changes in the international climate prompted an increase in European research funding, and with government bodies and research foundations offering grants to encourage studies into allies and enemies in Europe 'an anthropology of Europe was established and "normalised" in a single intellectual generation'. This is an exaggeration, for within the discipline in general European anthropology remained a fledgling research area, ill-defined and marginal to the mainstream. Moreover, as Davis (1977) noted, the pervasive attitude among Africanist and Asianist

---

9. There was also some loss of impetus to the incorporation of peasant studies in Europe within a wider problematic of backwardness or underdevelopment. This may have been facilitated by the economic boom in the years after the Second World War, which brought dramatic change and prosperity to many rural areas of Europe. The optimism of these years may have prompted a widening divergence between anthropological work in Europe and elsewhere. What prevailed in European anthropology was not a radical critique from the perspective of peasant studies (as occurred in Latin America and Asia, for example), but a certain methodological and theoretical continuity with earlier perspectives.

colleagues was that fieldwork in Europe was somehow inferior, and that 'real' anthropology involved studies of remote Third World peoples.

Nonetheless, the 1970s did witness the emergence of 'Europe' as a distinctive category of anthropological investigation. In the early 1970s, however, the contours of this new sub-discipline of an anthropology of Europe were only beginning to become visible. Freeman (1973), one of the first anthropologists to attempt to outline the scope and achievements of 'studies in rural European social organisation' (a title which was itself indicative of the rural bias and general lack of urban studies in early European ethnography), highlighted the distinctive character of European anthropology in the early 1970s.[10] Among the weaknesses she identified (many of which remain relevant to this day) were the overriding emphasis on small geographical entities, particularly isolated villages and so-called 'traditional' communities, and a corresponding failure to study larger regions or nations themselves, or to employ a more comparative framework (1973: 743).[11] Although anthropologists had been aware of the significance of taking into account the wider dimension and the State as early as 1954 (with Pitt-Rivers), the only proposal to gain ground as a way of dealing with the community–state relationship remained that of network analysis first utilized by Barnes in 1954.[12] In fact the analysis of patron–client relations (Wolf 1966b) and *caciquismo* became one of the central concerns of Mediterranean anthropologists.

Boissevain's (1975) essay entitled 'Towards a social anthropology of Europe' was perhaps the first systematic attempt

10. The four analytical concerns of particular importance to European researchers that Freeman highlighted provide an accurate portrait of European anthropology in the early 1970s: (1) definition and analysis of the 'peasantry', of its internal characteristics and external relations, including analysis of the folk–urban dialectic; (2) exploration of the values of 'honour' and 'shame' and of their implications for social behaviour and social status in European communities; (3) analysis of the relationships between neighbours, or the political relations between domestic groups, the assessment of such explanatory notions as 'the image of limited good' (Foster 1965) and 'amoral familism' (Banfield 1958), and investigation of such phenomena as envy and gossip in the field of social control – in short, those issues which Foster originally considered under the rubric of 'interpersonal relations in peasant society'; (1954) and Wolf's 'interstitial, supplementary, and parallel structures' (Wolf 1966b).

11. Freeman (1973: 745) also points out that, with the exception of Banfield's notion of 'amoral familism', Pitt-Rivers' analysis of patronage (1971 [1954], 1966), and Peristiany's work on honour and shame, none of the typically 'European' areas of enquiry grew out of European field research itself. Most were germinated, instead, from studies of Latin American peasantries and tribal societies in Africa and Asia.

12. See footnote No. 3.

to define an agenda for the emerging 'anthropology of Europe'. Beginning from a swingeing attack on the weaknesses of the structural-functionalist paradigm (a theme developed more fully elsewhere, and in his later work),[13] and a critique of the rarified, small-community studies typical of most earlier work. Boissevain argued that traditional anthropological concepts such as 'equilibrium, corporation, balanced opposition, reciprocity and consensus' – which had been developed for studying relatively undifferentiated, non-Western, tribal societies – societies without states or written histories – were of limited value for dealing with the complexity of European societies. Nor was the traditional research technique of participant-observation alone any longer sufficient. As he noted: 'The high degree of centralization, the interrelation between various levels of integration, the impact of multiple long-term processes, the sweep of change that can be documented across centuries still overwhelm many anthropologists. Consequently, many have sought refuge in villages, which they proceed to treat as isolated entities. They have tribalised Europe' (Boissevain 1975: 11).

In Boissevain's view, new concepts and research methods were needed. What was required was a framework for situating local events and processes in a wider regional, national and historical context; one that would also enable the anthropologist to examine the links between different levels of organization (local, regional, national; core and periphery). In short, an anthropology of Europe needed to focus on the interrelationship between local events and macro social processes of 'state formation, national integration, industrialization, urbanization, bureaucratization, class conflict and commercialization' (Boissevain 1975: 11) – processes whose origins lie beyond the community. However, his claim (1975: 16) that 'the contributors to this volume thus provide a first attempt at developing what could be called an anthropology of national and supra-national processes' was perhaps overstated, as few of the papers actually tackled these themes in any depth. Moreover, by justifying the case for an 'anthropology of Europe' in terms of lessons to be gained for 'poorer societies' further down the road to modernization, Boissevain moved perilously close to the old modernization paradigm. As in earlier instances where

---

13. Cf. Boissevain 1974. However, much of Boissevain's earlier work, was itself typically functionalist in style and theoretical orientation (cf. Boissevain 1966; 1969).

anthropologists (for example Gluckman) attempted to break new ground, they were thwarted by the constraints of structural-functionalist theory and methodology. Nonetheless, the volume provided a refreshing alternative to the polarizations and reifications typical of most traditional, ahistorical ethnographic studies of European societies, and the 'village-outwards' perspective adopted by most of the contributors paved the way for further work of this nature. Moreover, Boissevain's emphasis on 'processes' and 'relationships' between levels of organization avoided the need to try and reify Europe as a particular 'culture area', a concept which was increasingly central to anglophone anthropologists working in the Mediterranean.[14]

During the 1970s anthropological interest in Europe increased dramatically. By 1973 the number of social anthropological publications on Europe was almost equal to that of the of the entire previous decade (Freeman 1973: 743). Several factors fuelled this interest in Europe. One was the increase in postgraduate students of anthropology on either side of the Atlantic, and the fact that Europe represented a relatively unexplored frontier. Another was the shortage of research funds due to the increased number of applicants and the tightening of government purse-strings to counter student unrest. In this respect, Europeanists were at an advantage. As Boissevain (1975: 11) points out, 'it generally costs less to study a neighbour than to mount an expedition to the New Guinea highlands'.

Increased anthropological interest in Europe was also prompted by changes in the world economy and shifts in global political alignments. As Cole (1977) argues, anthropologists began to find themselves no longer welcome in the newly liberated post-colonial nations as anti-colonialist sentiment and suspicion of Western development projects spread throughout the emergent states of

---

14. A common denominator to most of those who shaped the anthropology of the Mediterranean as a 'culture area' was the fact that they conducted their research in the northern Mediterranean countries. The key features that were posited as characteristic of 'the Mediterranean' as a unit were only typical of those parts of Southern Europe which, although sharing Graeco–Roman and Christian traditions, were under Islamic rule for a number of centuries. We are referring to the southern parts of Portugal, Spain and Italy, as well as to Malta, Cyprus and many parts of the Balkans, including Greece. This point was made with force by Boissevain and Blok (1974). Unfortunately, that text received scant attention, with the consequence that the idea of the whole Mediterranean area as a cultural unit made constant progress. What should have been a construct identified with a cluster of cultural features which had a limited but meaningful geographical application became an unmanageable contraption which not only led many anthropologists astray, but generated countless sterile controversies.

Africa and Asia. With these doors closed, Western anthropologists increasingly turned their attention, and their careers, to rural Europe and the Mediterranean, one of the few areas still open to them.

While the idea of 'tradition versus modernity' continued to imbue European ethnographic studies throughout the early 1970s, some anthropologists began to explore new models. One alternative to functionalism was the 'action' approach, pioneered by Barth (1966; 1969), Goffman (1959), and Barnes (1972), and elaborated, in European anthropology, in the work of Boissevain and Bailey and their students. Their work focused on individuals and the stratagems they employ within a given socio-political framework. 'Action theory' covered a variety of approaches, including transactionalism, network analysis, systems analysis and game theory. What united them was an emphasis on the dynamic character of interpersonal exchanges. Instead of looking at the individual as a passive and obedient slave to group norms and pressures, Boissevain stressed that 'it is important to see him as an entrepreneur who tries to manipulate norms and relationships for his own social and psychological benefit' (Boissevain 1974: 6). The notion of the self-seeking entrepreneur manipulating social networks and cultural codes in order to maximize personal gain became a key premise of the transactionalist approach. As Bailey (1971: xi) summed it up in relation to his own work on the micro-politics of gossip and reputation management: 'The politicians ... who appear in this book are all caught in the act of outmanoeuvring one another, of knifing one another in the back, of tripping one another up, and they all appear to be engrossed in winning a victory over someone.' This approach facilitated the continuing emphasis on small-scale community studies, since it allowed politics to be defined as operative at the local level alone.

While some advocates saw transactionalism simply as a supplement to functionalist analysis, others claimed it had universal application and a much deeper theoretical significance. The extreme transactionalist position as developed by Barth (1959) held that the interaction of all these self-seeking individuals gives society its dynamic, which in turn is the basis for all social processes, including social change. What we call 'society' is thus, in effect, no more than the sum of these individual transactions. This approach ignored culture-area boundaries and historical specificities, and enabled an unproblematic shift from European contexts to others. The reason for this was the underlying assumption of universal patterns of behaviour, motivation and rationality. However, as critics pointed out, Barth could just as well be discussing Norwegian fishermen as the Yusufzai Pakhtuns, since their rationality and behaviour are seen as essentially the same and, in spite of ethnographic detail in the Pakhtun study, the local historical, class and other systemic constraints are ignored (cf. Asad 1972; Ahmed 1976). In spite of numerous studies in the European context, by universalizing a specific rationality and neglecting historical specificities, transactionalists made little impact on the development of an anthropology of Europe.

Despite these criticisms, Kapferer nevertheless felt justified in claiming (1976: 2) that transactionalism marked a 'paradigm shift' in social anthropology. For European anthropologists it did provide new research foci and a framework for analyzing elements of the complexity of European societies that had been invisible to functionalist analysis – even if its micro-perspective tended to obscure the wider picture. However, that shift of focus led to the elaboration of a number of new analytical concepts, as well as to a re-evaluation of some old concerns, such as 'patron–client relations', 'micro-politics', 'brokers', 'middlemen', 'informal and non-corporate groups', 'cliques', 'factions and action-sets' and 'instrumental friendship' (cf. Banton 1966; Bailey 1971; 1973; Blok 1974; Boissevain 1966, 1968, 1974; Gellner and Waterbury 1977; Wolf 1966b).

If one response to the critique of structural-functionalism was a theoretical shift of emphasis towards individual behaviour and 'informal' codes, another was towards a semiotic approach inspired by the work of Lévi-Strauss, Leach and Douglas. Here the primary objects of investigation were the deeper structures (cognitive and symbolic) underlying surface phenomena: the idea being that cultural arrangements can be 'read' as languages, reflecting an underlying classificatory code or symbolic order. Yet while this method had great appeal within the discipline in general, it had less impact in European anthropology than elsewhere, perhaps because the structuralist method was perceived to have greater analytical power in seemingly more 'bounded' societies, without written histories or complex state structures. However, the Oxford seminars which aimed at reassessing anthropological material through the structuralist framework provided an opportunity for researchers in European societies to locate their material within a broader comparative framework and obviate the limitations of 'the Mediterranean', or for that matter Europe. At the same time they facilitated the emergence of a fairly coherent body of research, particularly in Greece, where an interesting intellectual genealogy emerged (du Boulay 1974; Hirschon 1978; Dubisch 1983; Herzfeld 1987).

Within European anthropology the structuralist approach was used with some skill in interpreting indigenous beliefs concerning honour and shame (Blok 1981), the Greek vampire (Du Boulay 1974), the 'evil eye' (Herzfeld 1981) and Gypsy pollution taboos (Okely 1977). Structuralist methods were also adapted with variable success for analysing gender relations in Europe (Hirschon 1978; Okely 1977), though more often than not these resulted in reified sets of binary oppositions purporting to reveal complex principles of gender complementarity and fundamental symbolic ordering principles such as an 'inside – outside' dualism, or ancient structures of circular reciprocity (Ott 1981). Perhaps the most enduring impact of Lévi-Straussian structuralism on the anthropology of Europe has been, unsuprisingly, in the field of kinship studies, particularly as developed in France, Spain and elsewhere in Europe (see Goddard, this volume, chapter 3).

A third development arising from the critique of functionalism was towards a more global perspective, with a theoretical emphasis on the wider political, economic and historical contexts within which local social relations are embedded. Whereas traditional anthropological monographs had relegated history to the status of a minor background detail to be glossed over in cursory introduction to 'the setting', some of the more innovative anthropological studies in the 1970s adopted a more rigorous historical perspective (cf. Blok 1974; Cutileiro 1971) – an approach that Davis (1977) argued was specifically lacking but necessary in the anthropology of the Mediterranean.

Concomitant with these developments was a more radical reappraisal of anthropology in general. The critique of anthropology's colonial heritage further undermined certainties regarding the validity of dichotomies such as traditional/modern societies, primitive/complex, static/historical. The erosion of the exotic as the object of study strengthened the claims to legitimacy by anthropologists working in Europe. The radical critique furthermore helped to shift the anthropological gaze from the norms and values operating within small-scale societies towards the wider political and economic systems and their impact on local processes (cf. Cole 1977; Schneider and Schneider 1976; White 1980).

Yet none of the alternatives to structural-functionalism that arose during the 1970s in themselves either dominated or defined the character of 'European anthropology'. What they did do, however, was to broaden the scope of European anthropology. In this way, they helped to stimulate new and more imaginative ways of analysing social systems and cultural phenomena in Europe, but also led often to theoretical disunity, fragmentation, and competition. While anthropology in Europe benefited from this plurality of approaches, the anthropology 'of' Europe, alluded to by Boissevain and his colleagues, remained a largely unchartered and undefined project, but at least now it appeared a more feasible possibility with the introduction of perspectives which were more sensitive to historical and global determinations. And yet the bulk of research was still concentrated in the Mediterranean, as testified by Davis' comprehensive volume (1977), which brought together different aspects of research in this area.

The 1980s: The Re-Emergence of Europe?

If anything, what defines the 1980s and beyond is extreme complexity. Three major political factors should be taken into account in any attempt to characterize this period; the return of radical conservatism, with its associated neoliberal economic policies; the prospect of an ever wider and deeper European Community; and the collapse of 'real socialism' in Eastern Europe, with its inevitable spillover into political and academic debates concerning models of society. Within anthropology, the period was dominated by increasing relativism, uncertainty and preoccupations with issues of method.

Those approaches most associated with 'positivism' (structural-functionalism, structuralism, scientific Marxism, cultural materialism, etc.) came under heavy attack from an uneasy alliance of approaches within postmodernism, feminism, thirdworldism (cf. Llobera 1993) which tended to privilege the subjective moment in the process of research and give primacy to deconstruction, textuality and the politics of identity. The anthropological mirror was no longer science, but specific political agendas which the discipline was criticized for neglecting. While the conservatism of the anthropological profession may have prevented a more generalized upheaval within the discipline, there is little doubt that anthropology's scientific self-image was on the wane. This growing distrust of science was illustrated most notably in the 1988 meeting of the Group for Debates in Anthropological Theory, which voted decisively against the motion that 'social anthropology is a generalising science or it is nothing'.[15] Without a major change of direction, anthropology risks being relegated to a mere subheading of cultural criticism (cf. Llobera 1993).

Towards the end of the period under consideration the prospects for an anthropology of Europe were greatly enhanced, while the idea of an anthropology of the 'Mediterranean' was clearly receding. The momentum generated by the process of European integration, particularly the incorporation of 'Mediterranean' countries such as Greece, Spain and Portugal into the European Community (EC), undoubtedly played a major role in encouraging the conceptualization of Europe as a united whole. This tendency was further heightened with the political, cultural and (hopefully) economic return to Europe of the eastern European ex-Soviet satellites. While throughout the Cold War era political discourses typically emphasized the differences separating eastern and western Europe, or northern and southern Europe, the present trend in popular representations of Europe is to focus on similarities and areas of convergence. But it is not only the present (and the future) which is at stake; the past is also being reappraised in the light of what is considered quintessentially European. There has thus been a necessary search for the roots of Europeanness in history, religion, science and culture (Shore and Black, this volume, chapter 13).

An important ASA monograph, *Anthropology at Home*, was published in 1985 (Jackson 1985). The collection is concerned mostly with Europe, both West and East. At stake is essentially the issue of whether doing research in one's own culture, a European one to boot, is methodologically different from the traditional ethnographic pursuit in alien cultures. Perhaps one of the obvious conclusions is that 'the anthropologist at home' can no longer be a jack-of-all-trades, and that collaboration with folklorists,

15. This was a meeting organized by the Group for Debates in Anthropological Theory (GDAT) held at Manchester University.

sociologists, historians, etc. is the order of the day.

In their short survey of the 'ethnology' of France, Cuisinier and Segalen (1993) find it difficult to define the specificity of this discipline. Certainly, fieldwork figures prominently in their characterization of ethnology; they seem also to reject the regional approach in favour of a 'diversity of cultural identities' (1993: 121), some regional, some cutting across regions. On the other hand, in Cuisinier's *Ethnologie de l'Europe* (1993), the approach is different. The term 'ethnology' refers to a historically informed knowledge of the European ethnies, with their cultural patrimony and political projects and the conflicts that arise from their encounters.

Segalen (1989) emphasizes the importance of what she calls a 'European ethnological dialogue' (1989: 11) of the different anthropological approaches which exist across Europe. For Augé, in this edited volume, the anthropology of Europe becomes a sort of duty, because European societies are multiethnic, and only anthropology can cut through the singularity of these different groups. There are also a number of areas in which anthropology excels: questions of meaning, the self and the other, order and disorder, the nature of the social, etc.

Despite the ascendancy of Europe as an object of anthropological investigation, the 1980s also witnessed a revival of the idea of the 'Mediterranean' as a culture area, particularly in the work of David Gilmore (1982;1987). While even Pitt-Rivers, considered one of the founding fathers of Mediterranean anthropology, acknowledged the 'Mediterranean' to be merely a 'concept of heuristic convenience, not a culture area in the sense given this phrase by American cultural anthropology' (1977: viii), Gilmore (1987) and his colleagues persevered in the attempt to revitalize the Mediterranean as a relatively distinct homogenizing construct. However, apart from sharing the increasingly polluted waters of the Mediterranean Sea, there is little substance to the invented 'Mediterranean traits'. Too many anomalies had to be accommodated within the 'Mediterranean' straitjacket for this to be considered a useful concept, particularly when it is taken to include North Africa as well as Southern Europe. In fact, comparative analyses within the 'Mediterranean' framework were few and far between, and, after the 1960s comparisons between northern and southern shores were particularly rare. In any case, the most stimulating comparisons were not generated by any methodological rigour that the Mediterranean as a construct might provide, but rather underscored the brilliant qualities of an individual researcher (cf. Davis 1977).

Gilmore's insistence on the need to combine a variety of dimensions to define the cultural unity of the Mediterranean (1982: 184) seemed to find its forte in a resurrection of the honour and shame syndrome (1987: 3). Although some of the papers included in Gilmore's edited volume challenge the 'Mediterranean' in general and the adequacy of the honour and shame distinction in particular, the author concludes that the 'poetics of manhood' (Herzfeld *dixit*) 'would be most keenly appreciated by men in Sicily, or Andalusia, or Turkey, or Tunisia, rather than in other places distant from the Middle Sea' (1987: 16). The fact that the 'male contests' he is alluding to may not be so readily recognized by men in northern Portugal, or Catalonia, or Provence, or Lombardy, is simply ignored.

A totally different agenda, far from the appealing primitivism of honour and shame, was proposed in an important introduction to a collection of papers edited by Grillo (1980). Grillo argues that 'Europe constitutes a meaningful object of social investigation' (1980: 3), but that anthropologists in Europe have tended to focus on topics which ignore the potentially structuring factors. The persisting emphasis on rural community studies or on marginal and maverick social groups has been the stock and trade of the discipline's ventures in Europe. According to Grillo, a proper anthropology of Europe would have to tackle a number of issues hitherto ignored by the current practitioners. These include, *inter alia*: state formation, nation integration, industrialization, urbanization, bureaucratisation, class conflict and commercialization (ibid.:5). Inevitably, these tasks would lead the anthropologists, *pace* Boissevain, well beyond community studies and into collaboration with other disciplines, namely history, sociology, political science, etc. The distinctiveness of anthropology could still be preserved, provided that the discipline focus on 'total social facts' (Mauss) and emphasize the interstitial spaces between micro and macro, local and national, or the whole and its parts (Grillo 1980: 7).

The habits and practices of 'Mediterraneanist' anthropologists were challenged in an article by Llobera (1986), which reiterated criticisms previously advanced by Boissevain, Crump, Grillo and others, concerning the centrality of fieldwork. Llobera argued that many of the shortcomings of the subdiscipline, namely its fundamental ahistoricity and its reluctance to engage in constructive comparisons, followed from its preoccupation with fieldwork, a research technique many anthropologists had taken to be not only entirely unproblematic, but also the *raison d'être* of the discipline.

Llobera's paper also challenged the uncertainty within the discipline concerning the 'Mediterranean' as a cultural area. While many anthropologists paid lip-service to the idea that such a construct was bankrupt, in practice they continued to operate within its boundaries. By the end of the decade anthropologists were still attacking the non-viability of `Mediterraneanist' discourse (cf. Herzfeld 1987; Pina-Cabral 1989). Yet perspectives were changing. A sign of the new times is the predominance of the word `Europe' in the anthropological discourse; it is used as a term of reference for titles of books and articles, for research projects and for departmental specializations – whereas in the past the word `Mediterranean' would have been, in one way or another, a compulsory word in similar contexts. How far this was the result of internal dynamics (conceptual criticism of the construct) or external pressures (the influence of the European Community) is difficult to determine. In all probability it was a combination of both. Even those who, like Magnarella (1993), are still trying to conceptualize the Mediterranean, discuss the interface between different zones of the Mediterranean, and refrain from involving a single, uniform cultural area. However, it would still be premature to assume that the `Mediterraneanist' discourse is defunct. It will survive in often disguised and diluted forms, if only because there are vested interests both political and academic around it.

Anthropology and the Concept of 'Europe'

Any anthropology *of* Europe, as distinct from anthropology *in* Europe, must contend, at the outset, with two sets of questions. Firstly, what exactly is this entity called 'Europe,' how should we conceptualize it, and what are the distinguishing characteristics that set it apart from other regions of the world? Secondly, and perhaps even more problematic, to what extent does the concept of Europe constitute a meaningful object of anthropological enquiry? If we cannot even agree on a shared definition of the enigmatic and elusive term Europe, the prospects of being able to study it anthropologically might appear to be somewhat limited. Furthermore, in view of the differences and divergences which exist within European societies at all levels, does it make any sense to speak of Europe as a discrete unit or as a meaningful framework for comparative research? If so, we need to show that it is possible to delineate the 'external boundaries of the continent' and to demonstrate that 'the internal structure does not divide up into subdivisions which are unconnected or unrelated to each other' (Haller 1990).

At present there are two main reasons which suggest that Europe can be treated as a unit: increased economic interdependence between the different European states, and increased information exchange through the mass media as well as personal contact through tourism, study and work. At the same time it is also the case that these exchanges are intensifying at a global level. Perhaps the most significant factor to apply to Europe specifically is the increasing integration at a political level through agreements and treaties, and increasingly vigorous drives towards legislative and institutional standardization, particularly within the European Union (EU). But will increased integration within the EU act as a catalyst to greater homogeneity within Europe or will it exacerbate differences between EU members and non-members?

With the collapse of Soviet communism after 1989, market economies and liberal democracy have become dominant principles of organization for the whole of Europe, regardless of how long it might take for the former Soviet Bloc countries to implement these principles. However, this begs the question of whether such changes will result eventually in a significant levelling between eastern and western Europe or a more homogeneous and cohesive whole. A persistent factor of differentiation within Europe is the socio-economic level of development, as expressed not only in the per capita GNP but also in the 'quality of life' (standard of living, level of education, state of health, access to cultural facilities and life chances). So far, the various economic reforms and structural readjustment programmes carried out in the former Soviet bloc appear to have done little to ameliorate these differences (Brittan 1993).

There are also important historical and cultural differences which underlie the social organization of European societies, although there are some indications that these might be, if not receding, at least being attenuated. For example, with respect to religion it is possible to distinguish three major historical religious groupings: Catholic, Protestant and Orthodox Christianity. Linguistically, we can isolate three major groups: Romance, Germanic and Slavonic languages. Up to a point a correlation can be established between religion and language group, with the consequence that on the whole there is an overlap between Catholicism and Romance languages, between Protestantism and Germanic languages and Orthodoxy and Slavonic languages. To what extent we can establish other correlations, between say Protestantism, liberalism and economic development (Weber 1930; MacFarlane 1978) and say Orthodoxy, authoritarianism and economic underdevelopment (with Catholicism somewhere in between) is open to discussion (Haller 1990). Indeed, these linguistic and religious divisions are often seen to underlie the major ethnic cleavages and conflicts in contemporary Europe, from Northern Ireland and Belgium, to Bosnia and the Balkans (see Ruane, chapter 6 and Bowman, chapter 7, this volume).

Some anthropologists suggest that correlations can be made between 'anthropological phenomena' such as religion, family form and political orientation (see Todd 1985).[16] This proposition is problematic, but does nevertheless encourage a broader understanding of European societies and a historical perspective, without which the context in which these phenomena occur cannot be meaningfully grasped.

Answers to the question of 'what is Europe' hinge, in many respects, upon the problematic issues of classification and definition; yet these in turn are not only problems of semantics but of ideology and politics. Indeed, the concept of 'Europe' has been used and misused, and interpreted or misinterpreted from so many different perspectives that its meanings appear to be both legion and contradictory. This is not surprising, given that definitions of Europe are frequently both arbitrary and politically charged. There are interesting parallels here with the idea of nation. As Gervais (1993) points out in his study of England and 'Englishness' in

16. See the interesting discussion of differences within Europe explained along the lines of religion and family by E. Todd, 'Las Tres Claves de la Modernidad', E. Todd, 'Las Fronteras de las Fronteras' and I. Kerkhofs, 'Valores y Cambio' in *El Pais*, 25 January 1993, special edition 'Europa: el nuevo continente'.

literature, every image of 'the nation' is inescapably partial – a highly selective and edited version of that elusive whole, tailored for specific audiences and a particular end. Like the nation-state (against which it is often identified), 'Europe' can be seen as much as a creation of literature and myth as it is of power. Indeed, as Foucault's work on the relationship between knowledge, power and the rise of institutions illustrates, these elements are historically rather closely connected.

What is particularly interesting to note, both historically and sociologically, is the way in which the 'idea of Europe' as a political ideal and mobilizing metaphor has become increasingly prominent in the latter part of the twentieth century. Much of the catalyst behind this has undoubtedly been the the movement towards economic and legal union among the states of western and southern Europe. The growth of the European Union has rendered even more urgent and problematic the question of defining Europe. One effect of this, which has increased *pari passu* with the advance towards the millennium, has been a growing number of speeches and books by European leaders and intellectuals setting out their 'visions' of Europe. On closer inspection, however, what appears to be the voice of prophecy often turns out to be one of expediency. As Shore and Black observe, Article 237 of the Treaty of Rome states that 'any European country is eligible for membership to the EC', yet it fails to specify what 'European' means for countries outside the EC. Given the perceived economic and political advantages of membership, it clearly matters to some governments on which side of the 'European/non-European' divide their country falls.

To some extent, therefore, 'Europe' might be considered an example of what Turner called a 'master symbol': an icon that embraces a whole spectrum of different referents and meanings. But 'Europe' is also a discourse of power: a configuration of knowledge shaped by political and economic institutions that are themselves embedded in the disciplines and practices of government. Moreover, it is a discourse that has increasingly been appropriated by the European Community as a shorthand for itself. However vague or ill-defined the concept, to be 'European' or 'in favour of Europe' is increasingly taken to mean support for the European Community and its goal of 'ever-closer union'.

To see Europe in terms of discourses of power is simply to remind oneself that definitions are not always neutral, objective or disinterested. It also draws our attention to the power relations between observer and observed that such classifications often entail. Wallace (1990) illustrates this point cogently in his analysis of the different ways in which Europe has been defined in recent years. Here the boundaries of 'Europe' shift according to whether it is defined in terms of institutional structures, historical geography, or observed patterns of social, economic and political interaction. In each case, a different 'core' area emerges. Yet more problematic still is Wallace's emphasis on the importance of Europe as a distinctive cultural entity, one united by 'shared values, culture and psychological identity' (1990: 9–10). Advocates of this kind of 'cultural approach' point to Europe's heritage of classical Graeco–Roman civilization, Christianity, the ideas of the Enlightenment, and the triumph of Science, Reason, Progress and Democracy as the key markers of this shared European legacy. Significantly, these are all features which European Community officials emphasize as being particularly representative of 'the European idea' as they see it (Shore and Black, this volume, chapter 13; see also Shore 1993). There are also definitions of Europe which involve a subtext of racial and cultural chauvinism, particularly when confronted with Islam. For some, therefore, the definition and meaning of 'Europe' acquires saliency only when pitted against that which is 'non-European'.

If there is something that we can call Europe, understood perhaps as an ideal type, what characteristics does it exhibit? According to Zettenberg (1991) there are several self-regulating and autonomous institutions, associated with specific key values and types of freedom, which can be used to describe modern Europe. For Zettenberg, the economy is associated with prosperity and free trade; government with order and civic liberties; science with knowledge and academic freedom; religion with sacredness and religious tolerance; arts with beauty and artistic licence and ethics with virtue and the right to follow one's own conscience. The problem with these sets of correlations is that they are historical and conjunctural. Thus they apply elsewhere (notably the US), and have not at all times applied to what in other contexts we might consider to be European countries (were Spain under Franco, Italy under Mussolini, Greece under the Junta not *European* for the duration of these regimes?) As sets of ideals or aspirations they might well be at the forefront of European culture, as well as other national cultures, but they are not effective markers of the boundaries of Europe.

The Future of Europe and The Future of an Anthropology of Europe

The close of the twentieth century represents a momentous period in the history of Europe, but at present we can only have a hazy picture of what is likely to emerge in the future. As social scientists we have had to confront major international events: the collapse of Communism in eastern Europe, the end of the Cold War, increasing integration of the economies of the European Union, the breakdown of Yugoslavia and protracted war throughout Bosnia. We have simultaneously witnessed prolonged economic recession and mass unemployment, as well as increasing right-wing violence throughout eastern and western Europe. Yet we face these phenomena often bereft of suitable anthropological categories. Although many 'classical' anthropologists have contributed to the issues of nationality and nationalism (see Llobera, chapter 4, and Ruane, chapter 6, this volume), anthropology as a whole has been limited by its emphasis on small-scale units. Where progress has been made, largely through profitable exchanges with sociologists and social historians, this has been limited to developments appropriate only to the national state.

In the present circumstances, at a time of incessant change, the danger we face is that our short-term analyses may be dated by the time of their publication. Yet medium-term and long-term projections are difficult to muster when no clear trends seem to emerge. Tilly (1992), a leading historical sociologist, envisages a number of possible scenarios concerning the future of Europe. In the short term he predicts two different trends. Firstly, the proliferation of states matching the more bellicose and/or diplomatically successful populations that at present lack states of their own. This trend applies particularly to eastern Europe. Secondly, he sees the continuation of the long-term trend towards the consolidation into a decreasing number of more or less homogeneizing states; at the limit we are talking about a vast single European Community, with increased state-like powers and a certain sense of cultural identity.

However, in the long run Tilly sees the most important feature as the detachment of the principle of cultural distinctiveness from that of statehood. The implication of this is the creation of a strongly connected but multicultural Europe in which most individuals function bilingually (or trilingually) and exercise their right to territorial mobility in pursuit of opportunities and preferences. It also implies that the desire of ethno-nations to claim national independence within the framework of separate states will greatly diminish, because the European Union will offer all the advantages of being a free nation without the costs and inconvenience of being an independent state. The existing states, in whichever form they may exist, will cease to enforce cultural homogeneity and political dominance within their domain.

Tilly is well aware that this outlook may seem too optimistic given the lessons from history. That is why he allows for the possibility of two variants which might be realized within the long-term: a benign development, characterized by pluralism and diversity and with an absence of squabbles and attempts at domination, and a malign version, characterized by segmentation, hatred and parochialism, in the context of gross inequalities and violent ethnic conflicts.

All these possible developments identified by Tilly have relevance to the anthropological agenda for the future, concerned as they are with the interconnections between culture, identity and institutional frameworks. Our ability to meet the challenges of the future depends on our capacity to elaborate appropriate frameworks and concepts.

It is important that, while capitalizing on anthropology's ethnographic expertise, bringing awareness of local realities and grass-roots reactions, we expand our repertoire to enable fruitful systematic comparative analysis. Anthropologists have wrestled for generations with the problem of relating the local to the national or the global, and the temptation to succumb to the merits of the micro-study has frequently been overwhelming. But it is essential to persevere not only in locating the local within its wider context but in tackling the very institutions and practices which define and constitute the national and the supra-national levels in question. A historical dimension is important here not only in terms of coming to grips with the nature and shape of groups and institutions, but also in defining the overall object of study itself: that is, 'Europe'.

If Europe is considered as a unit, there follow a number of questions. For example, what are the political, cultural and economic consequences of mass immigration on Europe? What are the effects of global culture, particularly in the mass media, on European national cultures? How is increasing contact through tourism affecting traditional stereotypes about different European national and ethnic groups? We should also consider the impact of the global economy and the strategies of European and non-European transnational corporations, and the extent to which these might shape national and EU policies. Furthermore, what are the effects of the process of European integration on national identity and state sovereignty? Are there any institutions or policies which are helping to generate a European consciousness?

Given that 'Europe' itself is a disputed category, and yet one that has a bearing on many aspects of people's lives, one contribution of anthropology from an ethnographic point of view might be the exploration of what Europe means to different groups and individuals, and the many ways in which they conceptualize or talk about Europe in relation to their own identity. This is one of the themes that runs through a number of the contributions to this volume (Mandel; Chapman; Bowman; Ruane). If it is the *experience* of Europe that interests us, or Europe as a source of *identity* (Garcia 1993), then we need to be sensitive to the many different ways that this experience is mediated through other social factors such as religion, class, ethnicity, nationality and gender. In this respect, to speak of a single, all-constitutive 'Europe' becomes rather meaningless, or worse, encourages an essentialized vision of Europeanness as a quality that is somehow fixed, bounded, homogeneous and pure. Instead, we should recognize the plurality and diversity of the many different Europes that exist, and have existed, in any given time or context, and the ways in which these different meanings might be deployed to different effect. The way to see the different 'Europes' is as cultural conceptions advanced by diverse groups competing for hegemony in the political arena. This does not exclude the acknowledgment that some visions are more dominant than others.

The Scope of This Volume

The articles included in this volume originated from a conference held at Goldsmiths College, University of London, in June 1992 under the title 'The Anthropology of Europe: After 1992'. The aim of the conference was to explore old paradigms and new directions in European social anthropology, particularly in the areas of ethnicity, nationalism and gender. The implications of European unification both for the organization of European societies and for European anthropology were central themes underlying conference debates. Indeed the contributions to this volume reflect these concerns and in many ways represent a departure from conventional anthropological perspectives.

What many chapters have in common is an attempt to chart new research directions in European social anthropology in response to the changing character of European societies. Taking up the criticisms of European anthropology that were first highlighted by Boissevain and others in the 1970s, many contributors attempt to grapple with larger-scale social processes, including nationalism, migration, European Community institutions and state policy. Boissevain's chapter identifies three inter-related developments currently taking place that he suggests will feature prominently in anthropological research during the next few decades: changing patterns of production, movements of people and nostalgia for a sense of identity perceived as being eroded as a result of modernity and globalization. The theme of identity and boundaries and the relationship between migrants, conceptions of national identity and citizenship, is examined by Mandel, drawing on her ethnographic study of Turks in Berlin. Mandel argues that definitions of citizenship in Germany are conflated with notions of ethnicity and race, which produce and legitimize the category of outsider or *Auslander*.

Garcia explores the question of what it means to be a 'citizen' at national and supranational levels, arguing that Spain lags behind its European partners in terms of the rights and entitlements of its citizens. This she attributes to the history of the Spanish state and its weak relationship with 'civil society'. She draws an interesting parallel with the European Union, where there is also a problem of a lack of popular democratic participation. Attempts by the EU to create such a European citizenship are analysed by Shore and Black. As they show, a new iconography has been invented to lend legitimacy to the political aspirations of European Union institutions, but the reality of a 'citizen's Europe' has yet to be achieved.

The tension between the European Union and the member states is a theme that recurs in several chapters. Llobera's paper explores the contributions of Van Gennep and Mauss to the study of nationalism in Europe in the aftermath of the First World War. Many of the issues at stake, and particularly the impact of the principle of self-determination in multinational states and empires, are still relevant today, particularly in the light of the collapse of the Soviet Union and Yugoslavia.

Ruane argues that European integration is often perceived as heralding the end of the age of nationalism in Europe, yet nationalist concerns seem to have been incorporated into the very framework of the EU. This challenges the view of a post-nationalist Europe. Focusing on the Irish Republic, Ruane highlights the importance of nationalist ideologies and discourses and their implications for the future of Europe.

The boundaries of the new Europe are a problem explored by Chapman. Focusing on Poland, and the related questions of capital movements, trade barriers and the 'nationality' of transnational corporations, he illustrates some of the difficulties in establishing clear frontiers between the EU and non-community Europe, and the implications for those countries excluded from the Union.

If Ruane, Chapman, Shore and Black and others are concerned with the formation of a European state, Bowman explores the breakdown of a former federal state: Yugoslavia. Using a Lacanian perspective, he tries to explain the rise of ethnic hatred and violence that has come to epitomize the conflict in that country. For Bowman, ambiguity over ethnic and territorial boundaries, combined with the breakdown of authority (understood in a psychological as well as a political sense) has resulted in what many see as a descent into barbarism. From the perspective of the EU there is a temptation to disassociate the new republics from the project of Europeanism.

The problematic nature of national identities is also explored by Stanton in connection with Gibraltar's contradictory status as an outpost of the now defunct British Empire. As Stanton suggests, in a post-colonial world, becoming European poses problems for the Gibraltarians' already contradictory identity. The contradictions of this identity are to do with British identity, which is intrinsically linked to the concept and experience of empire. The question that emerges with the collapse of the British Empire is the content and meaning of being British and the disjunction between geopolitics and the remnants of a 'mirage of empire'.

In a different context, O'Brien explores the multiple identities which exist in a French Catalonian village. Her study illustrates the contextual nature of social identities, pointing out not only that women are more influential than men in reproducing ethnic identity, but also that they tend to shift towards a Catalan identity as they grow older. In fact, gender has been an important element in anthropological research in some areas of Europe, notably through studies focused on 'honour and shame'. But this framework has met with growing criticism, and its limitations in terms of providing a basis for comparative study have become increasingly obvious. Comas' contribution to this volume explores the advantages of an alternative framework to the comparative study of gender in Europe, based on a consideration of 'support and care'. She considers the sexual division of labour and the ideological elaboration of masculinity and femininity in rural and urban areas of Spain, arguing that these must be understood in relation to state policies and welfare provisions. The importance of linking local practices and beliefs with wider national and supranational levels of determination is further explored by Goddard. While on the one hand recognizing the importance of a historical and global contextualization of anthropological work, Goddard argues that a careful appraisal of (Mediterranean and non-Mediterranean) European anthropology offers important inroads into the development of a comparative study of European societies. Both Comas and Goddard emphasize the importance of studying gender, not only to explain inequalities between men and women, but because gender divisions are relevant to the production and reproduction of other encompassing manifestations of social difference.

Although this collection does not represent a coherent proposal for future work in European anthropology, our aim has been to explore, via critique and innovation, possible avenues for research. Although a number of different avenues would be beneficial to the discipline as a whole, we do argue for proposals that are cognizant of the importance of a historical approach and sensitive to the implications of national and global processes. The question of methodology is relevant here. Whilst recognizing the contribution of fieldwork and related techniques, we propose that anthropologists must broaden their methodological repertoire in order to grasp the complexities of history and of global determinations. Here an interdisciplinary approach would seem to be invaluable. Anthropologists working in Europe ignore at their peril the qualitative and quantitative methodologies offered by sociology and history. Blok (1992) suggests that anthropologists are generally unfamiliar with the methods, models and contributions of historians. And yet anthropologists would benefit from cross-fertilization with this discipline, which recognizes different levels theorization of the social and cultural spectrum, from microunits to macrounits (Tilly 1990). Similarly, if we take the case of sociology, of the introductions to three recent collections on the anthropology of Europe – Pina-Cabral (1992), Hastrup (1992) and MacDonald (1993) – only MacDonald makes mention of sociological texts. Historical sociology in particular has in the past twenty-five years made an outstanding contribution to explaining how European modernity came into being – a concern that would be central to the anthropology of Europe. But what would be the anthropologist's specific contribution to the study of European (and indeed other contemporary) societies?

It has been frequently stated that anthropological work is defined by its research technique, that is, participant observation in a face-to-face situation (traditionally in a small community). If anthropology often appears as just the sum of its ethnographies, and the knowledge of higher-level socio-cultural units (be they districts, regions, ethnonations, nation-states, multinational states, federations, world-system or wider social and cultural manifestations and traits) is problematic and approached with diffidence, this is largely a consequence of the limitations imposed by the centrality of this research technique.

What might have made sense among the Trobrianders and Tikopians of yesteryear is inadequate in relation to the Piedmontese or Bretons of today (not to speak of the European Union bureaucrats or transnational corporations). The issue here is that anthropologists should not be defined by their adherence to a specific way of collecting data, but by the scientific character of their projects. The question is not whether the anthropologist should or should not embark on fieldwork, but that the latter should not be the *fons et origo* of the discipline.

The legacy of the discipline is an acute sensitivity among its practitioners to the complexity and contradictory nature of social processes. Anthropologists are well aware of the specificities which global economic processes or wide-ranging ideologies may acquire for particular groups or localities. At the same time, they are well equipped to contextualize local beliefs and practices within a wider comparative framework, thus undermining any claims of universality that might underlie such beliefs and practices. Anthropologists have historically been concerned with those social groups or conditions which have for one reason or another been rendered 'peripheral' (Nugent 1988). They have often been the sole mediators for those rendered powerless and voiceless, although their role here has been scrutinized and – quite rightly – criticized. While taking on board these critiques, this continues to be an urgent task for the discipline, whether in the periphery of the world system or the peripheralized groups within Europe. At the same time, anthropologists have become intent on applying their skills to the study of those organizations and ideologies which may indeed have a hand in reproducing peripheralization, but whose main objective is to reproduce existing power structures, or indeed invent new ones. Thus anthropologists have before them a rich and varied field and a challenging and important task.

References

Ahmed, A. S. (1976). *Millennium and Charisma among Pathans*, London: RKP.

Almond, G. and Verba, S. (1963). *The Civic Culture. Political Attitudes and Democracy in Five Nations*, Princeton: Princeton University Press.

Arensberg, C. M. (1963). The Old World Peoples: The Place of European Cultures in World Ethnography. *Anthropological Quarterly*, **36**, (3), 75–99.

Asad, T. (1972). Market model, class structure and consent: a reconsideration of Swat political organisation. *Man*, **7**, (1), 74–94.

Bailey, F. (ed.) (1971). *Gifts and Poison: The Politics of Reputation*, Oxford: Blackwell.

Bailey, F. (ed.) (1973). *Debate and Compromise. The Politics of Innovation*, Oxford: Blackwell.

Banfield, E. (1958). *The Moral Basis of Backward Society*, New York: Free Press.

Banton, M. (ed.) (1966). *Social Anthropology of Complex Societies*, ASA Monograph 4, London: Tavistock.

Barnes, J. A. (1954). Class and Committees in a Norwegian Island Parish. *Human Relations*, **7**, (1), 39–58.

Barnes, J. A. (1972). *Networks in Social Anthropology*, Reading.

Barth, F. (1959). *Political Leadership Among the Swat Pathan*, London: The Athlone Press.

Barth, F. (1966). *Models of Social Organisation*, Occasional Paper No.

23, London: RAI.

Barth, F. (1969). *Ethnic Groups and Boundaries: The Social Organisation of Cultural Difference*, London: Allen & Unwin.

Benedict, R. (1946a). *Patterns of Culture*, NY: Penguin.

Benedict, R. (1946b). *The Chrysanthemum and the Sword*, Boston: Houghton Mifflin.

Blok, A. (1974). *The Mafia of a Sicilian Village*, Oxford: Blackwell.

Blok, A. (1981). Rams and Billy Goats: A Key to the Mediterranean Code of Honor. *Man*, **16**, (3), 427–40.

Blok, A. (1992). Reflections on Making History. In *Other Histories* (ed. K. Hastrup), London: Routledge.

Boissevain, J. (1966). Patronage in Sicily. *Man*, **2**, 18–33.

Boissevain, J. (1968). The Place of Non-groups in the Social Sciences. *Man*, **3/4**, 542–56.

Boissevain, J. (1969). *Hal Farug. A Village in Malta*, New York: Holt, Reinhart and Winston.

Boissevain, J. (1974). *Friends of Friends: Networks, Manipulators and Coalitions*, Oxford: Blackwell.

Boissevain, J. (1976). Uniformity and Diversity in the Mediterranean. In *Kinship and Modernisation* (ed. J. Peristany), pp. 1–11, Rome: Center for Mediterranean Studies.

Boissevain, J. (1977). Towards a Social Anthropology of Europe. In *Beyond the Community: Social Processes in Europe* (ed. J. Boissevain and J. Friedl), pp. 9–17, The Hague: Department of Education and Science, The Netherlands.

Boissevain, J. and Blok, A. (1974). Western Mediterranean Folk Cultures, *Encyclopaedia Britannica*, 15th edn, **2**, 852–4.

Bott, E. (1955). Urban Families: Conjugal Roles and Social Relations. *Human Relations*, **8**, (4), 345–84.

Bott, E. (1957). *Family and Social Networks*, London: Tavistock.

Brittan, S. (1993). Economic Viewpoint: The Painful Road to Capitalism. *Financial Times*, 30 September, p.18.

Campbell, J. K. (1964). *Honour, Family and Patronage. A Study of Institutions and Moral Values in a Greek Mountain Community*, Oxford: Clarendon Press.

Cole, J. (1977). Anthropology Comes Part-Way Home. *Annual Review of Anthropology*, **6**, 349–378.

Crockatt, R. (1987). The Cold War, Past and Present. In *The Cold War, Past and Present* (eds R. Crockatt and S. Smith) pp. 3–23, London: Allen & Unwin.

Cuisinier, J. (1993). *Ethnologie de l'Europe*, Paris: PUF.

Cuisinier, J. and Segalen, M. (1993). *Ethnologie de la France*. Paris: PUF.

Cutileiro, J. (1971). *A Portuguese Rural Society*, Oxford: Clarendon Press and OUP.

Davis, J. (1977). *People of the Mediterranean: An Essay in Comparative Social Anthropology*, London: RKP.

Dubisch, J. (1983). Greek Women, Sacred or Profane. In Women and Men in Greece: a society in transition (eds Mackrakis and Allen). *Journal of Modern Greek Studies*, **1**, (1).

Du Boulay, J. (1974). *Portrait of a Greek Mountain Village*, Oxford: Clarendon Press.

Du Boulay, J. (1978). The Greek Vampire: a study of cyclic symbolism in marriage and death. *Man*, (NS) **17**, 219–38.

Foster, G. M. (1965). Peasant Society and the Image of Limited Good. *American Anthropologist*, **67**, (2).

Foster, G. M. (1973) [1962]. *Traditional Societies and Technological Change*, (2nd edn). NY: Harper and Row. First published in 1962 as *Traditional Cultures and the Impact of Technological Change*.

Freeman, S. (1973). Introduction to European Social Organisation. *American Anthropologist*, **75**, 743–50.

Friedl, E. (1958). Hospital Care in Provincial Greece. *Human Organization*, **16**, (40), 24–7.

Friedl, E. (1959). The Role of Kinship in the Transmission of National Culture to Rural Villages of Mainland Greece. *American Anthropologist*, **61**, 30–8.

Friedl, E. (1962). *Vasilika*, New York: Holt, Rinehart and Winston.

Garcia, S. (ed.) (1993). *European Identity and the Search for Legitimacy*. London: Pinter.

Gellner, E. and Waterbury, J. (eds) (1977). *Patrons and Clients*, London: Duckworth.

Gervais, D. (1993). *Literary Englands: 'Versions of Englishness' in Modern Writing*, Cambridge: Cambridge University Press.

Gilmore, D. (1977). Patronage and Class Conflict in Southern Spain. *Man*, **12**, 446–58.

Gilmore, D. (1982). Anthropology of the Mediterranean Area. *Annual Review of Anthropology*, **11**, 175–207.

Gilmore, D. (ed.) (1987). Introduction to *Honour and Shame and the Unity of the Mediterranean*, Washington: American Ethnological Association.

Goddard, V. (1986). Honour and Shame: The Control of Women's Sexuality and Group Identity in Naples. In *The Cultural*

Construction of Sexuality (ed. P. Caplan), London: Routledge.

Goffman, I. (1959). *The Presentation of Self in Everyday Life*, New York: Doubleday.

Grillo, R. D. (ed.) (1980). *'Nation' and 'State' in Europe. Anthropological Perspectives*, London: Academic Press.

Haller, M. (1990). The Challenge for Contemporary Sociology in the Transformation of Europe. *International Sociology*, 5, 183–204.

Hastrup, K. (1992). *Other Histories*. London: Routledge.

Herzfeld, M. (1981). Meaning and Morality: A Semiotic Approach to Evil Eye Accusations in a Greek Village. *American Ethnologist*, 8, 560–74.

Herzfeld, M. (1987). *Anthropology Through the Looking-Glass*, Cambridge: Cambridge University Press.

Hirschon, R. (1978). Open Body/Closed Space: the transformation of female sexuality. In *Defining Females* (ed. S. Ardener), London: Croom Helm.

Jackson, A. (ed.) (1985). *Anthropology at Home*, London: Tavistock.

Kapferer, B. (ed.) (1976). *Transaction and Meaning: Directions in the Anthropology of Exchange and Symbolic Behaviour*, Philadelphia: Inst. for the Study of Human Issues.

Kay, C. (1989). *Latin American Theories of Development and Underdevelopment*, London: Macmillan.

Kenny, M. (1963). Europe: The Atlantic Fringe. *Anthropological Quarterly*, 36, (3), 100–19.

Kenny M. and Kertzer, D. (eds) (1983). *Urban Life in Mediterranean Europe: Anthropological Perspectives*, Urbana and Chicago: University of Illinois Press.

Llobera, J. R. (1986). Fieldwork in Southwestern Europe, *Critique of Anthropology*, 6, (2), 25–33.

Llobera, J. R. (1993). Reconstructing Anthropology: the task for the nineties. In *Despues de Malinowski* (ed. J. Besterd), Tenerife: Actas del VI Congreso de Antropologia.

Lowie, R. H. (1954). *Toward Understanding Germany*. Chicago: Chicago University Press.

MacDonald, S. (ed.) (1993). *Inside European Identities*, Oxford: Berg.

MacFarlane, A. (1978). *The Origins of English Individualism. The Family, Property and Social Transition*, Oxford: Blackwell.

Magnarella, P. (1993). Conceptualising the Circum-Mediterranean, *Journal of Mediterranean Studies*, 2, (1), 18–24.

Nugent, S. (1988). The Peripheral Situation, *Annual Review of Anthropology*, 17, 79–98.

Okely, J. (1977). Gypsy Women: models in conflict. In *Perceiving Women* (ed. S. Ardener), London: Croom Helm.

Ott, S. (1981). *The Circle of Mountains*, Oxford: Clarendon Press.

Parsons, A. (1967). Is the Oedipus Complex Universal? A South Italian "nuclear complex". In *Personalities and Culture* (ed. R. Hunt), Austin, Texas: University Press. 352–99.

Peristiany, J. G. (1974) [1966]. *Honour and Shame. The Values of Mediterranean Society*, Medway Reprint; originally printed in Chicago: Chicago University Press.

Pina-Cabral, J. (1989). The Mediterranean as a Category of Cultural Comparison. *Current Anthropology*, **30**, 399–406.

Pina-Cabral, J. (1992). Against Translation. In *Europe Observed* (eds J. Pina-Cabral and J. Campbell), 1–23, London: Macmillan.

Pitkin, D. S. (1963). Mediterranean Europe. *Anthropological Quarterly*, **36**, (3), 120–9.

Pitt-Rivers, J. (1963). Mediterannean Countrymen: *Essays in the Social Anthropology of the Mediterannean*, Paris/The Hague: Mouton.

Pitt-Rivers, J. (1966). Honour and Social Status. In (1974 [1966]) *Honour and Shame. The Values of Mediterranean Society* (ed. J. G. Peristiany), Chicago: Chicago University Press.

Pitt-Rivers, J. (1971) [1954]. *The People of the Sierra*, (2nd edn), Chicago and London: University of Chicago Press. First published 1954, London: Weidenfeld & Nicholson.

Redfield, R. (1971) [1956]. *Peasant Society and Culture: an anthropological approach to civilization*, Chicago: Chicago University Press.

Redfield, R. (1973) [1960]. *The Little Community. Peasant Society and Culture*, Chicago: Chicago University Press.

Schneider, J. and Schneider, P. (1976). *Culture and Political Economy in Western Sicily*, London and New York: Academic Press.

Segalen, M. (ed.) (1989). *L' autre et le semblable. Regards sur l'ethnologie des sociétés contemporaines*, Paris: Editions du CNRS.

Shore, C. (1990). *Italian Communism. The Escape from Leninism: an anthropological perspective*, London: Pluto Press.

Shore, C. (1993). Inventing the "People's Europe": critical perspectives on European Community "cultural policies". *Man. Journal of the Royal Anthropological Institute*, **28**, (4), 779–800.

Tilly, C. (1990). Future History. In *Interpreting the Past, Understanding the Present* (eds S. Kendrick and D. McCrone), London: Macmillan.

Tilly, C. (1992). The Future of European States, *Social Research*, **59**, (40), 705–18.

Wallace, W. (1990). *The Transformation of Europe*, London: Pinter.

Weber, M. (1930). *The Protestant Ethic and the Spirit of Capitalism*, London: Allen & Unwin.

White, C. (1980). *Patrons and Partisans: A Study of Two Southern Italian Comuni*, Cambridge: Cambridge University Press.

Wolf, E. (1966a). *Peasants*. Englewood Cliffs, NJ: Prentice-Hall.

Wolf, E. (1966b). Kinship, friendship and patron–client relationships in complex societies. In *The Social Anthropology of Complex Societies* (ed. M. Banton), pp. 1–22, London: Tavistock.

Zettenberg, H. (1991). The Structuration of Europe. *Journal of Public Opinion Research*, **394**, 309–12.

Chapter 2

Towards an Anthropology of European Communities?[1]

Jeremy Boissevain

Current social developments in Europe are increasing the total number of its constituent communities. As these communities seek to establish and defend their identities, there is growing political, economic and symbolic activity within and between them. This paper points to some of the developments that may well be overlooked in the rush to assess the impact on anthropology of the European Community. It also suggests some of the ways these may influence theoretical developments in the social anthropology of Europe.

Changing Theoretical Interests

Twenty years ago a number of social and cultural anthropologists working in Europe were turning away from functionalist-inspired community studies, which, by their narrow village-centred approach, were tribalizing Europe. While retaining the local-level base, these new studies began to move beyond individual communities in an attempt to understand the configurations they formed with higher levels of integration (cf. Bax 1976; Blok 1974; Boissevain and Friedl 1975; Schneider and Schneider 1976; Verrips 1977, 1980). Many of the studies from this period were down-to-earth monographs which dealt with specific political and economic themes from a historical perspective focused on power relations.

1. I am grateful to Gerard Hersbach and Cris Shore for helpful comments on an earlier draft of the present discussion.

Generally, they paid relatively less attention to ritual or symbolic activities.

A decade later, in the 1980s, a significant shift in interest was evident. Often focusing on ritual, many studies were concerned with the analysis of symbolism and symbolic behaviour (cf. Cohen 1982, 1985, 1986). I do not intend to explore here the epistemology of the shift in focus from the social to the cultural and cognitive, that is, why much of social anthropology has become cultural anthropology. Other contributors will address these questions. It no doubt has much to do with the charisma and power of leading anthropologists who had largely given up fieldwork to focus on myth, ritual, pollution and the Bible: Claude Lévi-Strauss, Edmund Leach, Mary Douglas, Clifford Geertz and Victor Turner. Be that as it may, the change in accent is also related to other influences.

Theoretical shifts are not only influenced by great teachers. They also reflect developments in the societies in which theoreticians live. Although Firth (1954) and Leach (1954) by the early 1950s had begun questioning the value of structural-functionalism in interpreting their own field data, the demise of this theoretical paradigm was hastened by its inability to provide adequate insights into the anti-colonial revolts and class-based conflicts prominent during the late 1950s and 1960s. But in spite of Kuhn's work (1970), the influence of social processes on theoretical developments is still often ignored, and shifts in theoretical focus are attributed solely to academic debate. The influence on debate of developments in the society in which that intellectual activity takes place is largely ignored.

For example, Victor Turner, in his postlude to Manning's 1983 collection, *The Celebration of Society*, asked, 'But why, I repeat, have anthropologists, folklorists, . . . begun, of late, to flock to the field of ludic studies?' (1983a: 188). His answer was that, finally, anthropologists had begun to see the light: 'It is gradually being brought home to us that we have been in error, in "bracketing off" such celebrations as "mystification," "false consciousness," "lower stages of cultural evolution," "ideological confusion," and similar pejorative evaluations based on consciousness of our own cognitive superiority' (ibid.: 190–1).

He thus suggested that the change in focus was the result of a process internal to the community of scholars conceived as an isolate. But at the same time that this theoretical shift was taking place, a revitalization of pilgrimages and public celebrations was occurring throughout Europe, not to mention Asia, Africa and the Americas (Manning 1983; Boissevain 1992). Though Turner was well aware of these developments (1974: 210, 211, 223; 1983b: 110, 112, 124 n.2), it does not seem to have occurred to him that the growing attention to ludic celebrations could also have been stimulated by the increasing number of such festivities in the societies in which the anthropologists and folklorists lived and worked.

Shifts in scientific paradigms cannot be fully understood unless they are examined against the social fabric of the societies in which they occur. The shift from social to cultural anthropology, from post-structural-functional transactionalism and political economy to symbolism and deconstruction, was related to social developments that were occurring outside academe during the 1970s and 1980s. The shift in scholarly focus occurred at a time that there had been a long pause in the armed combat which had been endemic in western Europe. This peace, which permitted contemplation, proved conducive to the questioning of given authority, of the benefits of continuing industrial growth, of the effects of expanding communication possibilities, of the rapid globalization of culture. One of the consequences of this reflection and introspection was a revalorization of traditions abandoned in the post-Second World War rush for material prosperity. Ludic rituals and symbols that linked the present to an idealized pre-industrial life-style provided a sense of belonging and identity, and became increasingly important during the 1970s and 1980s (cf. Boissevain 1992; Hewison 1987).

In short, growing scholarly interest in the analysis of symbols and rituals, rather than exclusively the product of academic debate, was also a reflection of the growing general interest in ritual and symbolic activity in the societies in which anthropologists themselves lived and worked. Theoretical debate and paradigmatic shifts follow the outline of the underlying social reality of the societies in which they occur.

It follows that social developments taking place in Europe today will influence the anthropology of tomorrow. It is consequently useful to examine some of the social processes affecting contemporary European societies.

Three interrelated developments are taking place that I think will influence the activities of anthropologists working on Europe during the next decade or so. These are the changing patterns of production, the movement of peoples and the nostalgia to which I have already alluded.

Changing Production

During the past two decades there has been a marked change in patterns of economic activity that has challenged the dominant position of West European manufacturers. The increase in production costs following the energy crisis of the mid-1970s led to the transfer to developing countries of many low-skilled (and often polluting) production processes. In addition, consumers, for various reasons (including the growth of more sophisticated advertising and the media), became increasingly dissatisfied with mass-produced, standard products and demanded varied and customized goods, for which they were willing to pay more. To meet this challenge, European manufacturers were obliged to produce more specialized, higher-quality products (Brusco 1982: 171; Sabel 1982: 199). This heralded what Charles Sabel has called the 'End of Fordism' (ibid.: 194–231), the end of the dominance of assembly-line production of goods destined for the mass market. Where Fordism centralized production, separated conception from execution and substituted unskilled for skilled labour, specialization required the opposite: decentralization, a reduction in scale and collaboration between designers and skilled producers. Unskilled labour became increasingly redundant. Miniaturization, computers and robots combined to produce massive lay-offs, not only in industry but also in labour-intensive white-collar sectors such as banking and publishing (see also Gershuny 1978).

These developments have resulted in the emergence in western Europe of an impoverished under-class of structurally un- or underemployed, many of whom are forming loose communities and developing distinctive subcultures. The alarming growth of this under-class has also been furthered by the dismantling of the costly welfare net put in place during the 1960s and 1970s. Aspects of these subcultures surface at weekends and at the solstices, when vandalism, violent racial xenophobia, joy-riding, the winter misery of the homeless and rituals at Stonehenge capture headlines. Respect for, if not the legitimacy of, European states is being weakened by their inability to provide a growing segment of their citizens with work, shelter and the level of benefits to which they have become accustomed.

Another consequence of changing modes of production is the growing awareness in Europe that there are strikingly different ways of doing much the same thing. Differences between Japanese and British automobile production have been discussed in the press. Less explored but equally fascinating questions include, for example: How were small family enterprises in Prato able to put the British reused woollen industry out of business (Boissevain 1984)? What exactly is the relation between kinship, share-cropping and the immensely successful high-technology cottage industries of central Italy that have made this region the wealthiest in the country (Bamford 1987)? Why are immigrants of Asian extraction generally more successful business entrepreneurs than Afro-Caribbean immigrants (Boissevain and Grotenbreg 1988; Ward 1988)?

Insiders and Outsiders: The Struggle for Identity

Even as long-established European nations integrate their economies, they are multiplying and becoming increasingly heterogeneous. At least two processes are responsible for this. First, European nation-states are losing their power to contain the struggle of minority groups for political identity. Second, everywhere there is movement of newcomers – immigrant labourers, refugees, tourists – into fairly homogeneous, settled communities. These developments are obviously not of the same order, but all establish populations of insiders and outsiders, and thus stimulate struggles for identity and the control of cultural and social boundaries.

Restive Minorities

The ethnic ferment in central and eastern Europe following the spectacular dissolution of the Communist regimes is a more recent powerful example of the inability of weakened states to control the identities and political ambitions of minorities. The fission of Yugoslavia, the Soviet Union and many of their constituent republics and provinces along ethnic fault-lines is creating new states. Their struggle to achieve statehood possibly will fuel aspirations for greater autonomy of west European minorities who have not yet been able to (re)gain political legitimacy. The struggles to divide social entities regarded as social and cultural wholes are bitter. They are causing massive population movements, as waves of new political refugees seek protection in western Europe, creating new groups of outsiders, and thus new boundaries to be defended.

Regional Ferment

The post-war period has been, at least for western Europe, a time of unprecedented peace and relative stability. For decades, the nation-states have not had to rally citizens against a common, outside enemy. Just as this stability furthered theoretical introspection, so it has also promoted localism by permitting the refocusing of attention and resources on rivals and boundaries closer to hand, on parochial and regional interests. This, in turn, has resulted in pressure for decentralization, for more regional autonomy. These regional movements have played an important part in stimulating the effervescence of public rituals as resources are channelled into local cultural manifestations. For example, in Andalusia there has been and explosive growth of the pilgrimage to the shrine of El Rocio, and in the Ladin-speaking area of the Italian Dolomites there has been a revitalization of carnival. Both events have become important vehicles of regional identity and cultural pride (Crain 1992; Poppi 1992).

Immigration

Other lines of cleavage are created by the continuing influx into western Europe of unskilled workers from Asia, the Mediterranean and Caribbean regions and, more recently, central and eastern Europe. Originally recruited as short-term 'guest workers' to fill positions on the lower rungs of the industrial ladder, many have now moved up a few rungs and been joined by their families. Western Europe has become an immigration destination. These immigrants have been disproportionatly affected by the structural unemployment. As their numbers and knowledge of how the system works have grown, so has their competition with the majority population for increasingly scarce jobs, welfare benefits and housing. This competition has furthered latent xenophobia and racism, which throughout Europe has become more open. The mounting, open racial violence in Germany during 1992 and 1993 has captured the headlines; but racial tension elsewhere in western Europe has also been rising as the stream of economic and political refugees grows.

Escalating ethnic unrest and overt racism is part of a vicious circle: it is aggravated by the inability of the states to redress the problem of structural unemployment which lies at the root of much of the discord. It is further exacerbated by the policy of most states to cut back on social benefits in order to stem budget deficits caused by rising welfare payments to growing numbers of unemployed. Furthermore, European Community treaties on immigration and minority groups and the European Convention on Human Rights have undermined the ability of EC states unilaterally to attack their minority populations by dealing severely with restive ethnic groups.

Rural and Urban Migrants

Another type of migration that creates strain, albeit of a different order, between established and outsider groups is the movement between urban and rural areas. During the 1950s and 1960s the rural poor moved to cities in search of (better-paid) work. At the same time, affluent urbanites began buying the rural cottages and farms vacated by the migrants for use as weekend homes. Beginning in the 1970s, increasing numbers began acquiring holiday/retirement houses farther away, in poor rural communities in Scandinavia, central France, Italy and elsewhere along the Mediterranean and, I suspect, more recently, in eastern Europe.

The friction and discrimination caused by the arrival of rural migrants in French, Italian and Spanish cities has been widely discussed. The effect of urban migrants on rural areas is less well documented (but see Brunt 1974). There are few studies of the impact of holiday-home owners (some exceptions are Esmeyer 1982; Gilligan 1987; Ireland 1987) or of the winter migration of growing numbers of less affluent elderly north Europeans to empty holiday accommodation in Spain and Malta. Nevertheless, the phenomenon of a second residence is widespread and growing.

For example, by 1984 in Gaiole in Chianti, one-third of the housing stock was owned by outsiders, mostly British and German but also Florentine and Roman (Verster 1985). In Malta, old 'character houses' vacated by villagers who have moved to new houses are being acquired by foreigners and wealthy Maltese townies in search of more tranquil and 'traditional' surroundings. Thus in many villages the core area is being slowly abandoned by natives and reoccupied and gentrified by wealthy outsiders who live next to natives who cannot afford to move (Boissevain 1986). If in Malta this has given rise to few incidents, arson attacks on holiday homes in Wales and Corsica demonstrate that the relations between locals and outside holiday-home owners can become fraught with tension.

Tourism

Ever-increasing hordes of tourists are streaming into the ancient cities, countryside and peripheral areas of Europe. In 1990, some 187 million tourists travelled to West European countries. Of these visitors, more than eight out of ten came from other European countries. (See Table 2.1. Owing to the unavailability of comparable statistics, the table underrepresents the totals, since it does not include Scandinavian destinations and often shows arrivals at accommodation rather than at frontiers). It is clear, however, that hundreds of millions of outsiders are annually entering, lodging in and exploring European countries. Each year their numbers increase.

The motives that impel tourists to undertake costly and sometimes gruelling journeys are hotly debated. Some see the tourist as a contemporary pilgrim fleeing the superficiality of modern society in a quest for 'authenticity' (MacCannell 1976). Others view tourists as engaged in a sacred journey to a world free from the constraints of work, time and conformity, a ludic interlude that renews the traveller to be able to cope again with the strictures and structures of everyday life (Graburn 1977). It is obvious, I think, that it is not possible to attribute a single motive to the millions of tourists. They have different motives and, globally speaking, their tastes are changing. Just as consumers became increasingly dissatisfied with standard, mass-produced goods, and demanded more varied and customized products, so today's tourists are rejecting standard mass package tours. More and more are seeking individualized holidays that cater for their desire for learning, nostalgia, heritage, and for a closer look at the Other. Not sun, sea and sand, but culture and nature have become the objects of the post-modern post-tourist (Urry 1990).

Regardless of their motives, tourists are outsiders who penetrate established communities for short periods and impinge upon indigenous populations. In some places tourist curiosity has fostered an awareness of local culture. In Malta, for example, tourist interest in parish celebrations has helped to make these

Table 2.1: 1990 Tourist Arrivals at European Frontiers

Country	Total Arrivals	Market Share from Europe %	Change in Total Arrivals 1989–1990 %
Austria*	19,011,397	87.76	4.4
Cyprus	1,600,170	82.23**	10.3
France	53,157,000	83.36	5.9
Germany*	15,626,858	68.55	6.6
Gr. Britain***	18,021,000	60.42	3.9
Greece	8,873,310	88.92	9.8
Ireland	3,666,000	84.53	5.2
Italy*	20,862,965	74.08	1.4
Luxembourg*	820,476	91.10	−6.1
Malta	871,675	90.91	5.2
Netherlands*	5,795,100	80.94	11.3
Portugal	8,019,919	92.56	12.7
Spain*	12,251,352	84.91	−12.2
Switzerland*	10,523,964	72.58	4.3
Yugoslavia*	7,879,529	92.96	−8.7
Total	186,880,715	82.39	3.6

* = Arrivals of tourists from abroad in all accommodation establishments.
** = 1989
*** = Visitor departures at frontiers.
Source: World Tourism Organization 1992

more acceptable to the middle-class urban élite, who had looked down upon them as old-fashioned, rustic affairs. Yet these events formed part of the indigenous cultural legacy. This heritage became particularly important to a new nation searching for its cultural identity after imitating the drama and art of its foreign masters for more than 450 years. Thus, partly thanks to tourist interest, religious pageantry is beginning to play a new role in Malta. It is being accepted by government, many young intellectuals and, somewhat more grudgingly, by some members of the urban middle class as an important national asset. Increasingly it is figuring alongside sun and sea as part of the image that Malta projects of itself to qualify as an Other worth visiting. The general interest that tourists have shown in the country has increased Maltese self-confidence (Boissevain 1991).

There has been surprisingly little friction along the Mediterranean coast in summer between the mass tourist intent on celebrating sun and sea, and locals trying to do much of the same thing. Both are celebrating a brief period of freedom, a bit of anti-structure (a bit of the Other?) at the same time. But as the tourist gaze increasingly moves away from seaside ghettos in search of culture and unique events, it is reaching into backstage regions, gradually penetrating the daily lives and private domains of the hosts.

Cultural tourists, now growing bolder, are also setting out on their own to look at what has been sold to them. For example, in the Austrian village of Stuhlfelden, German tourists slipped uninvited into a private party and were observed peering into closed rooms and cupboards. The indignant hosts, keenly aware of the community's dependence on German visitors, were afraid to say anything (Droog 1991). In September 1993, Maltese friends celebrating the annual festa of St Leonard in Kirkop discovered two Germans peering about inside their house. The curious couple had come to the village with a festa tour, and had simply opened the glass inner door and walked into their brightly lit front room. Our friends politely showed them out. Then, to protect their privacy, they closed the wooden outer door that is always left open during the festa to display festive furnishings and decorations to passers-by.

Other anthropologists have recently reported the stumbling about of tourists in domestic back regions in Sardinia, Austria, the Lofoten Islands (Odermatt 1991; Puijk 1992). To protect themselves from such intrusion, but also to celebrate their own identity and re-create community sentiment eroded during the frenetic, competitive holiday season, host populations are closing certain attractions to tourists or celebrating when tourists are absent (cf. Boissevain 1991; Cruces and Diaz de Rada 1992; Crain 1992; Poppi 1992). Such episodes will multiply as cultural tourism is marketed to the masses. While intellectuals and guides in tourist destinations look forward to increasing cultural tourism, in the long run I think it will create more friction and have a greater impact on local culture than mass seaside tourism, where visitors were content to remain enclosed in ghettos.

Nostalgia

Another trend characteristic of today and likely to continue into the future is a romantic longing for an idealized past. Around the beginning of the 1970s a number of developments took place which affected attitudes towards the present and influenced thinking about the past. Established authority and the belief in continuing economic growth and its benefits were challenged, almost simultaneously, by the 1968 Paris student revolt; the anti-Vietnam War demonstrations in the United States; the sobering analysis of the Club of Rome's *The Limits of Growth: A Report on the Predicament of Mankind* (1972); the publication of Schumacher's *Small is Beautiful: A Study of Economics as if People Mattered* (1973); and, spectacularly, by the 1973 energy crisis and OPEC's challenge to the industrialized West. Seen collectively, these amounted to a serious reappraisal of just what the frenetic economic boom of the 1960s and the post-war drive for modernization had achieved. A concern for a new concept, the 'quality of life', emerged. This new look led to the reappraisal and idealization of, among other things, community customs and rituals and the 'traditional' community-centred rural way of life, abandoned in the quest for modernization. This reappraisal, in turn, has created an interest in the environment, history and traditional rituals, not to mention organic foods, working men's clothes, stripped pine furniture, home brewing, children's games, and farmhouse holidays. In Malta, for example, farming and craft implements, even ploughs and entire carts, have joined the classical statues, urns and swords that traditionally adorned the hallways and courtyards of the middle classes.

Nostalgia is being commoditized. The number of heritage parks and costumed pageants celebrating past events has multiplied spectacularly (Hewison 1987). For example, no less than £127.2 million was invested in heritage and museums in Britain during the first six months of 1988 (Urry 1990:105). Heritage and museums has become an industry. While until the early 1970s most British museums were publicly owned, 56 per cent of recently opened museums have been private ventures (ibid.:106).

The heritage industry purports to present history. But since 'traditional' artefacts are displayed and events are staged in part to mark boundaries and (re)establish community solidarity *vis-à-vis* growing numbers of outsiders, as well as to earn money, they invariably present an idealized, non-controversial, generally accepted version of the past. The past of most European communities was characterized by class conflict, exploitation, violence and factionalism. Authentic history, if displayed, would divide, not unite communities.

Sue Wright, for example, has described how in response to requests from local activists in a depressed district in north-eastern England, she and a colleague attempted to re-create community spirit by piecing together local history and symbols in a celebratory framework. Their efforts were only partly successful. Their invented galas were welcomed, but the authentic (critical) history that they had injected to stimulate reflection on the district's development problems was swiftly eliminated. Local residents and, in particular, politicians, found authentic history too politically divisive to be acceptable (Wright 1992).

Conclusions

Recent economic and political upheavals in eastern Europe and the steadily rising standard of living in western Europe have thus combined to increase ethnic and class heterogeneity, by bringing various categories of new Others – unemployed homeless locals, migrant labourers, political refugees, tourists – into established communities. This process will be accelerated as the Maastricht Treaty takes effect. The introduction of outsiders with widely different customs into relatively homogeneous neighbourhoods has created suspicion, jealousy and fear, and will continue to do so. Established natives have reacted by closing ranks, by attempting to re-establish contact with each other, by redefining and projecting the essence of their own identity through rituals, but also increasingly by means of violence. This action to establish clear boundaries between 'us' and 'them' is redefining existing communities and creating new communities. Everywhere in Europe 'communities' are multiplying and there is renewed concern with local identity and concomitant symbolic and physical activity at the interface between these multiplying communities.

While it is difficult to predict developments, it seems likely that the anthropology of Europe, at least for the next decade, will be influenced by the effects of the trends that I have attempted to set out. Thus, many of the next generation of anthropologists working in Europe will examine the emerging subcultures of the many new communities; they will explore the new modes of production; they will examine the nature of the escalating dialectic of racism and xenophobia that is engulfing Europe; they will examine the symbolic and political economic techniques communities use to confront each other and to mark and to protect their borders; they will try to understand the habits and motives of tourists and the reactions of the hosts; and they will further explore the nostalgia gripping 'post-industrial' society.

It is even more difficult to foresee the theoretical course such studies will take. What is certain is that there will be changes, if only because many in each generation seek to free themselves from the hegemony of the preceding generation (cf. Boissevain 1974). It is likely, therefore, that the present intense concern with symbolism, deconstruction and reflexivity will give some ground to a greater interest in the pragmatics of survival. When confronted with structural unemployment, growing homelessness, racist violence and neighbours who slaughter each other, a concern with speculative symbolic analysis and academic rhetorical techniques pales. Political and economic dimensions, recently somewhat neglected, may therefore become more important, as they were following the Second World War and decolonization. Their analysis can be enriched by insights developed during the past decade of intense cognitive and reflexive exploration. Perhaps this will occur with less concern for Self and more regard for Others. But I hold no crystal ball.

References

Bamford, J. (1987). The Development of Small Firms, the Traditional Family and Agrarian Patterns in Italy. In *Entrepreneurship in Europe. The Social Processes* (eds R. Goffee and R. Scase), pp. 12–24, London.

Bax, M. (1976). *Harpstrings and Confessions. Machine-Style Politics in the Irish Republic*, Assen/Amsterdam.

Blok, A. (1974). *The Mafia of a Sicilian Village, 1860–1960. A study of violent peasant entrepreneurs*, New York.

Boissevain, J. (1974). Towards a Sociology of Social Anthropology. *Theory and Society*, 1, 211–30.

Boissevain, J. (1984). Small Entrepreneurs in Changing Europe. In *Ethnic communities in business. Strategies for economic survival* (eds R. Ward and R. Jenkins), pp. 20–38, Cambridge.

Boissevain, J. (1986). Residential Inversion: The Changing Use of Social Space in Malta, *Hyphen*, 5, 55–71.

Boissevain, J. (1991). Ritual, Play and Identity: Changing Patterns of Celebration in Maltese Villages. *Journal of Mediterranean Studies*, 1, 87–100.

Boissevain, J. (ed.) (1992). *Revitalizing European Rituals*, London.

Boissevain, J. and Friedl, J. (eds) (1975). *Beyond the Community: Social process in Europe*, The Hague.

Boissevain, J. and Grotenbreg, H. (1988). Culture, structure, and ethnic enterprise: the Surinamese of Amsterdam. In *Lost Illusions. Caribbean Minorities in Britain and the Netherlands* (eds M. Cross and H. Entzinger), pp. 221–49, London.

Bouquet, M. and Winter, M. (eds) (1987). *Who From Their Labours Rest? Conflict and practice in rural tourism*, Aldershot.

Brunt, L. (1974). *Stedelingen op het platteland. Een antropologisch onderzoek naar de verhouding tussen autochtonen en nieuwkomers in Stroomkerken* (Urbanites in the Countryside. An anthropological study of the relation between locals and newcomers in Stroomkerken), Meppel.

Brusco, S. (1982). The Emilian Model: productive decentralization and social integration. *Cambridge Journal of Economics*, 6, 167–84.

Cohen, A. P. (ed.) (1982). *Belonging. Identity and Social Organization in British Rural Cultures*, Manchester.

Cohen, A. P. (1985). *The Symbolic Construction of Community*, Chichester, London.

Cohen, A. P. (ed.) (1986). *Symbolising Boundaries. Identity and*

Diversity in British Cultures, Manchester.
Crain, M. (1992). Pilgrims, *Yupeez* and Media-Men: The Transformation of an Andalusian *Romeria*. In *Revitalizing European Rituals* (ed. J. Boissevain), pp. 95–112, London.
Cross, M. and Entzinger, H. (eds) (1988). *Lost Illusions. Caribbean Minorities in Britain and the Netherlands*, London.
Cruces, F. and Diaz de Rada, A. (1992). Public Celebrations in a Spanish Valley. In *Revitalizing European Rituals* (ed. J. Boissevain), pp.62–79, London.
Droog, M. (1991). 'En Dan Word Je Weer Gewoon Mens.' Het opleven van feesten in een Oostenrijkse dorp (`And then you become human again.'The revival of celebrations in an Austrian village), unpublished MA dissertation, Department of Anthropology, University of Amsterdam.
Esmeyer, L. (1982). *Marginal Mediterraneans: Foreign settlers in Malta, their participation in society and their contribution to development*, Amsterdam.
Firth, R. (1954). Social Organization and Social Change. *Journal of the Royal Anthropological Institute*, **84**.
Gershuny, J. (1978). *After Industrial Society. The emerging self-service Economy*, London.
Gilligan, H. (1987). Visitors, Tourists and Outsiders in a Cornish Town. In *Who From Their Labours Rest? Conflict and practice in rural tourism* (eds M. Bouquet and M. Winter), pp.65–82, Aldershot.
Graburn, N. H. H. (1977). Tourism: The Sacred Journey. In *Hosts and Guests. The anthropology of tourism* (ed. V. Smith), pp. 17–31, Philadelphia.
Hewison, R. (1987). *The Heritage Industry*, London.
Ireland, M. (1987). Planning Policy and Holiday Homes in Cornwall. In *Who From Their Labours Rest? Conflict and practice in rural tourism* (eds M. Bouquet and M. Winter), pp.65–82, Aldershot.
Kuhn, T. S. (1970). *The Structure of Scientific Revolutions* (2nd edn), Chicago.
Leach, E. R. (1954). *Political Systems of Highland Burma*, London.
MacCannell, D. (1976). *The Tourist. A new theory of the leisure class*, New York.
Manning, F. E. (ed.) (1983). *The Celebration of Society: Perspectives on contemporary cultural performances*, Bowling Green.
Odermatt, P. (1991). Over de Nuraghen en Wat Verder Over de Zee Kwam. Een onderzoek naar het toerisme in Sardinië'

(Concerning Nuraghe and other things that came across the sea. A study of tourism in Sardinia), unpublished MA dissertation, Department of Anthropology, University of Amsterdam.

Poppi, C. (1992). Building differences. The political economy of tradition in the Ladin Carnival of the Val di Fassa. In *Revitalizing European Rituals* (ed. J. Boissevain), pp.113–36, London.

Puijk, R. (1992). Tourism and modernization in a Lofoten fishing village, paper presented at the 2nd Conference of the European Association of Social Anthropology, Prague, 28–31 August 1992

Sabel, C.F. (1982). *Work and Politics. The division of labor in industry*, Cambridge.

Schneider, J. and Schneider, P. (1976). *Culture and Political Economy in Western Sicily*, New York.

Turner, V. (1974). *Dramas, Fields, and Metaphors. Symbolic action in human society*, Ithaca and London.

Turner, V. (1983a). The Spirit of Celebration. In *The Celebration of Society: Perspectives on contemporary cultural performances* (ed. F. E. Manning), pp. 187–91, Bowling Green.

Turner, V. (1983b). 'Carnaval' in Rio: Dionysian drama in an industrializing society. In *The Celebration of Society: Perspectives on contemporary cultural performances* (ed. F. E. Manning), pp.103–24, Bowling Green.

Urry, J. (1990). *The Tourist Gaze. Leisure and travel in contemporary societies*, London.

Verrips, J. (1977). *En boven de polder de hemel. Een antropologische studie van een Nederlands dorp 1850–1971*, Amsterdam, 1977.

Verrips, J. (1980). The polder and the heavens above: An anthropological study of a Dutch village 1850–1971, *The Netherlands' Journal of Sociology*, **16**, 49–67.

Verster, A. (1985). Tweede Huis Toerisme in de Chianti' (Second house tourism in the Chianti), unpublished MA dissertation, Department of Anthropology, University of Amsterdam.

Ward, R. (1988). Caribbean business enterprise in Britain. In *Lost Illusions. Caribbean Minorities in Britain and the Netherlands* (eds M. Cross and H. Entzinger), pp. 204–20, London.

World Tourism Organization, (1992). *Yearbook of Tourism Statistics*, **2**.

Wright, S. (1992). Heritage or Critical History: The Re-Invention of Mining Festivals in North-East England. In *Revitalizing European Rituals* (ed. J. Boissevain), pp. 20–42, London.

Chapter 3

From the Mediterranean to Europe: Honour, Kinship and Gender

Victoria A. Goddard

This chapter addresses two areas of work that have contributed to the development of the anthropology of Europe. The first concerns the literature on honour and shame which was – and, for many, still is – central to the definition of the area of study. However, in this case, the area of study was not Europe but the Mediterranean. As was explained in the Introduction, the Mediterranean has been poorly delimited and theorized. Anthropologists have on the whole been reluctant to elaborate a clear definition of the area, and have instead followed a haphazard and contradictory approach, aimed at deriving a unity from the intrinsic characteristics of the data. Historians have been more successful here, and some anthropologists have taken their work as a point of departure for their own work, and as a validation of the area as an appropriate object of study (Braudel 1973; Davis 1977). Nevertheless, the general lack of rigour in defining the Mediterranean has undermined the potential contribution of workers in this area.

The first section of the chapter will examine some of the limitations of the Mediterranean literature on honour and shame in order to propose a broader comparative perspective than that offered by the concept of 'the Mediterranean'. The second section considers the study of kinship, which, as anthropologists inevitably point out, has been central to the discipline since the nineteenth century. However, studies of kinship in Europe raised a number of difficulties for anthropologists, not least because of the discipline's conceptual baggage and theoretical concerns, which were ill-suited to the analysis of European societies. Because of these difficulties, the study of kinship has focused largely on the family.

Although studies of the family were pioneered in urban research in Europe (e.g. Firth 1956; Firth, Hubert and Forge 1969; Bott 1957),[1] here too there was a significant shift away from studying within a European context and towards a Mediterranean one. Although here work on the family and kinship has had a lower profile than honour and shame, it has also been considered a central item on the research agenda. In a series of seminars held in Nicosia in 1970 to mark the birth of the new Mediterranean Centre, Peristiany identified the theme of Mediterranean family structures as one of the main foci of Mediterranean anthropological research because 'It provides an excellent tool for the investigation of "traditional" values and institutions and a useful introduction to the study of social change' (Peristiany 1976: 1). Yet general conclusions regarding the nature of kinship in European societies appear to break down the assumed `unity of the Mediterranean' cultivated by the honour and shame literature. It is this contradiction, latent within Mediterranean and European anthropology, which will be explored in this chapter.

Anthropological research in the Mediterranean has been largely concerned with small-scale communities and traditional cultural values. Assumptions regarding traditional society underscored work on both honour and kinship. Social change was generally seen as resulting from the impact of external modernizing forces which were either accommodated or resisted. While these assumptions provided an implicit basis for the continuity and legitimation of work in the Mediterranean, they have arguably limited the scope of inquiry.

Furthermore, within both these areas of research, gender ideals and gender roles constitute a significant, if not a central, consideration. In fact, the unity of the Mediterranean has often been predicated on the basis of the specific character of gender ideals that are purported to predominate here. This is the case with the earlier literature on honour and shame (Peristiany 1965; Campbell 1964) and is also stated more explicitly in some of the recent literature, particularly in the work of Gilmore (1987a). But although ideals of masculinity and femininity and related behaviour are

---

1. Firth's research in Britain was part of an innovative and ambitious collaborative arrangement with David Schneider, who carried out parallel research in the United States.

extensively documented and discussed, this is not done in the light of theories of gender. Rather, the material congeals around the pole of meaning of 'honour', generally understood to be male reputation, and gender difference remains assumed and untheorized. Gender issues are also prominent in discussions of kinship in the area. Peristiany (1976) argued that the different degrees and forms of integration of women into the different family types identified by anthropologists in the Mediterranean area provided important criteria for defining and characterizing these societies. The status of women has often been used as a gauge of the relative modernization and progress of individual societies and cultures (Goody 1983; Moors 1991). This, and the assumptions that inform this approach, have affected the development of the anthropology of Europe, and particularly that of the Mediterranean. Consequently, we find a paradox, whereby male and female positions and domains are exposed, yet remain untheorized in relation to gender.

It is from the perspective of gender that these two fields will be discussed, with a view to opening up exploration of more rigorous and more effective frameworks for comparison. The aim is to outline a critique of the category of the Mediterranean as an object of study. While Europe represents a more appropriate unit of analysis and comparison, we should be aware of some of the dangers involved in an uncritical acceptance of Europe as the alternative object of study. The paper suggests that gender provides a link between studies of kinship and studies of honour and shame, and that by integrating these fields progress can be made towards generating new proposals for anthropological research. These would enable us to suggest themes for research within Europe, whilst recognizing the value of comparisons on a wider basis.

Honour, Shame and the 'Mediterranean'

Peristiany's edited volume on honour and shame (1965) assumes that the Mediterranean is a relevant area of analysis, where patterns of behaviour allow for comparison and the drawing of general conclusions. These essays assert that in a wide-ranging area, from southern Portugal to Turkey and southern France to north Africa, people are preoccupied with reputation (apparently to a greater extent than elsewhere), and that this concern is embodied in concepts of honour and shame. The emphasis in the literature has been generally on honour – shame being seen as a rather residual category – and on male honour in particular. Later generations of anthropologists have raised many doubts and questions regarding these characterizations (Lever 1985; Llobera 1986; Goddard 1987; Herzfeld 1980; Pina-Cabral 1989) and many chose to circumvent these concepts altogether (Reiter 1975; Hirschon 1978), or to seek alternatives or modifications to improve a general framework (Herzfeld 1987; Giovannini 1987) or to take account of local specificities (Abu Zahra 1970, 1974; Wikan 1984; Loizos and Papataxiarchis 1991). Yet in spite of the problems raised, as late as 1987 the Mediterranean was re-proposed – or some might say confirmed – as a valid unit of analysis, which was to be defined, precisely, in terms of the honour and shame complex (Gilmore 1987b).

One of the consequences of a persistent anthropological focus on honour and shame has been a narrow restriction in the anthropologists' concerns. The reification of honour pre-empted the need for explanation and analysis. On the contrary, a number of institutions and practices have been attributed to the code of honour when they required an explanation in their own right. A second, and related problem, is that debates regarding the Mediterranean have taken place within an enclosed and self-contained discourse, and have effectively resisted the impact of inputs and developments originating in other areas of anthropological enquiry. Thus, although discussions regarding honour and shame revolve principally around gender relations and the construction of gender identities, there has been little exchange between the abundant material gathered under the auspices of honour and the impressive developments that have taken place in the study of gender within anthropology. It is significant that, with the exception of some of the early classical works on the Mediterranean, the by now bulky literature on honour and shame is noticeably absent from Moore's comprehensive introduction to the anthropological study of gender (Moore 1986). Another aspect of the self-contained nature of the honour theme is the inability of much anthropological work in the area to confront the global processes which impinge on local phenomena, a limitation compounded by the tendency to select rural or small-scale communities for the purposes of research.

Many anthropologists have felt uncomfortable with the

constraints and limitations of the dominant anthropological discourse on the Mediterranean. Giovannini, for one, has made a number of attempts to expand and refine the terms of the debate. Furthermore, her efforts have been guided by an awareness of gender difference as a social phenomenon rather than as an outcome of natural characteristics. Her suggestion that we focus on chastity as a circum-Mediterranean code represents an attempt to break with the limitations of the focus on honour (1987). In relation to her work in a Sicilian town she recognizes the impact of wider-ranging institutions, such as the State and the Church, and processes of socio-economic change, which she sees as playing an important role in conditioning cultural codes and behaviour (Giovannini 1981). She also emphasizes the importance of class and of the 'politics of gender'. However, her approach remains enclosed within the terms of definition of a Mediterranean culture area, and this inhibits the possibility of a fuller understanding of regional and national factors. In a later piece (1985), where she discussed the establishment of a small factory in a Sicilian village, Giovannini located the issues within a wider literature which went beyond the terms defined by Mediterranean anthropology and the honour code. This provided new opportunities for comparative analysis, linking State policies, entrepreneurial strategies and gender relations.

Giovannini argued that entrepreneurs in the area, already encouraged by State subsidies aimed at developing the South, were able to draw on local gender stereotypes to justify advantageous employment strategies. Furthermore, these stereotypes were an obstacle to the organizing capacity of women as workers. Giovannini links her own observations to the work of Nash (1985) and Safa (1980) to conclude that employment in industry did not bring about any automatic transformation in gender roles, or indeed in women's consciousness as workers and as women. On the contrary, she suggests that employment strategies may well reinforce pre-existing patterns of gender subordination.

What is significant here is that her discussion relates to a transnational enterprise, whose territorial mobility allows for investment patterns closely aligned with conditions which it deems to be favourable to its operation. Although several conditions are relevant (access to markets, to skilled labour for specialized operations, favourable terms regarding taxation, etc.), the pursuit of cheap and, preferably, passive labour is an important consideration. Women constitute a very high proportion of this cheap, malleable labour force. Indeed, similar conclusions to Giovannini's have been proposed elsewhere, not only in relation to factories in peripheral and semi-peripheral countries of Asia, Africa or Latin America but also in core areas, including areas of Europe. Harris' analysis of multinationals in Co. Mayo, Ireland, is particularly relevant here (1988).[2] As in the Sicilian case, factory production was established in Co. Mayo as a result of a combination of government incentives to industry and the opportunities offered by 'green labour', i.e., workers, in this case women, with little or no previous experience of wage labour and therefore little if any experience of unionization. Both Harris and Giovannini address the question of women's organization and militancy at work, but propose different explanations. Giovannini suggests that the capacity of women to organize is undermined by cultural symbolizations of women as 'virgins' or 'whores', which are ultimately divisive. Harris points out that the level of militancy of the Co. Mayo workers is determined by their own assessment of the conditions of existence of the firms which employ them. Given the unhappy memory of their mothers' and grandmothers' lives of struggle and hardship and their own negative experiences of making ends meet in the absence of locally available work, they are concerned to preserve their jobs, and therefore abstain from protest relating to issues which have a direct bearing on a firm's choice of location (for example comparatively relaxed legislation regarding health and safety). Yet the definition of gender roles is important here as well, not only in providing the specific commodity of (cheap) female labour but also in conditioning peer-group consensus. Thus, Harris explains the lack of enthusiasm regarding demands for child day-care facilities for women factory workers in terms of 'the ambiguities they themselves experience about the relation between maternity and paid employment and, also, from the social pressures imposed by their kin and friendship networks outside of work'(Harris 1988: 156).

Giovannini's approach, rooted in the idea of a Mediterranean cultural unity, ultimately confirms the view of traditional values

2. Although within a global framework Europe as a whole may be seen as a 'core' area, Europe is itself internally differentiated into 'core', 'periphery' and 'semi-periphery' (see Seers *et al.* 1979; Rokkan and Urwin 1983). It is significant that the examples discussed are provided by cases in peripheral, and heretofore rural, areas of Europe.

blocking progress. Harris, on the other hand, recognizes the importance of conceptualizations of gender roles, but locates these more effectively in their spatial and historical context. Nevertheless, both authors illustrate the fact that *women* workers have specific characteristics, not only in relation to their distribution in the labour-force, but also in connection with the factors that impinge on their attitudes and actions as workers. In fact, the significance of the cultural constraints affecting women workers is far from negligible. In the Sicilian town these arise from what Giovannini identifies as the elevation of 'woman' into a dominant symbol (Giovannini 1981). 'Woman' is conceptualized in positive terms as 'mother' and 'virgin', with the Virgin Mary as the paramount ideal. In opposition to these are the negative symbols of 'whore', 'witch' and 'stepmother'. But despite her efforts at elaborating a more comprehensive approach to the question of gender behaviour, Giovannini's horizon is still limited by the assumption of Mediterranean values, implicitly connected to the idea of 'traditional society'. Because of this she fails to contextualize these symbols adequately, and instead envisages them as pertaining to an autonomous symbolic level (associated with tradition) which may affect other areas of social life (for example, the process of modernization). Giovannini thus describes rather than explains, and what she describes are symbols operating within the field of traditional culture rather than within the domain of the 'politics of gender'. It would be more appropriate to consider the symbolic as an integral aspect of different practices. In the case of 'work', the symbolic can be seen as constituting not only the place and role of gendered subjects within specific tasks and industries, but the work-space and process of production and work itself (see Willis 1979; Hearn and Parkin 1987; Magaud and Sugita 1990).

By extending the comparative framework, the validity of Mediterranean values as an explanatory framework is undermined. If Mediterranean tradition cannot account for the ways in which women are conceptualized, the examples outlined might be read as suggesting that greater insights may be afforded by a consideration of the role of religion. This is a tempting alternative to an explanation based on Mediterranean values, given that, within a pseudo-evolutionary perspective, religious thought is often conflated with 'tradition', in opposition to secularization, rationalization and modernization. Furthermore, the view of the

Virgin Mary as ideal woman, and the symbolization of women
which Giovannini describes, coincide with the symbolism and
teachings of the Catholic Church. Both Ireland and Italy have a
history of Church influence and intervention in national politics.
In particular, the Roman Catholic Church has had a significant
impact on State policy regarding family and sexuality, with
important implications for women (Caldwell 1978). But this line
of enquiry demands a careful analysis of the relationship between
Church and State in each specific instance, rather than a reliance
on 'traditional religiosity'. A historical dimension is crucial here,
for, as Giovannini herself points out for the case of Italy, State
legislation has altered significantly since the 1970s. In fact, there
are strong indications that the Catholic Church has lost some of
its power to influence government, and, more importantly, popular
opinion, as illustrated by the defeat of the Church position in the
referenda concerning both the divorce law and the abortion law
in Italy in 1974 and 1981 respectively (Nanetti 1988).[3]

The importance of Catholicism (or religion in general) at both
institutional and individual levels should not be underestimated.
But Catholicism on its own cannot provide a satisfactory
explanation for the behaviour of women in the labour market.
Significant parallels are to be found in women's employment
patterns and attitudes to work in settings which differ markedly
in this respect. Pearson (1988) points out that the high concentration
of women in the assembly phases of production in the UK
electronics industry is comparable to figures from areas as diverse
as the USA, Mexico and South-East Asia. The South Wales case
studied by Pearson again shows parallels with the Irish and Sicilian
material, in that multinationals were able to interact here with
existing gender divisions. So here too the employment of 'green
labour' facilitated the implementation of new forms of labour
management, and discouraged unionization and militancy.

3. Changes in legislation are uneven and respond to very complex and often contradictory
factors. Irish legislation is seen as less 'progressive' than that of Great Britain in some areas, such
as abortion or divorce, whereas it is more 'progressive' in others. In 1993 Irish legislation equalized
the age of consent for homosexual and heterosexual partners at 17. On 18 February 1994 the British
Parliament voted against the equalization of the age of consent between heterosexuals and
homosexuals at 16, and instead brought the age of consent for homosexuals down from 21 to
18. In this respect Britain lags behind many other European countries. There is also a perceived
lag, publicized in the media, between the decisions taken by Parliament (e.g. *re* homosexual rights
and hanging) and the opinion of voters. This is seen to raise issues of democracy and the role of
government, which becomes particularly complex in relation to issues which are defined as
pertaining to 'morality'.

Giovannini's questions regarding the weak militancy of the Sicilian women in her study can usefully be inserted in a wider framework. The implicit juxtaposition of Northern Europe and the Mediterranean, possibly inspired by the unstated contrast between a traditional Mediterranean and a modern North, has tended to reinforce the status of tradition (in this case the values of honour and shame or associated ideas) as explanation for a range of individual and institutional patterns. On the other hand, in this case, an explicit juxtaposition reveals important continuities. These support a critique of honour and shame as concepts with explanatory value, and force us to broaden, and deepen, our inquiry. Thus careful historical analysis, taking into account specificities of secular and religious institutions, provides an important backdrop to the analysis of gender and identity. We are then better placed to identify the specificities of local contexts. We can thus avert the risk of reifying into 'tradition' what in fact may be issues of power, domination and inequality.[4]

On the other side of the Mediterranean, parallel observations have been made with regard to Islam. The North African experience (and indeed, by historical legacy, that of part of Southern Europe as well) could be understood as deriving much of its character from Islam, its teachings and institutions. Such an explanation would be supported by assumptions regarding the opposition between traditional-religious versus modern-secular, and would furthermore reinforce certain assumptions regarding the opposition between Christianity and Islam, where the relative autonomy and oppression of women often plays a central role (Goody 1983).[5] But simplistic conclusions regarding both the impact of Islam and the relative status of women in Islamic cultures have been forcefully challenged. Wikan (1984) provides important insights in her data on Cairo and Oman by focusing on shame rather than honour, the latter being the discourse of official rhetoric and of arenas of male competition. Shame, on the other hand, is a point of reference in everyday life. By exploring shame, she shows

4. This is not to deny the significance of 'tradition'. In fact an appeal to 'tradition' can legitimize a practice or institution, or provide the basis for challenging them. But, echoing the structural-functionalists' discomfort with the evolutionists' use of 'survival' as an explanation of existing practices, I would argue that 'tradition' does not in itself provide the explanation for such practices, and the meaning and content of tradition must itself become the object of scrutiny.

5. Goody says: 'The Islamic world has often been looked upon as a purgatory for women, in implicit contrast to Christian Europe, a continent in which some see pre-industrial England as the particular paradise for the female sex (Macfarlane 1978)' (Goody 1983: 27).

that the system of values and their application is flexible, for the assessment of a woman by her peers is a complex matter, where sexual behaviour and indeed other behaviour is contextualized rather than judged in absolute terms. Local practices respond to a number of factors, and are more fluid and more 'autonomous' than the explanations in terms of 'honour' or Islam allow for.

Abu-Zahra (1970) argues that Islam itself varies historically and contextually (see also Al-Shahi 1987). She criticizes Antoun's explanation (1968) of the code of female modesty in terms of Quranic teachings, which he sees as having a constraining effect on women. Abu Zahra not only points out the sections of the Quran which claim equality for men and women (see also Tillion 1983; Goody 1983); but, more importantly, she warns of the very significant gaps which may exist between the erudite readings of the Quran by specialists and intellectuals on the one hand and popular views and practices on the other. There are wide variations in the interpretations of sacred texts and significant linguistic variations throughout North Africa and the Middle East which impinge on the meaning of the holy message. Furthermore, when we privilege Islam as an explanation of social and cultural phenomena, we risk neglecting the role of State policies and interventions. Abu Zahra points to the different national Personal Status Codes, whose contents vary from country to country. These official codes may not adhere to Islamic law, and may contradict the practices current in specific regions or villages, and thus provide a significant alternative framework or point of reference. What these criticisms suggest is that the relationship between dominant religious institutions, State institutions, and local practices is a complex and uneven one, thus making quite problematic the task of characterizing specific cultural areas.[6]

It is therefore misleading to focus on religion as the sole or primary cause of gender ideologies, without contextualizing the relationship between religion and the State and considering its contents and meanings in different localities and for different groups. But the links between State, religion and gender ideologies,

---

6. Another important consideration is the history of women's organizations and political movements. Moors (1991) suggests that the ommission of studies and/or discussions of feminism in Middle Eastern societies is a symptom of 'orientalism', where the status of women in Muslim societies takes on special significance. For an interesting discussion of the complex dialogues between feminism, Islam, and the West in Turkey see Sirman (1989). See also Kandiyoti (1989) for a discussion of the use of images of woman within State discourses.

flagged by a number of anthropologists, do remain an important consideration. For J. Schneider (1971) the weakness of the state in Southern Europe is identified as a central factor in the formation and centrality of codes of honour. Other anthropologists have argued that strong social concern with women's sexuality and roles reflects the production of boundaries and identities in response to specific State ideologies, as well as to commoditization and capitalist exploitation (Goddard 1987; Sant Cassia 1992). The exploration of the links between gender, family or household, State and religion, provides an interesting focus for comparative analysis, as illustrated by Asano-Tamanoi's comparison of Catalonia and Japan (Asano-Tamanoi 1987). She argues that whereas in Japan the State effectively incorporated men and women as household members, both within State ideologies and in connection with State-sponsored capitalist expansion, in Catalonia the household constitutes an impenetrable entity that beholds centralized authority with suspicion. What these works point to is the importance of integrating these different levels and fields – the local and the global, the personal and the public, the family and the State, which draws us away from a focus on traditional values as a dominant framework for the explanation of social behaviour.

In the early 1960s considerable effort was expended on the creation of an area of study which, though originally seen as integral to an anthropology of Europe, eventually established itself as a quasi-autonomous field of study (see Introduction): the Mediterranean. Central to defining the Mediterranean area was the question of values and their relation to gender difference. This resulted in the collection and discussion of a wealth of empirical data on men and women's behaviour, attitudes and outlook; but the data remained locked into the concept they were meant to define. Thus, an implicit or explicit reference to 'tradition', seen as opposed to the modernity characteristic of Northern Europe and the United States, restricted the field of enquiry and the depth of explanation of a number of institutions and practices. On the other hand, a focus on gender, problematizing gender difference, offers the opportunity of a broader – yet more focused – comparative framework. The explicit juxtaposition of North and South breaks down oversimplifications regarding the status of local tradition and of tradition versus modernity. From such a juxtaposition, it is clear that the problem of gender and work, for example, responds to more complex determinations. The perspective invites us to consider a number of different factors pertaining to the fields of the economic, the political and the ideological.

Gender and the Study of Kinship

While a focus on 'honour' led to generalizations regarding circum-Mediterranean culture, thus suggesting a unity between the southern areas of Christian Europe and Islamic North Africa and the Middle East, kinship studies often stressed the different histories and characteristics of the societies on the two sides of the Mediterranean (Goody 1983). The societies of North Africa shocked the anthropological world by their total disrespect for anthropological expectations. Here the preference was for lineage endogamy or 'keeping the girls of the family for the boys of the family' as Tillion (1983) put it. On the other hand, European societies were also seen to deviate from anthropological expertise and expectations, being characterized by a cognatic system. Anthropologists trained within the British tradition, so firmly anchored in African lineages, were frustrated in their efforts when working in the European context. Here they felt obliged to abandon the study of larger groups and to focus instead on the family and on marriage.

As in the case of honour and shame, a number of assumptions dictated the agenda for research that, coupled with the methodological difficulties already mentioned, discouraged the development of anthropological studies of kinship in Europe. The major influence here was the Parsonian view according to which societies evolved from a peasant social structure, where kinship was an important aspect of social organization, towards a modern society, where kinship lost most of its social functions and became exclusively the locus of sentiment, manifested in the expressive role of the family. Thus, from this perspective, kinship is seen to disappear in modern societies (Bestard 1986: 14, 20).

Strathern attributes this 'vanishing' to the Euro-American view of kinship, specifically the 'English' folk model, which she sees as informing anthropological theories. According to this model kinship is grounded in biology and is concerned with the 'basic facts of life'. As in the case of gender, the facts of kinship were seen to belong to the realm of nature, so that the anthropologist's role was limited to recording and explaining the variations found on a single, natural, theme (Strathern 1992a). Consanguinal relations were considered to be particularly close to the natural model and were seen as 'a virtual fact of nature, a universalism in human arrangements' (Strathern 1992a: 102). Cognatic kinship thus represented the background against which unilineal systems were constructed, and the cognatic systems of Europe appeared as a mere reflection of natural relations, seeming to offer the anthropologist very little potential for the construction of models (ibid.: 103).

Furthermore, in the post-Parsonian view, European kinship was considered to be qualitatively and quantitatively different from systems encountered elsewhere, for here, in contrast to primitive societies where family and kinship were clearly 'embedded', kinship belonged exclusively to the private, domestic sphere. This interpretation limited further the possibilities of exploring the conditions of production and reproduction of kinship and the reproductive strategies of wider groups, as well as the significance of kinship systems within contemporary European societies.

But in spite of these limitations developments did take place. In particular, Lévi-Strauss' distinction between elementary and complex systems of kinship and marriage offered the opportunity of locating contemporary European societies within the field of the comparative study of kinship systems. Héritier (1981) took up the challenge, and her work on semi-complex and complex systems helped place European kinship on a continuum with other systems, legitimizing and facilitating rigorous anthropological study. Her work, and that of others largely inspired by her, showed that over time there were significant patterns to the systems of marriage exchanges. The approaches that emerged from these insights were historical in orientation, and relied on a combination of oral accounts, family memory and official records and statistics, as well as the more conventional fieldwork methods (Segalen 1986; Segalen and Zonabend 1987; Zonabend 1984; Bestard 1986).

The importance of a historical approach becomes especially clear when we consider the tradition of research into the history of marriage, family and household in Europe (Flandrin 1979; Anderson 1980; Laslett and Wall 1972). A historical perspective also contributes to a clearer understanding of the central issues, and encourages the questioning of assumptions which underlie our approach to these phenomena, which is perhaps an especially important exercise in the European context (Rapp 1987).[7]

From the other side of the Channel, Goody challenged claims regarding the uniqueness of European kinship and society, implicit in the anthropologist's silence and explicit in much historical work, particularly that of MacFarlane (1978). Goody also espoused a historical approach to kinship; but rather than applying this to one region, he looked for systems in transformation over time and space (1983, 1991). He too is primarily concerned with marriage, but his focus is the transmission of property, specifically the impact of transmission of property to daughters. Here Goody stresses the influence of Church and State on local practices.[8]

But, as Segalen and Zonabend (1987) argue, there is more to kinship than the transmission of patrimony. It is also to do with the transmission of memory and the construction of identity. One of the most interesting developments within the field of studies of complex alliances in European settings is the understanding of kinship and marriage as constituent elements in the formation of identities, whether personal, local or regional (Zonabend 1984; Bestard 1986). Here again kinship links up with wider processes and institutions, reflected in the way family history evades, accommodates or transcends History – in the sense of events at the level of State and Church. At the same time, kinship is a central arena for the constitution of individual identities and for generating language, symbols and instruments for the construction of personal and more encompassing identities (Bestard 1986; O'Brien, this volume, chapter 9).

Kinship studies in Europe have demonstrated the significant variations over time and space that occur in the arrangement of relations between marriage partners, kin and affines. Although issues of property are frequently important considerations in these arrangements (and these have been studied in detail; see Friedl

7. For example, in Segalen's historical account of the peasant household in France (1983) the units of analysis – the household and the family – are problematized and therefore explored, as are gender relations. Indeed, this work contradicts many assumptions and simplifications regarding the peasant household, and indicates that there are significant regional variations in household form and patterns of exploitation of the land, as well as in the internal and external relationships which underpin them. Associated with these variations are different configurations of gender relations and different distributions of power within the household. Neither the household nor gender relations can be considered fixed and natural.

8. Both Christianity and Islam imposed conditions of limitation on local lineage groups, aimed at breaking down the autonomy and patrimony of such groups. Responses to these pressures ranged from lineage endogamy in North Africa (see also Tillion 1983) to a number of different patterns of endowment.

1963; Loizos 1975; Davis 1973, 1975; Du Boulay 1983; Sant Cassia 1992), the transmission and reproduction of 'symbolic capital' (Bourdieu 1977) is also significant, being central to the construction of identities. Wider-ranging identities, such as nationalism, borrow from the symbolic repertoire of kinship, and indeed of gender.

Because both gender and kinship are associated with the realm of nature, they are at one and the same time powerful sources of images and yet seriously under-theorized areas of study (Collier and Yanagisako 1987). This is particularly the case in the 'too-familiar' context of the study of European societies. The link between gender and kinship has been made explicitly and implicitly from a number of very dissimilar perspectives. For Collier and Yanagisako gender and kinship are constructed in a mutual relationship, and they are 'realized together in particular cultural, economic, and political systems'(1987: 7). This mutuality, though evident in so much of the literature, has not been fully recognized. Instead, the naturalization of both gender and kinship has pre-empted proper treatment and encouraged their conceptualization as two discrete fields, rather than as constituting a single field as envisaged by Collier and Yanagisako. As they suggest, 'both "gender" and "kinship" studies have been concerned with understanding the rights and duties that order relations between people defined by difference'. But difference has been understood as arising from natural rather than social facts (Yanagisako and Collier 1987: 29).[9]

In the anthropology of Europe, and of the Mediterranean in particular, the links between systems of kinship and marriage and gender identity have been recognized and discussed, though in many cases only minimally explored. However, as early as 1972, in his discussion of honour in Algeria and elsewhere in North Africa and the Middle East, Bourdieu explicitly linked the quality of honour to ideals of manliness. These ideals were in turn related to power, from which women were excluded except within the confines of an unofficial or even clandestine domain. Bourdieu's account of the kinship system is a gendered one to the extent that his analysis incorporated gender and power differences as an integral aspect of the system. He argued that many distortions in

9. Collier and Yanagisako recognize their indebtedness to D. Schneider's work on 'American Kinship', which criticized the biological model that he saw as pervading kinship studies. Instead, he promoted the study of kinship as a symbolic system. Collier and Yanagisako wish to suggest a parallel critique in relation to studies of gender (1987: 29).

the data resulted from the anthropologists' acceptance of the 'official' male version, neglecting the unofficial reading which comes from a female perspective. He suggested that men and women used and interpreted the same field of genealogical relationships in different ways. A consideration of both the 'official' and 'unofficial' versions revealed, for example, that the arrangement of marriages did not conform to a normative structure in any simple way, as many anthropological works imply. Instead, marriages depended 'on the state of the practical kinship relations', mobilized by men on the one hand and by women on the other. Thus, power relations, between groups and between women and men, determined the final outcome in each case.

Gender and Personhood

Howell and Melhuus (1993) argue that kinship studies lost their centrality within the discipline during the 1970s and 1980s and, especially towards the end of the 1980s, studies of personhood came to occupy the central arena. Here again gender was a central yet neglected consideration (1993: 7). Personhood and kinship, and the relationships that may hold between them, have been explored quite prominently in some ethnographic areas. Specifically, Strathern's discussion of the Melanesian Garia (1992a) is directly relevant, as this is a society which, like European societies, is cognatic. Nevertheless, the Garia conceptualize personhood in ways which differ radically from those current in Western cognatic societies, and the comparison encourages reflection on the characteristics of European systems and ideas, and the relation between the two:

Strathern suggests that for the Garia the person is composite and androgynous. The person is in fact constituted by and through relationships. This is the case not only for the cognatic Garia, but for other Melanesian societies as well, where the person is a cognatic entity, to be disassembled at death or in other life-crisis situations. The person is seen as embodying social relationships, which are integral to his/her being. There is thus a continuity between person and society which, she argues, is absent in Western European models. Here, the person is thought of as separate from or even opposed to society. Strathern suggests that the folk model of 'English' kinship sees kinship as incapable in itself of explaining social phenomena because of its incompleteness: the achievements of kinship have to be completed by 'society'. Similarly, the person is seen as an incomplete individual – completion has to be realized through socialization and through social relationships. Where kinship's socializing role ended, society took over. And in contrast with other systems, the cognatic system is seen to produce differentiation and heterogeneity. In English kinship unique individuals are produced as a hybrid, constituted by a specific combination of inherited genetic traits and completed by the experience of social relations.

Strathern's discussion of cognatic systems and personhood in Melanesian and Euro-American systems reveals not only the difficulties involved in comparative analyses, but also the complexities of the interrelations of kinship and person and conceptualizations of society and of the self. There is of course no simple correspondence between personhood and kinship type. Nevertheless, it is still useful to explore the ways in which kinship systems and family forms, residence patterns, or household relations are involved in the production and reproduction of personhood. Gender is an obvious consideration here, being an integral aspect of personhood in European societies.[10] According to Rapp, the Euro-American family 'is still the primary locus for the reproduction, transmission and transformation of cultural notions of gender and generation' (Rapp 1987: 125; also Barrett and McIntosh 1985). Rapp argues that this family type forms individuals with notions of gender which are tied to ideas of motherhood, and in particular with maternity, and of a fatherhood which is seen as revolving around economic responsibility. At the same time, `childhood' is imbued with ideas of progressive development.

This implies that the way the family is conceptualized and the way in which roles within it are constructed are generative of ideas of self and of relative power and exclusion that characterize the *different* selves that are created from this context (see Rubin 1975). The impact of ideals of motherhood on gender identity (especially but not only female identities) is, arguably, especially important in generating difference built on the basis of gender discontinuities.

10. However, as Strathern (1992a) points out, there is no one-to-one correspondence between gender identity and notions of personhood, and a particular individual may not have a singular gender identity. Howell and Melhuus (1993) also point out that more than one concept of personhood may exist in any given society.

For Irigaray, the symbolic universe expressed through family and kinship has particularly significant consequences for women's subjectivity. 'Motherhood' provides the focus for a definition of 'woman' which runs through the entire Western philosophical tradition. Whereas 'man' is recognized as separate and separable from 'father', there is no space within (male-centred) discourse for 'woman' disassociated from 'mother' (Irigaray 1977).

These considerations shed new light on Giovannini's Sicilian material. We are now further removed from Mediterraneanness and are closer to an understanding of these constructs of gender, and related symbols and images, as variants of a more pervasive discourse about social relations and conceptualizations of personhood and society (cf. Goddard 1988; Sant Cassia 1992). Furthermore, the difference created by this discourse is itself generative of differences in power, so that power is intrinsic to subjectivity and personhood.

There is a danger that, by concentrating on family and kinship, we may reproduce the conception of family and kinship as pertaining to an enclosed, private sphere, removed from, or even opposed to 'society'. This means not only that we reproduce ideological discourses regarding the family, but also that we limit and distort interpretation. For example, Loizos and Papataxiarchis (1991) express dissatisfaction with analyses of gender in Greece which over-emphasize the family as the domain for the definition and realization of gender relations. Instead, they propose the exploration of concepts of gender expressed beyond the family and outside marriage, where they may assume different forms, possibly challenging ideas of masculinity or femininity current in the language of kinship and family. Undoubtedly, there are many contexts where individuals and groups are able to shift and alter the conditions of their identity and sexuality, and these provide a useful focus of study. But the limitations they identify derive not so much from the anthropologists' overemphasis on kinship, as from a particular conceptualization of kinship: as distinct and opposed to the public arena or to the politico-jural domain (Collier and Yanagisako 1987).

It is more productive to see the family as 'an uncertain form whose intelligibility can only come from studying the system of relations it maintains with the sociopolitical level' (Donzelot 1980: xxv). From this perspective the family becomes a point of intersection of a number of often contradictory discourses and practices. For however the family might be thought about (as natural and permanent or as breaking down and in crisis) sociologically the family is seen as changing, as in a state of flux, as are the relationships that constitute it. In addition, this perspective obviates the dangers of studying the family as an isolated entity, to be understood exclusively in its own terms, abstracted from its historical context. On the contrary, there is an evident continuity between family and kinship relations and other relations that we can describe as social, economic or political.

The family has been at the heart of debates regarding social change, specifically the development of capitalism in areas of Europe, and indeed the successful development or otherwise of capitalism world-wide. The family has frequently been singled out not only as a relevant factor or indicator of social change, but also as a causal factor of this change and of the character of socio-political structures. The debates that have taken place in social history have largely revolved around the question of the specificities of the European or the English family and their consequences for the development of capitalism (Laslett and Wall 1972; MacFarlane 1978; but see also Anderson 1980; Goody 1983, 1991). However, the relationship between family form, individual orientations and social ideologies is hardly straightforward.[11]

This relationship has been explored by Todd (1985), who develops Le Play's classification of family types in Europe, concentrating on two central criteria, those of liberty and of equality, and their implementation within different family types. For Todd, the family reproduces people and values. The latter are absorbed unconsciously and automatically by each new generation from the preceding one, feeding into individual views and behaviour. Todd believes that the nature of what he calls the 'elementary' or 'human' relations that in each family type are produced between its members is then reflected in 'second' or 'social' relations. Thus, an egalitarian family structure will generate not only egalitarian sentiments between siblings but also a predisposition towards an egalitarian ideology in relation to politics and government.

---

11. Poster (1978) warns against the dangers of determinism, and argues that, in order to avoid a simple reduction of subject to family form, when studying the family we must incorporate a psychoanalytic dimension. In spite of the methodological difficulties, we should strive to understand the 'emotional structures' as well as the material implications of different family systems.

From Todd's perspective, 'the ideological system is everywhere the intellectual embodiment of family structure, a transposition into social relations of the fundamental values which govern elementary human relations...' (Todd 1985: 12). Just as MacFarlane explains the origins of English individualism and hence capitalism through the character of the English family, so Todd explains the French Revolution as an extension of values pertaining to the family type characteristic of the Paris region (1985: 14). He identifies two kinds of individualism: the liberal (but not egalitarian) Anglo-Saxon individualism generated by an absolute nuclear family type and the liberal and egalitarian 'Latin' individualism, associated with the egalitarian nuclear family type characteristic of many areas of France and Southern Europe as well as Latin America. These have different implications for the ideological and institutional characteristics of these societies. Whereas mass politics is now universal, Todd sees its form as depending on the orientations generated by different family types. Thus, he explains historical differences across Europe: National Socialism by Germany's authoritarian family, stressing discipline and inequality; Soviet Communism by the Russian community family, based on equality, discipline, parity between brothers and an authoritarian father-figure.

Strathern (1992b) also addresses issues pertaining to the relationship between family and society, between individuals and social structures, albeit with far greater caution. In relation to English kinship specifically, she stresses its characteristics of diversity and discontinuity. In the English system at least there is no simple reproduction and no direct continuity of form or type. Even ideas about change and continuity are discontinuous, since each generation embodies different ideas of change and tradition. Whereas the older generation come to stand for continuity and traditional values, the new generations are associated with change and a greater degree of individualism. 'Out of the fact and direction of generation, the antitheses between convention and choice or relationships and individuality acquire a temporal dimension. . . . Increased variation and differentiation invariably lie ahead, a fragmented future as compared with the communal past' (1992b: 21). Thus the way past, present and future are seen, and the way individual and society are conceptualized, is relational. Generational discontinuity might play a part in how we conceptualize history, and thus in the relationship between self and society.

Davis (1989) points to the usefulness of the generational dynamic discussed by Lisón-Tolosana in his work on Belmonte de los Caballeros. Here changes in context are significant. In Belmonte the 'controlling generation' had been adolescents and army recruits during the Spanish Civil War, and had thus experienced dramatic conflicts and dangers. Their experiences shaped their attitudes to politics, which were cautious. On the other hand, the emerging generation grew up in a quieter, repressive but apolitical world, and their attitude was more assertive, seeking greater freedom and independence. The relationship between the two generations was one of opposition. This oppositional relationship constituted the history of Belmonte between 1900 and 1961, a history of reactive response, of reinterpretation and discontinuities. Davis contrasts this generational form of history, which in Belmonte's controlling generation was a history of 'never again', with the genealogical and 'always so' view of history (belonging to the Zurwaya tribesmen of Libya) and the national (the Libyan State's) version of historical events which he encountered in his own research. These different histories reflect not only differences in context but also in the nature of the social relations (within families and generations, lineages, nations and states) which, as Davis points out, produce history.

'Being' is thus a product of context and of specific relationships. Generation and gender are powerful sources of difference as well as of symbols which speak of difference, discontinuity and inequality. Here again, content and meaning are contingent on the numerous relations and situations which produce them. Todd and others argue that different types of family or indeed of nuclear family involve different configurations of relations and patterns of power-distribution which have implications for gender relations. And if, as Irigaray suggests, motherhood represents the dominant theme in discourses of womanhood which generate and reproduce inequality, it would be important to explore the specific combinations of factors and relations effecting the elaboration of motherhood, and the extent to which and the ways in which these ideas might be deployed in other discourses.

Material and non-material factors combine to affect ideas of personhood. This is explored by Sant Cassia (1992) in his study of the family, and in particular of the transmission of property, in Athens in the late eighteenth and early nineteenth centuries. Sant Cassia shows how the ways in which exchanges of property and goods, together with values and morals, impinge on a number of domestic arrangements and on dominant ideals of motherhood and, more generally, parenthood. As a result of changes in the sphere of exchange, parenthood became central to ideas of personhood. Sant Cassia argues that in nineteenth-century Athens rapid commodification spilled over into the marriage circuit by commodifying dowries. The idea that women were themselves thereby becoming commodities was resisted through the growth and elaboration of a cult of motherhood, which was in turn reflected and expressed within the realm of religious doctrine. Marriage and parenthood became, in nineteenth century Athens, the principal channels for the definition and realization of the self. This was markedly different from earlier conceptions of personhood, which had relied heavily on genealogy and descent. The emphasis on parenting and especially on motherhood was also reflected in the growth of Greek nationalism, which used womanhood, and particularly motherhood, as metaphors for the nation.

The shifts that Sant Cassia traces at the level of the material exchanges in the economy and the marriage circuit represent significant points of change for conceptions of the person. To the process of commodification he introduces the concept of civil society, 'as a causative or shaping agent on the nature of exchange' (1990: 247). For Sant Cassia 'civil society' ultimately shapes the person, influencing and defining circuits of exchange, setting the context of the various spheres of action such as the public and the private, and the terms of exchanges, including marriage. The outcome is the co-existence of two types of morality in Greece: the competitive morality of the public – and male – arena and the morality of self-sacrifice associated with the family (ibid.: 250).

Civil Society and the Study of Kinship[12]

Gramsci (1973) outlined two superstructural 'levels' which he considered central to the understanding of society: 'civil society', 'the ensemble of organisms commonly called "private"' (p. 12), and

---

12. The concept of 'civil society' has a long trajectory in Western political discourse, and its content and meaning have varied significantly. For a useful overview of the use of this concept see Giner (1985) and Gamble (1981). For the purposes of this article my own use will be restricted to the work of A. Gramsci on this topic.

the State or 'political society'. The arena of 'political society' is to do with the State's use of coercion to enforce consensus; 'civil society' is the arena for the function of 'hegemony'. Both functions are for Gramsci 'organizational and connective'. Furthermore, the contents and the boundaries of civil society and political society shift historically, and are thus specific to time and place.

The connectiveness emphasized by the Gramscian perspective has been used to criticize current uses of the public/private dichotomy in the study of gender and to develop an appropriate model of the complexities and contradictions of women's activities in the realms of the family, the labour market and the state. Showstack Sassoon (1987) turns to Gramsci to move beyond the impasse reached by the 'domestic labour debate' and to avert the shortcomings of analyses which reduce the family to the needs of reproduction of capitalism. Showstack Sassoon points out that the relationship between women and the labour market is mediated in contemporary societies by the interventions of the State, which impinge on the family and on women's family labour. Thus, when analysing women, family and work, the intertwining of the domestic and the productive, civil society and the State becomes of central importance. The precise forms of institutions and of social relations are consequent upon the historical trajectory of each country, and of the groups that constitute it. This means that national variations can be considered while simultaneously recognizing common international trends and more general characteristics of late capitalism (Showstack Sassoon 1987:18).

A further advantage offered by the concepts of civil society and of hegemony is that they constitute a framework for seeing power relations outside the field of coercive state structures. This of course is especially relevant to the analysis of gender and kinship. More generally though, they provide space for the question as to 'how will each single individual succeed in incorporating himself into the collective man, and how will educative pressure be applied to single individuals so as to obtain their consent and their collaboration, turning necessity and coercion into "freedom"?' (Gramsci 1973: 242).

It has already been suggested that an approach such as that of Donzelot, which stresses the characteristics of the socio-political domain, is valuable for the study of family and kinship. Developing further the recognition that kinship is not an isolated field, the use of the concept of 'civil society' offers a basis for comparative work.

From this perspective the specific and the local can be understood within the context of changes taking place in a number of different sites. By locating kinship and family within civil society we are emphasizing the links between forms and relations within kinship and wider relations and processes.

It is increasingly clear that when looking at Europe, either historically or synchronically, we are dealing with multiple forms of domestic arrangements, marriages and inheritance patterns. Given the variety of arrangements, Balbo (1987) rejects the usefulness of the term 'family' and suggests that it be replaced by the concept of 'survival units'. Her observations regarding the inaccuracy of seeing 'the family' as nuclear and of this as constituting the norm are well taken. But as she points out, the term 'family' is a charged one. And it is precisely this which makes 'the family' or rather discourses about 'the family' interesting and important.

Balbo points to homosexual unions, single-parent units, couples living in communal arrangements, etc. Strathern's work too shows that there is complexity and differentiation, here seen as characteristic of English kinship. But this diversity does not pose an absolute obstacle to comparative work. The concept of civil society could provide the basis for such a comparative exercise by broadening the analysis out from kinship *strictu sensu* and including other sets of practices and ideas. Barrett and McIntosh's (1985) distinction between familial ideologies and family forms is relevant here, in that notwithstanding statistically significant differences at the level of family and household composition, familial ideologies (which may be somewhat more stable and pervasive than any particular morphology of the units themselves) are important in shaping a number of institutions at the level of the State and of civil society, as well as in providing points of reference and markers for individual experience and subjectivity.[13]

Europe as a useful (though not exclusive) framework for such comparison can be justified not only in terms of common or overlapping histories but also to the extent that the nations and states that constitute it share a number of ideals regarding the

---

13. Barrett and McIntosh distinguish between 'familism' and 'familization' on the one hand, and 'familialism' and 'familialization' on the other. The first two terms refer to politically pro-family ideas and to the strengthening of families themselves. The second pair of terms refer to ideologies modelled on what are thought to be family values and the rendering of other social phenomena like families (1985: 26).

nature of civil society, the role of the State and the forms and intentions of intervention, although the shape and extent of these vary significantly (see Comas d'Argemir, this volume, chapter 10). It is to be expected that increasing harmonization under the auspices of the European Community will result in greater convergence, not only in terms of ideals but, increasingly, in terms of institutions and policies. This is not to say that local practices will be homogenized or adhere strictly to these ideals. On the contrary, local interventions may vary and discourses and practices may take on specific meanings, even, possibly, meanings of resistance to such homogenization. Indeed the different incursions of the State into civil society, the changes in the shape of what it constitutes, may be resisted or accommodated in ways which further differentiate specific localities or particular groups. In fact, one of the expectations of greater European integration is that it will result in an enhancement of the us/them dichotomy, in relation to both external and internal others. It is precisely the tensions resulting from these contradictory processes, the transformations and the disjunctions between different discourses and practices, between civil society and the State, between these and practices and ideas in the fields of kinship, family and personhood which are of interest to the anthropologist, and where s/he can make a significant contribution.

Conclusion

There are precedents within European, and particularly in Mediterranean anthropology, for locating gender and personhood at the heart of family and kinship. The literature has often linked the study of family to ideals of personhood, largely as a result of the anthropologists' emphasis on personal reputation when working in this region. Pitt-Rivers for example suggests that a man's association with his family and his ability to defend it are the most important aspects of the group's assessment of his reputation (1965: 51). At the same time, honour is the central and connecting principle behind the contributions to Peristiany's collection on *Mediterranean Family Structures* (1976).

Peristiany identified family structures as a central area of Mediterranean research. Like Fortes and Evans-Pritchards' collection on African systems of kinship and marriage, Peristiany's collection is concerned with establishing a valid and coherent area of study. The essays included in the volume cover a wide geographical area and a broad range of themes. Indeed, the collection represents a number of different perspectives and problems, from the study of shepherds to the study of shanty-town dwellers. What the contributors illustrated was the variety of social arrangements, which could not be confined easily to any single formula or proposition. It is hard to see how any clear definition of an area, whether based on geographical criteria, on culture or religion could be accomplished, given the level of generality pursued and the empirical disjunction and lack of fit between the competing criteria for such a definition. The rich diversity of the contributions undermines Peristiany's implicit reference to cultural unity, and his task of bringing the various contributions together in his introduction is a difficult one. There is a tension here between the individual anthropologists, aware of the complexity of their case, and the efforts at generalization and at forging a unity which must have appeared as a necessary step towards academic legitimation. In fact, Peristiany has few general conclusions to offer, and his ultimate strategy is to provide a focus by looking at the relationships between women and kinship: the degree of integration of women in the different types of family and the impact of this on 'the intensity of their identification with their husbands' honour' (1976: 2) is, he suggests, a Mediterranean-wide problem, and also appears as the gauge of modernization and change. For Peristiany 'The relationship between degree of social integration, affective orientations and feminine conception of honour would well repay study in the Mediterranean area' (1976: 12). Thus, the question of honour, and indeed of gender, is once again the lens through which the unity of the Mediterranean is visualized.

Different kinship systems and different family forms can be expected to create different types of space for men and women, young and old, and to impinge on female and male subjectivities. More generally, these systems inform processes of acquisition of what Bourdieu calls 'the semi-learned grammars of practice' (1977: 20). Gender ideals and roles, generational relationships, ethnic and class relations, all these are apprehended through lived-in kinship. We should not take this to mean that there is a blanket correspondence between family forms and personality types or socio-political ideologies. As Strathern (1992b) points out, the

English kinship system produces individuals and it produces differentiation. In different ways and to a varying extent we can expect degrees of individuation, differentiation, change and heterogeneity elsewhere. But patterns are discernible. To begin with, heterosexuality is privileged, and marginalizes alternative sexualities and identities, as individuals and relationships are saturated with idioms derived from kinship. Such a privileging of heterosexuality coincides with the significance of parenthood and particularly motherhood as points of reference for the constitution of gender identities. Male and female ideals are intimately tied to ideas about performance in the field of kinship. Here the distinction suggested by Barrett and McIntosh (1985) is particularly useful, for whatever the arrangements of conviviality or commensality, of socialization and authority, familialism informs the processes whereby these differentiated individuals are developed, as well as providing discourses of community and nation with strong symbolic referents. Undoubtedly, beyond the idiom of kinship there are other sources of identity construction and other alternative, even contradictory, elements are available for the elaboration of other practices. Yet there is a continuity here between the person, kinship structures, civil society and the State, both in terms of how reproduction, sexuality and gender inform wider discourses such as nationalism and because there is no clear break in the continuum of actions and ideas, as has been suggested by the opposition between the public and the private or the politico-jural and the domestic domains.

The growing anthropological literature in the area, and in particular the heritage of work carried out in Southern Europe on gender and reputation, offers the possibility of developing that integrated field proposed by Collier and Yanagisako on the one hand and Howell and Melhuus on the other. The suggestion that gender can provide a bridge between until-now disparate areas of study is particularly suggestive. Howell and Melhuus' reference to the anthropology of the person is important. Although the category of the person frequently appears to be abstracted from gender, feminist philosophers and linguists have shown how this construct encompasses and subsumes women under what is essentially a male category.

Gender (at least in the European case, if the Mediterranean literature has any validity) is integral to the construction of subjectivities and to the organization of family and kinship. But the potential insights of perspectives which use gender as the pivot around which individuals and kinship structures might be analysed also have implications for wider identities and their mobilization in the political field. Thus not only can we further our understanding of gender and individual identity, but we are also led directly to the question of history and the changing shape of civil society. And it is here (and not in honour and shame, or a European family type) that we find the springboard for comparative analysis within Europe and between Europe and other areas. For it is in the historical evolution of the continuities and contradictions between ideas and practices of family, gender, individual and society that we can locate our understanding of different societies.

Both the studies derived from a Lévi-Straussian perspective and Goody's work on Eurasian systems go a long way in breaking down assumptions about the discontinuities between Europe and others, and the consequent discontinuities between the anthropology of European societies and the discipline as it has developed elsewhere. Recent studies have accentuated these insights, and the parallels and differences between, for example, English and Melanesian kinship have become clearer and have offered fresh insights. The work of anthropologists in the field of kinship studies in Europe has therefore been extremely productive, and the anthropologist is now well placed to develop a fruitful field. However, taking our cue from Goody, we should bear in mind that Europe as a valid focus or unit of study must be problematized and assumptions of uniqueness avoided, for they have in fact thwarted the anthropological effort here, segregating the discussion and parochializing the terms of reference.

Tillion characterized Mediterranean societies in terms of 'the republic of cousins' (1983). This she contrasted to the 'republic of brothers-in-law' which she saw as characteristic of 'so-called savage society' and the 'republic of citizens' for those societies located in 'the modern sector' (1983: 13). Another way of discussing the qualitative differences between these types could be in terms of the nature of the relations which govern civil society and the relation between civil society and the State. The history and the nature of the interconnections between State, civil society and religion in European and North African countries show significant differences, as well as obvious parallels. A pressing question is that of the relative secularization of the State and of civil society. Given that sexual behaviour, gender roles and women's status are an important focus for secular and religious discourses and interventions, the study of gender and kinship must take into account the contradictory messages and processes unleashed by the relation between State and civil society.

Mediterranean anthropology explored some of the issues relating to the links and gaps between locality and national state, although these attempts have been limited by an emphasis on networks, particularly in the literature on patron–client relations. Ineffectual state bureaucracies have frequently been put forward as causal to certain characteristics of the Mediterranean, from patronage and *mafia* to the code of honour. Anthropologists have been well placed to examine the tensions which may exist between state structures and local relations and between national and local ideologies (Silverman 1975; Pratt 1980; Davis 1989), a tension which can produce 'good patriots' but 'rebellious citizens' (Herzfeld 1985: 26). This of course is an important issue when considering how civil society is constituted and how individuals and groups may or may not respond to or be incorporated into civil society. The question of national and local histories is important here both in terms of how state ideologies might attempt to encompass groups (Davis 1989) and how localities construct a 'social memory' which defines the boundaries and character of localities and their relation to the State as well as to history (Collard 1989; SEGRG 1992; also Zonabend 1984).

The comparison of Northern and Southern shores of the Mediterranean, pioneered by Mediterranean anthropologists, is both feasible and fruitful, given historical convergence and differences. This is not only so in the fields of kinship and gender, but applies also to national identity and the nature of civil society (cf. Davis 1987). The comparison is the more fruitful if it escapes the constraints of the anthropological focus on the honour code. Thus, groups or individual men and women can be located in their practices and relationships (where discourses of honour or tradition may or may not play a part), while these are understood as aspects of wider processes. A systematic comparison which takes account of specific histories, concrete forms and relations between State, religion and civil society, would avoid reproducing the assumptions underlying 'the Mediterranean'. In relation to gender, the continuities and differences revealed by a comparison of European and North African cases can only enrich our understanding; but this must be accomplished on the basis of rigorous and clearly defined terms of comparison, and not within the complacent climate generated by a reliance on Mediterranean values and tradition.

A similarly productive, and urgent, exercise would be a comparison between Western and Eastern Europe. Gramsci argued that, at the time of his writing, in most advanced countries civil society had become a very complex structure. The history of these countries could be summarized as one of increasing secularization of the State and civil society. On the other hand, speaking for Russia up to the Second World War, Gramsci described a situation in which 'the State was everything, civil society was primordial and gelatinous' (1973: 238). The very specific transformation of State and civil society in Russia or elsewhere in Eastern Europe since that period and the rapid and dramatic changes that have affected the ex-Comecon countries make for very particular configurations of relations and ideas in connection with the State and civil society, with important implications for gender and kinship relations and ideologies.

The argument of this chapter is that we have much to glean from Mediterranean anthropology. The way forward, however, is not to reproduce the terms and concepts of that specialization but instead to broaden the analysis in two senses. One is that gender and kinship should be understood as relevant to personhood, while located within the broader contexts of civil society and indeed in connection with the construction of far-reaching identities such as nationalism. Secondly, that Europe rather than the Mediterranean should constitute the central scope of comparative analysis, although this should not be a restrictive focus. Indeed, there is much to be gained by placing European societies within a wider context of study, just as recent anthropologists have placed European kinship and marriage on a continuum with other systems, bringing Europe into the anthropological universe.

References

Abu Zahra, N. (1970). On the Modesty of Women in Arab Muslim Villages. A Reply. *American Anthropologist*, **72**, 1079–88.
Abu Zahra, N. (1974). Material Power, Honour, Friendship and the Etiquette of Visiting. *Anthropological Quarterly*, **47**, (1), 120–38.

Al-Shahi, A. (ed.) (1987). *The Diversity of the Muslim Community. Anthropological Essays in Memory of Peter Lienhardt*, London: Ithaca.

Anderson, M. (1980). *Approaches to the History of the Western Family. 1500–1914*. London: Macmillan.

Antoun, R. (1968). On the Modesty of Women in Arab Muslim Villages: a Study in the Accommodation of Tradition. *American Anthropologist*, **70**, 671–97.

Asano-Tamanoi, M. (1987). Shame, Family, and State in Catalonia and Japan. In *Honor and Shame and the Unity of the Mediterranean* (ed. D. Gilmore), Washington: American Anthropological Association Special Publication No. 22.

Balbo, L. (1987). Crazy quilts: rethinking the welfare state debate from a woman's point of view. In *Women and the State* (ed. A. Showstack Sassoon), London: Routledge.

Barrett, M. and McIntosh, M. (1985). *The Anti-Social Family*, London: Verso.

Bestard, J. C. (1986). *Casa y Familia. Parentesco y reproducción domestica en Formentera*, Palma de Mallorca: Institut D'Estudis Balearics. English transl. 1991 *What's in a Relative? Household and Family in Formentera*, Oxford: Berg.

Bott, E. (1957). *Family and Social Networks*, London: Tavistock.

Bourdieu, P. (1977). *Outline of a Theory of Practice*, Cambridge: Cambridge University Press. First published 1972 in Switzerland: Librairie Droz.

Braudel, F. (1973). *The Mediterranean and the Mediterranean World in the Age of Philip II*, London: Collins.

Caldwell, L. (1978). Church, State and Family: the Women's Movement in Italy. In *Feminism and Materialism. Women and Modes of Production* (eds A. Kuhn and A. M. Wolpe), London: RKP.

Campbell, J. K. (1964). *Honour, Family and Patronage. A Study of Institutions and Moral Values in a Greek Mountain Community*, Oxford: Clarendon Press.

Collard, A. (1989). Investigating 'social memory' in a Greek context. In *History and Ethnicity* (eds E. Tonkin, M. McDonald and M. Chapman), London/NY: Routledge.

Collier, J. F. and Yanagisako, S. J. (1987). Introduction to *Gender and Kinship. Essays toward a Unified Analysis* (eds J. F. Collier and S. J. Yanagisako), Stanford, California: Stanford University Press.

Davis, J. (1973). *Land and Family in Pisticci*, London: Athlone Press.

Davis, J. (1975). An Account of Changes in the Rules of Transmission of Property in Pisticci 1814–1961. In *Mediterranean Family Structures* (ed. J. G. Peristiany), Cambridge: Camridge University Press.

Davis, J. (1977). *Peoples of the Mediterranean. An Essay in Comparative Social Anthropology*, London: RKP.

Davis, J. (1987). Family and State in the Mediterranean. In *Honor and Shame and the Unity of the Mediterranean* (ed. D. Gilmore), Washington: Special Publication of the American Anthropological Association No. 22, 22–34.

Davis, J. (1989). The Social Relations of the Production of History. In *History and Ethnicity* (eds E. Tonkin, M. McDonald and M. Chapman), ASA Monograph 27, London: Routledge.

Donzelot, J. (1980). *The Policing of Families. Welfare versus State*, London: Macmillan. Original publication 1977 Les Editions de Minuit.

Du Boulay, J. (1983). The Meaning of Dowry Changing Values in Rural Greece. *Journal of Modern Greek Studies*, **1**, (1), 243–70.

Firth, R. (ed.) (1956). *Two Studies of Kinship in London*, LSE Monographs in Social Anthropology No. 15.

Firth, R., Hubert, J. and Forge, A. (1969). *Families and their Relatives. Kinship in a Middle-Class Sector of London*, London: RKP.

Flandrin, J. L. (1979). *Families in Former Times*, Cambridge: CUP.

Friedl, E. (1963). Some Aspects of Dowry and Inheritance in Boeotia. In *Mediterranean Countrymen: Essays in the Social Anthropology of the Mediterranean* (ed. J. Pitt-Rivers), Paris: Mouton.

Gamble, A. (1981). *Introduction to Modern Social and Political Thought*, London: Macmillan.

Gilmore, D. (1987a). The Shame of Dishonor. *Honor and Shame and the Unity of the Mediterranean* (ed. D. Gilmore), Washington: Special Publication of the American Anthropological Association No. 22: 2–21.

Gilmore, D. (ed.) (1987b). *Honor and Shame and the Unity of the Mediterranean*, Washington: Special Publication of the American Anthropological Association No. 22.

Giner, S. (1985). *Comunió, domini, innovació*, Barcelona: Laia.

Giovannini, M. (1981). Woman: A Dominant Symbol within the Cultural System of a Sicilian Town. *Man*, **16**, 408–26.

Giovannini, M. (1985). The Dialectics of Women's Factory Work in a Sicilian Town. *Anthropology*, **9**, (1/2), 45–64.

Giovannini, M. (1987). Female Chastity Codes in the Circum-Mediterranean: Comparative Perspectives. In *Honor and Shame and the Unity of the Mediterranean* (ed. D. Gilmore), Washington DC: Special Publication of the American Anthropological Association No. 22. pp 61–74

Goddard, V. (1987). Honour and Shame: the Control of Women's Sexuality and Group Identity in Naples. In *The Cultural Construction of Sexuality* (ed. P. Caplan), London: Tavistock.

Goddard, V. (1988). *Women and Work: the case of Neapolitan outworkers*, Unpublished Ph.D thesis, University of London.

Goody, J. (1983). *The Development of the Family and Marriage in Europe*, Cambridge: CUP.

Goody, J. (1991). *The Oriental, The Ancient and the Primitive. Systems of Marriage and the Family in Pre-Industrial Societies of Eurasia*, Cambridge: CUP.

Gramsci, A. (1973). *The Prison Notebooks*, London: Lawrence & Wishart.

Harris, L. (1988). Women's Response to Multinationals in County Mayo. In *Women and Multinationals in Europe* (eds D. Elson and R. Pearson), London: Macmillan.

Hearn, J. and Parkin, W. (1987). *'Sex at Work'. The Power and Paradox of Organization Sexuality*, Brighton: Wheatsheaf.

Héritier, F. (1981). *L'Exercise de la Parenté*, Paris: Editions du Seuil.

Herzfeld, M. (1980). Honor and Shame: Problems in the Comparative Analysis of Moral Systems. *Man*, **16**, 339–51.

Herzfeld, M. (1985). *The Poetics of Manhood. Contest and Identity in a Cretan Mountain Village*, Princeton: Princeton University Press.

Herzfeld, M. (1987). 'As in your own house': Hospitality, Ethnography, and the Stereotype of Mediterranean Society. In *Honor and Shame and the Unity of the Mediterranean* (ed. D. Gilmore), Washington: Special Publication of the American Anthropological Association No. 22. 75–89.

Hirschon, R. (1978). Open Body/Closed Space: the Transformation of Female Sexuality. In *Defining Females* (ed. S. Ardener), London: Croom Helm.

Howell, S. and Melhuus, M. (1993). The Study of Kinship, the Study of the Person; a study of gender? In *Gendered Anthropology* (ed. T. Del Valle), London, New York: Routledge.

Irigaray, L. (1977). *Ce Sexe qui n'en est pas un*, Paris: Editions de Minuit.

Kandiyoti, D. (1989). Women and the Turkish State: Political Actors or Symbolic Pawns? In *Woman-Nation-State* (eds N. Yuval-Davis and J. F. Anthias), London: Macmillan.

Laslett, P. and Wall, R. (1972). *Household and Family in Past Time*, Cambridge: Cambridge University Press.

Lever, A. (1985). Honour as Red Herring. *Critique of Anthropology*, **6**, (3), 83–106.

Llobera, J. R. (1986). Fieldwork in Southwestern Europe. *Critique of Anthropology*, **6**, (2), 333–49.

Loizos, P. (1975). Changes in Property Transfers among Greek Cypriot Villages. *Man*, **10**, 502–23.

Loizos, P. and Papataxiarchis, E. (eds) (1991). *Contested Identities. Gender and Kinship in Modern Greece*, Princeton: Princeton University Press.

MacFarlane, A. (1978). *The Origins of English Individualism. The Family, Property and Social Transition*, Oxford: Blackwell.

Magaud, J. and Sugita, K. (1990). *A Propos d'une comparaison franco-japonaise: le retour des réseaux*. Paper presented to the Séminaire franco-brésilien: Autours du 'modèle' Japonais.

Moore, H. (1986). *Feminism and Anthropology*, Oxford: Polity Press.

Moors. A, (1991). Women and the Orient: A Note on Difference. In *Constructing Knowledge. Authority and Critique in Social Science* (eds L. Nencel and P. Pels), London: Sage.

Nanetti, R. (1988). *Growth and Territorial Policies: the Italian Model of Social Capitalism*, London/New York: Pinter Publishers.

Nash, J. (1985). Segmentation of the Work Process in the International Division of Labour. *Contemporary Marxism*, **2**, 25–45.

Pearson, R. (1988). Women's Employment and Multinationals in the UK: Restructuring and Flexibility. In *Women's Employment and Multinationals in Europe* (eds D. Elson and R. Pearson), London: Macmillan Press.

Peristiany, J. (ed.) (1965). *Honour and Shame. The Values of Mediterranean Society*, London: Weidenfeld & Nicolson.

Peristiany, J. (ed.) (1976). *Mediterranean Family Structures*, published in association with the Social Research Centre, Cyprus, Cambridge: CUP.

Pina-Cabral, J. (1989). The Mediterranean as a Category of Regional Comparison: A Critical View. *Current Anthropology*, **30**, (3), 399–406.

Pitt-Rivers, J. (1965). Honour and Social Status. In *Honour and Shame. The Values of Mediterranean Society* (ed. J. D. Peristiany),

Chicago/London: Chicago University Press.

Poster, M. (1978). *Critical Theory of the Family*, London: Pluto Press.

Pratt, G. (1980). A Sense of Place. In *'Nation' and 'State' in Europe: Anthropological Perspectives* (ed. R. Grillo), London: Academic Press.

Rapp, R. (1987). Toward a Nuclear Freeze? The Gender Politics of Euro-American Kinship Analysis. In *Gender and Kinship. Essays toward a Unified Analysis* (eds J. F. Collier and S. J. Yanagisako), Stanford: SUP.

Reiter, R. (1975). Men and Women in the South of France: Public and Private Domains. In *Toward an Anthropology of Women* (ed. R. Reiter), New York: Monthly Review Press.

Rokkan, S. and Urwin, D. (1983). *Economy, Territory, Identity. Politics of Western European Peripheries*, London: Sage.

Rubin, G. (1975). The Traffic in Women: Notes on the 'Political Economy' of Sex. In *Toward an Anthropology of Women* (ed. R. Reiter), New York: Monthly Review Press.

Safa, H. (1980). Class Consciousness among Working-class Women in Latin America: Puerto Rico. In *Sex and Class in Latin America* (eds J. Nash and H. Safa), New York: Bergin Press.

Sant Cassia, P. (with C. Bada) (1992). *The Making of the Modern Greek Family. Marriage and Exchange in 19th Century Athens*, Cambridge: Cambridge University Press.

Schneider, D. and Homans, G. (1955). Kinship Terminology and the American Kinship System. *American Anthropologist*, **57**, 194–208.

Schneider, J. (1971). Of Vigilance and Virgins: Honor, Shame and Access to Resources in Mediterranean Societies. *Ethnology*, **10**, 1–24.

Seers, D., Schaeffler, B. and Kiljunen, M. L. (eds) (1979) *Underdeveloped Europe*, London: Harvester Press.

Segalen, M. (1983). *Love and Power in the Peasant Family. Rural France in the 19th Century*, Oxford: Blackwell.

Segalen, M. (1986). *An Anthropological History of the Family*, Cambridge: Cambridge University Press.

Segalen, M. and Zonabend, F. (1987). Social Anthropology and the Ethnology of France: The field of kinship and the family. In *Anthropology at Home* (ed. A. Jackson), ASA monograph 25, London: Tavistock.

SEGRG (1992). The relevance of Gender for the Anthropology of Europe: Gender and the Politics of Difference. Conference on 'The Anthropology of Europe: 1992 and After', London:

Goldsmiths College.

Showstack Sassoon, A. (1987). Introduction: the Personal and the Intellectual, Fragments and Order, International Trends and National Specificities. In *Women and the State* (ed. A. Showstack Sassoon), London: Routledge.

Silverman, S. (1975). *Three Bells of Civilization: the Life of an Italian Hill Town*, NY: Columbia University Press.

Sirman, N. (1989). Feminism in Turkey: A Short History. *New Perspectives on Turkey*, **3**, (1), 1–34.

Strathern, M. (1992a). *Reproducing the Future*, Manchester: Manchester University Press.

Strathern, M. (1992b). *After Nature: English Kinship in the Late 20th Century*, Cambridge: Cambridge University Press.

Tillion, G. (1983) [1966]. *The Republic of Cousins. Women's Oppression in Mediterranean Society*, London: Al Saqi Books. Original publication *Le Harem et les Cousins*, Paris: Editions du Seuil.

Todd, E. (1985). *The Explanation of Ideology. Family Structures and Social Systems*, Oxford: Blackwell. Original publ. *La Troisième Planète, structures familiales et Systèmes Idéologiques*, Paris: Editions du Seuil.

Wikan, U. (1984). Shame and Honour: a Contestable Pair. *Man*, **29**, 635–52.

Willis, R, (1979). Shop Floor Culture, Masculinity and the Wage-Form. In *Working Class Culture* (eds J. Clarke, C. Critches and R. Johnson), London: Hutchinson.

Yanagisako, S. J. and Collier, J. F. (1987). Toward a Unified Analysis of Gender and Kinship. In *Gender and Kinship. Essays toward a Unified Analysis* (eds J. F Collier and S. J. Yanagisako), Stanford, California: Stanford University Press.

Yuval-Davis, N. and Anthias, F. (eds) (1989). *Woman-Nation-State*, Basingstoke: Macmillan.

Zonabend, F. (1984). *The Enduring Memory. Time and History in a French Village*, Manchester: Manchester University Press.

Chapter 4

Anthropological Approaches to the Study of Nationalism in Europe. The Work of Van Gennep and Mauss

Josep R. Llobera

Introduction

The neophyte anthropologist who is interested in studying the national question in Europe will inevitably experience a sense of despair when he/she discovers the meagre theoretical legacy left by our classical ancestors in this area of knowledge (even when the word anthropological ancestor is understood in a generous manner). It is true that Durkheim and the Durkheimian tradition offer more possibilities than are usually acknowledged. I have myself explored in some detail Durkheim's contribution to the study of the national question (Llobera 1994). In addition, the work of Maurice Halbwachs (1980, 1992) in the area of the *mémoire collective* has obvious implications for the study of the nation; after all, the nation has strong, though complex, historical roots, and any attempt to unravel the symbolic and emotive use of the past can throw light on its nature.

An author who seems to have been totally ignored in all the anthropological attempts to recover what the past of the discipline has to offer on the study of nationalism is Arnold van Gennep. The main purpose of this paper is to present van Gennep's contribution to the study of the national question; I will also examine in some detail Mauss's inquiry on the nation. No doubt the important event which exercised the mind of these two leading anthropologists in this direction was the partial application of the principle of self-determination after the First World War to the constituent parts of the Austro-Hungarian and Ottoman empires. The fact that both contributions remained unfinished and fragmentary (particularly that of Mauss) may be the result of the appearance of more pressing anthropological pursuits – as Henri Lévy-Bruhl (1953–4) suggests for Marcel Mauss – or simply that the task was more difficult and complex than they had anticipated.

In van Gennep's case the contribution is substantial: it consists of a book and four articles. The book, the first volume of a *Traité comparatif des Nationalités*, was entitled *Les éléments exterieurs de la Nationalité*, and was published in 1922 (1922a); two other promised volumes – *La Formation de la Nationalité* and *La Vie des Nationalités* – were never published. The articles were published between 1920 and 1922. They relate nationality to a variety of factors: class (1921a), land (1921b) and religion (1922b); there is also a study of the formation and maintenance of Georgian nationality (1920). Why van Gennep's contribution should have been silenced or not recognized by the anthropological community is not an issue that is easy to explain. He suffered the fate of many other French social scientists who were eclipsed by the Durkheimian School.

Marcel Mauss's contribution is centred around 50 pages of text comprising fragmentary notes on a treatise of *La Nation* (1969a); the writings date from 1920 or 1921 and were published in *L'Année Sociologique* in 1953–4. Mauss published a short paper on 'La Nation et l'internationalisme' in 1920 (Mauss 1969b).

Arnold van Gennep

Van Gennep's book presents itself as a scientific study of the nationality (*nationalité*) based on a comparative study of a large number of empirical cases – which he labels the 'ethnographic method'. The geographic horizon is essentially European, and the study uses not only published material but also fieldnotes collected by the author over a four-year research period in southern Poland, while travelling in different parts of Europe, and on two scientific expeditions to North Africa (p. 9). What is at stake for van Gennep is to map out the different factors that give rise to what he calls 'nationalitarian forces' (*forces nationalitaires*); this process, which started in Western Europe, spread elsewhere as soon as the conditions for the appearance of national sentiments were in place (p. 10).

Nationalities are taken to be normal social phenomena, even if the author may deplore the fact that nationalitarian sentiments are sometimes used to justify conflict, violence, war, and massacres. What interests van Gennep are the strong notions and sentiments associated with nationalities, particularly when they are oppressed by an alien state. To ignore the role of nationalities at the level of world politics is the same as pretending that strong passions do not exist (p. 11). Nationalitarian sentiments are extremely powerful, and often take precedence over economic arguments (p. 12).

I have already indicated that van Gennep takes nationalities as given, and to a certain extent he also accepts as part of social life nationality struggles – even if he hopes to contribute transactional and negotiated solutions to the violent confrontations among nationalities. In other words, for van Gennep nationalities are here to stay, even if he does not enter into the question of whether they have a natural right to exist. This 'special political phenomenon is the result of a combination of ideas, sentiments and wills' (p. 12); it is a dynamic phenomenon, a 'tendential movement', and hence essentially unstable, which is affected by a variety of forces, some of which promote cohesion, others which encourage dissociation (p. 13). In the final instance, what matters is is to be able to map out the main features that distinguish nationalities from other systems of mass grouping' (ibid.).

Van Gennep's decision to focus on 'nationalities' rather than 'nations' is not without theoretical consequences. The term 'nationality', as it was used in France and elsewhere in the nineteenth and early twentieth centuries, indicated the will to exist as a nation of a group of people united by a community of territory, language, culture, history, etc. Closely connected, but independent, was the principle of nationalities, which asserted the right of these groups to constitute themselves in politically independent states. Van Gennep was well aware that it was difficult, if not impossible, to put forward a scientific definition of nationality. Initially what was meant by 'nationality' was the 'set of characteristics that constitute a nation' (p. 16); later the word was used to refer to a special collective formation. To avoid ambiguity van Gennep suggested the term 'nationalitarian' (*nationalitaire*).

Van Gennep observed that what seemed to defeat the majority of theoreticians who had tried to tackle the nationality question was the great variety and fluidity of its phenomenal forms. Most definitions of 'nationality', faced with the impossibility of agreeing about the list of elements which constitute it, abandoned any attempt to provide an objective, morphological approach to the matter and concluded that it was a fact of the collective consciousness; this reduction of nationality to a psychological phenomenon is the equivalent of saying that we cannot define what a nationality is; we can only ascertain that there is a 'nationalitarian way of thinking' *(manière de penser nationalitaire)*. There is a tradition, which in France is identified with the work of Renan, that identifies the nationality with a phenomenon of collective psychology. Most authors who had written on nationality during the period of the First World War shared this conception. Van Gennep mentions, in particular, Henry Hauser's *Le Principe des nationalités*, Israel Zangwill's *The Principle of Nationalities* (1917), Bernard Auerbach's *Races et Nationalités d'Autriche-Hongrie* (1917) and René Johannet's *Le Principe des Nationalités* (1918). A great deal of the confusion exhibited by these authors stems from their inability to distinguish clearly between nationality and the State.

Van Gennep insists that nationality and State are different realities, which obey different principles. The State is a political reality, while it is possible to conceive of a nationality independently of the State. Just because France and a few other countries have a national identity which is clearly and historically associated with a State, it does not follow that the same should happen elsewhere. In fact, these countries are exceptions; Europe is a mosaic of nationalities. This we may not like, and from a practical point of view we might prefer that the population of Europe belonged to a single race, had a single language and had the same aspirations. However, 'we are left with a variety of groups which do not want to be assimilated to each other or to be absorbed by a single one of them' (p. 24). The objective of anthropology is to study, and if possible, to explain them (ibid.).

The author who seems to have come closest to van Gennep's vision of the nationality is the Bulgarian J. Ivanov, who defines it as

> a human collectivity, with a moral and physical individuality and with common traditions and aspirations. The elements that constitute and maintain the national individuality are: unity of race, geographic boundaries, language, religion, political unity, way of living and common cultural manifestations; the larger the number of these elements present in a nationality, the more its organisms are united and the more vigorous and ardent is the national sentiment that animates it. (p. 27)

Nonetheless, this definition, say van Gennep, lacks a reference to the conscious element, which is crucial in any definition of nationality. Furthermore, it is not sufficient to list the elements that constitute a nationality; it is important to know how they combine and what happens if one or more is absent.

According to van Gennep the sentiment of nationality already existed in pre-modern times. As he put it: 'a history of nationalitarian sentiment would be, properly speaking, a history of patriotism' (p. 33). Now, the latter takes different forms in accordance with the type of political organization in which it appears; in pre-modern times it was in the main dynastic; later on, at the time of the French Revolution, it became 'national' in the political sense of the term. But when we find a reasonably homogeneous human group which is unable to govern itself, and one of the key aspects of its collective consciousness is the will to self-determination, then we can talk about a 'nationalitarian' sentiment. What is modern is not the nationalitarian sentiment but the belief that a culturally defined group (van Gennep does not use this expression) has the natural right to govern itself. Of course, it is a fact that states have managed to create a sense of of patriotism out of culturally and linguistically diverse populations either through homogenization (France) or through the creation of state identity (Switzerland). In both cases, these were long-term processes, taking place over a few centuries. There is no doubt that what we see developing is a sense of loyalty towards the State (which becomes the *patrie* for peoples who might be otherwise culturally diverse).

Van Gennep is adamant that the nationalitarian sentiment precedes modernity, and he quotes a variety of cases in which the existence of such sentiment can be reasonably assumed. A particularly poignant document he refers to is that of the Polish scientist, Jacobus Szadek, who in 1464 laid down the basic nationalitarian principles. Claiming for the King of Poland, Kasimierz IV, the land of Pomerania (among others) from the Germans, he argued that it had been inhabited and governed by Polish people, who had given Polish names to mountains, rivers, towns, etc., long before the Teutonic Knights had existed. Furthermore, the lands had belonged to the Kingdom of Poland since its inception, and had been subject to Polish sovereignty. Finally, the argument was raised that the population of these lands could not be subjected to an oppressive, alien tyranny (p. 36).

It would appear that if the full expression of the principle of self-determination of peoples came only with the French Revolution, there are plenty of instances that suggest that it existed long before that time. In fact, what dominated the history of Europe since Roman times was what van Gennep called 'the Oriental conception of ethnic politics' (p. 39), which subordinated peoples to foreign rule. It was precisely the early anthropological development of an interest in ethnicity that contributed to highlighting the traditions of self-rule in the Celtic, Germanic and Slav worlds. In fact, these decentralizing traditions, which emphasized the rights to autonomy and freedom of cities, provinces, principalities and small kingdoms, never disappeared completely from the European horizon. Only with the advent of absolutism did this principle take a turn for the worse. It is on the basis of comparative human science that the European past can be recovered; the nationalitarian principle is a European legacy that was destroyed by an oppressive State modelled on the Oriental empires (p. 42). Van Gennep saw the emerging Soviet system as an extreme application of the Asiatic model, in that a heterogeneous mass of people was subjected to an alien oligarchy supported by a janissary army (the Bolsheviks).

Van Gennep defined colonialism as 'the application of the Oriental principle of domination to populations who are considered more or less civilized (due to the possession of more advanced means of destruction)'. He believed that the end of colonialism was near, and that this was due precisely to the spread of the nationalitarian principle to Asia and Africa. That the human sciences were not alien to these developments should be a source of pride for anthropologists (p. 43).

The application of the nationality principle will not suppress natural antagonisms, but perhaps will contribute to make massacres less common; at least one of the reasons for wars will be phased out. To what extent this principle might be a step backward from the universalism of the Enlightenment is one question that van Gennep asks himself. The idea of universal fraternity would possibly require the homogenization of languages, religions, political systems, etc. Only an evil empire could do that, and the Bolsheviks were the ideal candidates to try it. Van Gennep believed that the opposition between humanity and nationality is arbitrary, and that there is no reason why nationalities cannot live in peace with each other once they are free (p. 45).

I have already indicated that van Gennep did not manage to

articulate a comprehensive theory of nationality, and that at most he succeeded in mapping out the external factors that determine it.

There is, first, an outer layer of symbols of nationality which van Gennep just mentions. Traditionally, group differentiation was often achieved by means of manipulation of the body (tattoos, paintings, scarifications, mutilations, etc.); the modern equivalent of such procedures is national or regional dress. This is an easily distinguishable sign that allows a rapid classification of people in terms of friends or foes; it may also be used as a symbol of protest against an oppressive state. The process of European cultural homogenization has made dress a less relevant element of nationality, although in its folklorized form it still plays a certain role. The symbolic value attached to dress has been transferred in modern times to flags. Dress and flag are both about colours and about specific combinations of them (p. 53). The strong emotional value attached to flags as nationalitarian symbols (not only as military ones) finds no parallel in other elements. Whether the choice of flag be totally arbitrary or historically informed, a conscious decision is needed to adopt a given flag as the colours of a nationality. On the other hand, the spirit of a nationality may express itself through certain aspects of material culture, particularly the type of villages and houses (p. 56).

Among the controversial symbols of nationality van Gennep finds customs, traditions, rituals, etc. The reason is simply that some of these cultural manifestations cut across different countries; nonetheless, there is a sense in which people perceive them as theirs. Writing may also become a symbol of nationality, as is the case with the Serbs' and Croats' adopting different alphabets to transcribe their distinct, but closely related, languages. Van Gennep insisted that this issue was particularly relevant for Eastern Europe.

None of this outer layer of symbols of the nationality constitute either individually or collectively the core of the nationality. It has been shown that their disappearance does not mean the end of the 'emotive and reflective complex that constitutes the nationality' (p. 68). Among the external symbols of the nationality that van Gennep finds essential are language and territory.

Language is 'the most striking and pugnacious symbol of differentiation, continuity and collective cohesion' (ibid.). How early it was perceived that the existence of a variety of languages within the same state could be a cause of dissociation and how early the importance of language as a nationalitarian element was realized are topics that van Gennep explores in some detail. On the whole, he considers both as part of the thrust of modernity. I believe that he is wrong in that respect, and that we can find substantial manifestations of such occurrences prior to the dawn of modernity. Nonetheless, he is correct in emphasizing that the right of nationalities to preserve their language is a much more recent event, depending on 'the invention of the printing press, the establishment of linguistics as an autonomous discipline and the development of the railway system, which allowed for easy communications' (p. 73). These inventions were double-edged tools, which could be used both by the State and against the State. No doubt, the means at the disposal of the State to impose a language were far superior than those available to the oppressed nationalities (it was taught in schools and its use was made compulsory in the army, the administration, the judicial system, the press, etc.).

Van Gennep observed that the trend towards linguistic conformity that was predicted in the eighteenth century never materialized, and that the very opposite took place. The distinction between language, dialect and patois becomes more and more blurred; any dialect or patois can become, in the right circumstances, a nationalitarian language (p. 75). Nevertheless, small linguistic communities are always in danger of being absorbed by larger, linguistically close ones. Communities which speak closely connected languages tend to be in opposition to each other, because 'linguistic kinship appears to interested groups as a danger to their specific individuality' (p. 80). This may apply to dialects and patois as well. This opposition is the result of the fact that languages and dialects symbolize important psychological differences (p. 82).

Native, autochthonous languages are essentially an oral means to communicate at the familiar level, and hence strong emotions are attached to them. On the other hand, people may use other languages to engage in economic, social or political relations. Modern linguistic symbolism is the result of extending to the nationality what originally was typical of a smaller unit. In the absence of concerted action, administrative languages can displace native languages in a few generations if the economic needs or the state pressures are there. The importance of the mother tongue in determining nationality is exemplified by the use of official linguistic statistics. In the long run, linguistic censuses have accentuated the traits of both the dominant and the subordinated nationalities. The obsession of modern states with measuring the strength of maternal languages has been an important factor in highlighting the centrality of language in the constitution of the nationality. In van Gennep's words:

> If anything has contributed to spread among the masses the idea that the nationality is symbolized and recognized by the language, it is precisely the behaviour of governments in the elaboration of general or special censuses. By mid-nineteenth century the rural and urban masses did not clearly perceive this relationship. But the insistence of the census-takers on obtaining linguistic data and on influencing the answers, of governments on falsifying the results and of impassioned journalists, politicians and intellectuals on discussing them, has led to the idea, even in the most retarded countryside backyards, that to speak this or that language was to be in favour of or against the government. (p. 122)

Linguistic and other kinds of statistics are unreliable because they are open to easy manipulation by the State. Van Gennep offers a classic example of manipulation, which is as poignant today as it was seventy-five years ago. Macedonia is such an example. He looks at the claims of Bulgarians, Serbs and Greeks concerning this area. Bulgarians take language (without distinguishing between maternal language and language of use), religion (declaration of attachment to the Bulgarian exarchate Church) and the declaration of nationality as the basic facts of national consciousness. For Serbs what counts are the basic facts of dialect and spoken language, the resemblance of customs and religion. Finally, Greeks consider the so-called influence of Hellenic civilization, as it manifests itself in all sort of survivals (from the belief in vampires to the use of specialized Greek words, from popular tales to dress), as the decisive factor. Who, then, are, the Macedonians; are they Greeks, Bulgarians or Serbs? Or are they just Macedonians? The answer was as problematic when van Gennep was writing as it is today (p. 125). One must therefore conclude that the nationality is an entity which is too complex and dynamic to be enclosed in the confines of a statistical approach (p. 143).

Another symbol of group cohesion and persistence, as powerful as the linguistic one, is the territory (p. 143). This association between a people and a territory is not exclusively a modern phenomenon. Patriotic sentiments tend to develop as a result of the attachment of human beings to a particular land; these localized sentiments can be extended to the whole territory of the State or of the nationality. Oral and written literature have often expressed the force of the territorial symbolism. There are, of course, some cases of nationalities without a territory (the Gypsies, for example), but they are rare. The Jews, maintains van Gennep, are not one of them, because they have an ancestral territory and a strong symbolic association with it.

Closely associated with the territory is the problem of borders. 'Territory only acquires its full symbolic value when we know its boundaries' (p. 151). The idea of boundary exists in all societies from primitive to civilized. Different markers have been used to indicate boundaries: some natural, others artificial. These markers are often envisaged as sacred; to cross a boundary is to move from one world to another; it represents performing magic and a religious ritual. Often, limits are invisible: the ideal line traced between two physical markers; the 'symbol of the border' is a secondary symbol within the nationality sentiment (p. 152). The precision in delineating borders is a recent thing; in the past what was common was not an ideal line, or even a clearly defined geographic marker (river, mountain, etc.), but rather a frontier, a border area which was neutral (No Man's Land). Marches also belonged in this category. In any case, van Gennep criticizes the concept of 'natural borders', as well as the idea of natural linguistic borders. Neither mountains, nor rivers, nor seas nor forests are an obstacle for the expansion of a language. Van Gennep dedicates Chapters 7 and 8 of the book to tackling these issues.

In the context of the discussion on borders a number of related, important concepts appeared in the nineteenth century. Ideas like access to the sea, control of water sources, military strategy ('safe borders'), economic borders, etc. Van Gennep is convinced that the attempt by geographers to discover a causal link or a normal coincidence between nationalitarian or political boundaries, on the one hand, and natural boundaries, on the other, has failed. The concentration, dispersion and expansion of peoples follows its own logic, and it is not the geographic one, except in rare and passing circumstances (p. 174). Borders are changing symbols of human relationships. The attempt to correlate nationalitarian borders and geographic ones has created many political problems in the nineteenth and twentieth centuries.

The importance of the cartographic symbol, spread by school maps, is also remarked on by van Gennep. There is a patriotic feeling of pride in imperial maps (like those showing the British Empire in red). But ethnographic maps tend to be rather unreliable, often providing mixed information. In addition to the linguistic element, the nationalitarian border also incorporates other elements which are ethnographic (customs and buildings), psychological (religion, collective will), economic and strategic. Along with all these factors one must also consider the idea of historical borders, which van Gennep considered a dangerously volatile concept (p. 207).

Van Gennep introduces the idea of historical symbol to refer to the 'image that each people has of its past military and political greatness, an image which was traditionally perpetuated by heroic legends, war songs, live memories, etc., and that today is transmitted in uncritical history textbooks and illustrated with maps'.

Another important symbol is the name of the nationality (territory and inhabitants). Names come, go and return. At the time of writing his book van Gennep observed that names such as Serbs, Croats and Slovenes (which had existed for a thousand years) were being phased out and replaced by that of Yugoslavs; now the very opposite is happening. Some names of nations are rooted in past peoples with whom there is no ethnic or cultural link (Angles and English, Franks and French, etc.) Sometimes the names of territories remain unchanged, but the peoples who inhabit them change. The symbolic importance of the name is a survival from earlier times; the name is the most powerful symbol of the cohesion and the persistence of the group as an organized collectivity. Andrew Lang based on this essential value of the collective name his theory of the origins of totemism, and hence of religious and social organization. 'Deutschland über alles' and 'Rule Britannia' are but abridged formulae of the sentiment and image of the name. In modern times there is a tendency to favour a coincidence between the name of territory and that of its inhabitants: Poland is the land of the Poles, etc. Old, multinational countries fit rather badly in this scheme (p. 213).

The book concludes with the idea that

the superposition, and in favourable cases, the combination of all symbols analysed determine in the individuals and in the masses the formation of a tangible (sensible) representation of their nationality. This representation contains visual, auditive and sensorial elements, to which are added other more or less conscious and nuanced sentiments, according to the degree of individual and collective sensibility and education. (p. 217)

Van Gennep observed that symbols may lose part of their importance, particularly when the nationality is well established; on the other hand, nationalitarian symbols do not acquire their full value until the nationality is in danger or at war.

As I have indicated at the beginning, van Gennep's treatise stops at the external manifestations of the nationality; it provides only, as he put it, a plastic representation. However, it lacks a consideration of the internal materials from which the nationality is formed, how these materials are assembled and the framework that sustains them and keeps them in place. Without these it is very difficult to discern the general law which determines the origins, conduct and evolution of the nationality.

Marcel Mauss

There is little doubt that Marcel Mauss's interest in the national question was awakened by the nationalist turmoils associated with the First World War. As with van Gennep, his interest in the matter seems to have fizzled out a few years later. Mauss's main text on the national question – *La Nation* (1920) – is, as I have already noted, much shorter and less coherent (because it is made up of disparate fragments) than van Gennep's *Traité Comparatif des Nationalités*. The editor of the manuscript, H. Lévy-Bruhl, emphasizes three main characteristics : (1) it is written in the grand style, and aims to be a comprehensive and monumental treatise; (2) it tries to capture two nationalitarian trends, which are only contradictory in apperance, that is, fissiparity and union; and (3) while noting the importance of economic factors in the making of the nation, Mauss also takes on board elements like politics, language, religion and morality (Lévy-Bruhl 1953–4: 7). Unlike van Gennep, Mauss focuses on the nation, rather than the nationality, and envisages it as a total phenomenon. Now, nation and State are quite close in Maussian terminology, though the former is less juridical and more emotive than the latter (1969a: 572).

The nation, as an eighteenth-century concept, is constituted by the citizens of the State. This is essentially a French concept which developed with the Enlightenment, and more specifically with Rousseau, and culminated in the French Revolution. The concept of nation comes much later to the English tradition, which only knows of 'subjects', 'kingdom' and 'country', and thinks of the nation in these terms. Even the American revolutionaries were not altogether aware of the national character of their actions.

Here Mauss pinpoints a difference in national character between the English and Continentals (or at least French and Germans); while among the former the law precedes concepts and ideas, with the latter the opposite is the case (Mauss 1969a: 374–5). Patriotism *stricto sensu* flourished only in the context of the nation politically understood. Mauss is quite adamant that neither fidelity to the king (nor loyalty to the State) nor the hatred of foreign rulers can be equated with patriotism. What is at stake in modern, proper patriotism is its popular character. As he put it:

'Nations in formation, like Italy and Germany, and even more oppressed nationalities, like Poland, Bohemia, Hungary and Serbia, developed in succession a consciousness of their will to exist, to revolt and to reconstitute themselves ... And the nationality principle expressed symbolically this claim of nations to existence, to a complete existence' (ibid.: 575–6).

It would appear that in the course of the nineteenth century the concept of nation understood as the will of the people lost popularity in favour of the concepts of nationality and State; the former emphasizes the revolt against alien domination, the latter empties out society of its citizens.

Mauss's objective is to investigate which type of society can be labelled nation. In that he follows the Aristotelian distinction between *ethnē* (peoples) and *poleis* (states or nations). What determines the difference between *ethnos* and *polis* is the lack of integration and solidarity which characterizes the former. Nations show a high degree of vertebration and consciousness of themselves, which is absent or poorly developed in peoples. The imagery used by Mauss is biological, although he is aware of the dangers, and after a *tour de force* he arrives at the following definition of the nation:

'A nation is a society materially and morally integrated, with a centralized power which is stable and permanent, with clearly delimited borders, and with a relative moral, mental and cultural unity of its inhabitants, who consciously adhere to a state and its laws' (p. 584).

As can be seen, this is a rather restrictive definition of the nation, and makes of it a rather recent institution. The nation is thus essentially a Western European product, and it requires the following two conditions:

1. Society has to be integrated: that is, all segmentation by clan, city, tribe, kingdom or feudality has to be abolished. Ideally, there are no intermediaries between the nation and the citizen. In addition to that, nations have clear boundaries, without areas which depend on foreign rulers and without designs on the territory of other nations.

2. There must be economic unity. The idea of a national economy is essential for Mauss; economic life flows as far as the boundaries of the nation. The members of a nation are unified economically; protectionism and nationalism often coincide. A good case in point of economic nationalism was the creation of a national market as a precondition for the creation of a political nation in Germany in the nineteenth century.

The question arises as to whether these two factors are sufficient to define the nation. Mauss seems to answer in the negative, by saying the following:

> But this political unity, that is to say, military, administrative and juridical, on the one hand, and economic, on the other, and especially this conscious, constant, general will to create it and to transmit it to all and sundry, has only become possible by means of a series of considerable phenomena which have unified the other social phenomena, either at the same time, or before or after. A nation which deserves to be called a nation has its civilization, aesthetic, moral and material, and its language. It has its mentality, its sensibility, its morality, its will and its form of progress; and all the citizens who compose the nation participate in the Idea that directs her. (p. 591)

The process of individuation of nations and nationalities has taken place in the past two centuries; civilization has not become more uniform, but rather the opposite.

> This local, moral and juridical unity is expressed in the collective spirit
> by the idea of fatherland, on the one hand, and by the idea of citizen,
> on the other. The idea of fatherland symbolizes the sum total of duties
> that citizens have *vis-à-vis* the nation and its land. The notion of the
> citizen symbolizes the sum total of civil and political rights that the
> member of this nation has in correlation with the duties that he must
> accomplish. (p. 592)

These two ideas constitute the modern nation; the nation, for
Mauss, is made up of citizens who live consensually.

In a modern nation the tendency is to individualize its members
and reduce them to uniformity; the nation is homogeneous, like a
primitive clan, and it consists of equal citizens. It is symbolized by
its flag, while the clan had its totem. The nation has its cult, as the
clan worshipped its ancestral god-animals. Like a primitive tribe,
the nation has its dialect elevated to the dignity of a language, and
it has its domestic law, which is opposed to international law. Like
a clan, the nation claims the right to vendetta when offended. The
nation has its own currency, customs, borders and colonies; even
mentality and race are marked by individuation (p. 594).

Mauss insists that this process of individuation of the nation is
visible even in two very different, unexpected orders of
phenomena: in the higher forms of intellectual life (*mentalité*) and
in the forms of biological life (*race*). The use of a given language,
with its traditions, characteristics, literary forms, etc., contributes
to individuate the nation to a hitherto unforeseen extent. The
scientific literature often misses this process, because either it is
only predicated of primitive societies (which are then envisaged
as nations) or because the homogenization of the modern world
is assumed (p. 594). According to Mauss, modern European nations
believe in their common race, no matter how erroneous this
conception might be – after all, European populations are racially
mixed. There are constant references to the French or the English
race in the nationalist literature. And for many, race creates
nationality (though in fact the opposite is the case).

An important phenomenon which is typical of the nineteenth
century is the creation of national languages by nationalities that
did not previously have them. This usually applies to peoples who
had unwritten or forgotten languages. Language has often
preceded nationality. What we can see here is 'a will of the people

to intervene in processes which until recently had been left to unconscious variations and developments' (p. 598). For Mauss this should not be seen as 'artificialism'; linguistic nationalism is a strong sentiment, and peoples want to colour European culture with their language. In modern times language has created the nationality. States often want to impose the dominant language on populations with different languages; but the fact that this is felt as an imposition shows the progress that the principle of the autonomy of peoples has made (p. 599).

Finally, for Mauss a nation believes in its civilization, in its mores, in its technology and in its art. Nations have a high opinion of themselves, believing perhaps to be the most civilized and the best in the world. After this examination of different factors Mauss proposes a final, more sophisticated definition of the nation as 'a sufficiently integrated society, with central power (at least democratic to a certain degree), with the idea of national sovereignty and the boundaries of which are those of a race, a civilization, a language, a morality, in a word, a national character'. Of course, some elements may be absent, but in the complete nation all these elements coincide. There are few examples of complete nations (France being one of them), and Mauss believes these to be aesthetically more appealing.

Conclusion

In this chapter I have merely tried to present what I believe to be a wealth of anthropological analyses on the national question that have hitherto remained unexplored. If not an elaborate theory of the nation or of nationality, I think there are brilliant insights, finely tuned comparisons and detailed analyses in both authors. It should be said that van Gennep and Mauss approached the national question historically and with an ethnographic richness (in relation to both Western and Eastern Europe) that my paper has not been able to reflect appropriately. I have not been able to trace any reference to the work of van Gennep on nationality in the anthropological literature (or in the literature on the national question in general). As to Mauss, his definition of the nation was taken up by L. Dumont (1970); Dumont also elaborated Mauss's idea of moral integration to mean that the nation should be seen both as collection of individuals and as a whole. R. Grillo (1980) also quotes the Maussian text approvingly, but goes no further.

In a programmatic article published some years ago I stated that the tasks of a theory of nationalism in Europe involved three major objectives: (a) an understanding of the subjective sentiments of national identity, as well as the associated elements of consciousness; (b) an account of the genesis and evolution of the idea of nation from the medieval period to early modern times; and (c) a spatio-temporal explanation of the varying structures (ideologies and movements) of nationalism in the modern and contemporary periods (Llobera 1987).

If we consider who are the best-known contemporary anthropologists who have studied the national question in Europe, the names of Gellner and Dumont spring to mind. In some respects their approaches are very different, but they are equally innovative. Methodologically speaking, their approaches could be construed as exemplary, particularly for those anthropologists who are still pussyfooting around the verandas of their village 'communities'.

Although I believe that there are limitations and anomalies in Gellner's theory, he has gone a long way in providing a reasoned account for the emergence and pervasiveness of nationalism in modern times (Gellner 1983). His idea that the roots of nationalism are found in the specific structural needs of industrial society has appealed to a wide range of anthropologists (as well as social scientists). Gellner's insistence that nations are invented has also been widely accepted, among other things because, like the previous thesis, it confirms the generalized perception among many social scientists that nationalism is best explained in economic terms. However, Gellner has little to say about national sentiments and consciousness; in fact, this is a topic that social scientists have largely ignored. The work of van Gennep, but also the Durkheimian tradition in general, can be of assistance in providing a number of elements with which to build a theory of national consciousness. A rich and specific contribution stemming from van Gennep's book is his treatment of the symbols of nationality and their relationship to the creation of national consciousness. Again, for some unspecified reason the Durkheimians made little use of the concepts of collective consciousness and collective representations outside the realm of primitive societies, although Mauss recognized their wider applicability. A projection into modern society of some of the analytic frameworks used in *Les formes élémentaires de la vie religieuse* could help to clarify the meaning and importance of nationalist beliefs and rituals.

L. Dumont, who places himself in the Durkheimian tradition, has published a series of articles on the German and French national ideologies (Dumont 1986, 1991) which are much more limited in scope than Gellner's book. His writings have so far only influenced a limited but fervent and influential circle of anthropological admirers. By focusing on some key philosophical and literary texts, Dumont has claimed to have uncovered three basic principles of the German mind (universal sovereignty, introverted individualism and holism) which are the key to modernity. Dumont remains prisoner of the conviction that one can explain historical developments as complex as Nazism without reference to macro historico-sociological categories (Llobera, forthcoming).

A comparison between Gellner and Dumont highlights the limited explanatory framework of the élitist cultural structuralism of Dumont as against the sociological structuralism of Gellner. To be sure, Gellner's approach is also history-bereft, and that is its major scientific weakness. There is a sense, then, in which the Durkheimian tradition, seen through the eyes of Lévi-Straussian structuralism, can generate concise and elegant models that unfortunately have little connection to a reality that is historically much richer and more complex. What was perhaps acceptable for societies 'without history', is totally inappropriate for modern Europe. In some ways it is interesting to emphasize that both van Gennep and Mauss, but particularly the former, are much more concerned with history than our two contemporary anthropologists.

At a time when the collapse of the Communist régimes, the building of a united Europe and the weakening of the pseudo nation-states has put the national question once more in the foreground, I think that there is much that we can learn from the writings of van Gennep and Mauss.

References

Dumont, L. (1970) [1964]. Nationalism and Communalism. In *Religion, Politics and History in India* (ed. L. Dumont), Paris: Mouton.

Dumont, L. (1986). *Essays on Individualism*, Chicago: Chicago University Press.

Dumont, L. (1991). *L'idéologie allemande* Paris, Gallimard.

Gellner, E. (1983). *Nations and Nationalism*, Oxford: Blackwell.

Grillo, R. (1980). Introduction to *Nation and State in Europe* (ed. R. Grillo), New York: Academic Press.

Halbwachs, M. (1980). *The Collective Memory*, New York: Harper and Row.

Halbwachs, M. (1992) *On Collective Memory*, Chicago: Chicago University Press.

Lévy-Bruhl, H. (1953–4) Avertissement, *L'Année Sociologique*, troisième série: 5–7.

Llobera, J. R. (1987). Nationalism: Some Methodological Issues. *JASO*, **18**, (1), 13–25.

Llobera, J. R. (1994). Durkheim and the National Question. In *Debating Durkheim* (eds H. Martins and S. W. F. Pickering). London: Routledge.

Llobera, J. R. (forthcoming) The German Conception of the Nation. A Critique of L. Dumont's Writings on the German Question.

Mauss, M. (1969a). La nation. In *Oeuvres*, Paris: Minuit, Vol III: 573–625.

Mauss, M. (1969b). La nation et l'internationalisme. In *Oeuvres*. Paris: Minuit. Vol III: 626–39.

Van Gennep, A. (1920). La Nationalité géorgienne. Les causes de sa formationet de son maintien, *Revue de l'Institut de Sociologie Solvay*, 1re année, no. 3: 7–46.

Van Gennep, A. (1921a). Classe rural, noblesse et nationalité, *Revue de l'Institut de Sociologie Solvay*, 2e année, no.1: 200–22.

Van Gennep, A. (1921b). L'action du sol sur la formation des Nationalités, *Le Monde Nouveau*, 3e année, III: 1659–72.

Van Gennep, A. (1922a). *Traité comparatif des Nationalités. Les éléments extérieurs de la Nationalité*, Paris: Payot.

Van Gennep, A. (1922b). Religion et Nationalité, *Journal de Psychologie Normale et Pathologique*, 19e année, Janvier: 24–46.

Chapter 5

'Fortress Europe' and the Foreigners Within: Germany's Turks

Ruth Mandel

In this chapter I address a number of issues relating to questions of identity and boundaries – physical and social – affecting the population of migrants from Turkey in Germany. As a result of the end of the Cold War, the collapse of the Berlin Wall, and the unification of Germany, the situation of non-citizen foreign migrants has changed. The redrawing of the geopolitical map of Eastern and Central Europe necessitates a rethinking of domestic German relations as well. Thus, though most of my research was carried out in pre-unification Germany, I will touch on the current unified climate as well. But as so often happens with research of this sort, and particularly in this part of the world, history has caught up with, if not overtaken, the ethnography.

In the mid and late 1980s I spent over two years living in Berlin carrying out ethnographic research, primarily among the Turkish migrant community. West Berlin at that time was something of an overdetermined city-state, heavily symbolic of an array of contradictions. Physically surrounded by the German Democratic Republic, West Berlin stood at once for Western decadence and promiscuous consumption, as well as the 'free world' and Western liberal democracy. Encoded in innumerable ways, these ideas were broadcast to the Communist east twenty-four hours a day on the US military's Armed Forces Radio, as well as the national German television channels and radio stations. Most West Berliners accepted the Wall as an inevitable fact of life, and had little concern with or interest in what went on beyond it.

But even in the indifference shown it, the Wall helped to shape the preciousness of the *Zeitgeist* and culture that for many represented West Berlin. Divided into three sectors, West Berlin was ruled by a bizarre set of laws, customs and regulations, devised by the Allies after the Second World War. Artificially propped up by financial assistance from the West German government, the West Berlin economy was not otherwise viable. Now, all this has changed dramatically. The enormous US military presence will be gone by 1994. Traces of the Wall and the strip of no-man's-land alongside it are being erased at breakneck speed, in the massive urban renewal projects. (Berlin is perhaps the one spot in the Western world where the construction industry has not been devastated by the recession.) Two very separate countries have been merged together, not so much as equals, but, as the popular expression has it, as the West German colonization of East Germany. In many respects, East German society, identity and political culture have been forcibly eliminated. In the 'five new states', as the former GDR is now called, this has caused a national identity crisis and collective cognitive dissonance on a unprecedented scale. There has been a wholesale dismantling of the education system, the bureaucracy, the organization of recycling, the entire medical system based on polyclinics – in short, every aspect of life as it was known. In addition, on an individual level, eastern Germans who now operate in western environments must deal with the psychological pressures of sticking out, of being the 'bad' easterners, of having the wrong accents, taste, clothing, work ethics, habits, and the like.

Furthermore, the eastern Germans for the most part have been accustomed to life in an ethnically homogeneous society. Now they, especially those in Berlin, or those who live in close proximity to foreigner (often refugee) hostels, for the first time must deal with people they perceive as very different from them.

One of the most vexing problems facing the new and enlarged Germany is the question of the foreigners within. It has become increasingly apparent that now there are several classes of outsiders, or foreigners (in German, one word, *Auslander* describes both; see Forsythe 1989). Before unification the salient social identity opposition was between German and *Auslander* – usually a euphemism for Turk. Now, a new set of identities has emerged – Western vs. Eastern people. As mentioned above, the very real differences between them are manifested in a myriad of forms: in disparate sensibilities and experiences, as well as their separate and unequal economic situations and vocational prospects.

However, in many ways cross-cutting these formidable differences are the Turkish migrant workers and their families. On the one hand the Turks are more 'foreign' than the Germans of the eastern 'new states', yet in many cases the Turks are much better integrated into the western German social and economic structures. Consequently, they have become victimized, as they serve as targets for the anger, frustration and violence of some desperate, often eastern Germans.

A Historical Precedent

The contemporary period is not the first time that labour migration has been a controversial issue in Germany. In the late nineteenth and early twentieth centuries, between 1870 and 1914, industrialization in the west encouraged migration from the east (Bade 1987). German agricultural labourers from the *Junker* landed estates in the eastern regions moved to newly industrialized western areas. Consequently, Poles began to move *en masse* to fill the agricultural jobs. This period was marked by dramatic demographic shifts in the agricultural and industrial sectors. Whereas the German economy had been primarily agricultural until the mid-nineteenth century, by 1871 the rural segment had dropped to 64 per cent of the population; by 1900 it was 46 per cent, and the decrease continued thereafter. Between 1882 and 1907 the number of workers employed in industry rose from 4.1 million to 8.6 million, or by 110 per cent, while the actual population only increased from 45.2 million to 61.7 million, or by 37 per cent (Rhoades 1978: 556). The first wave of Polish migrants came for seasonal, agricultural work.

> By 1890, seasonal agricultural workers were required to register with the police and return to their home country during the winter off-season. The return trip, however, could be avoided simply by renewing the identification card. Many aliens, however, remained illegally in Germany without fulfilling this requirement. Although work contracts always stipulated that employment was seasonal, this rule was strictly enforced only during periods of recession. (p. 556)

Later the Poles moved into the industrial sectors further west, and many worked in the mining areas both in Germany and in Belgium.

By 1913 in the Ruhr region (Germany's central industrial area, then as now) there were 1,177 Polish associations. Polish banks, churches, newspapers, and trade unions flourished, to the point that, as early as 1886, 'cries of *Überfremdung* ('over-foreignization') arising from nationalist sentiment brought Bismarck to expel thirty thousand Polish workers and temporarily halt immigration' (p. 557; see also Brubaker 1992). In 1908 public use of the Polish language was banned, which led to the bizarre phenomenon of '"dumb assemblies" . . . in which nobody said a word, but [at which] leaflets in Polish were read communally' (Castles and Kosack 1973: 20).

Max Weber, in his *Antrittsrede* (inaugural address) of 1885, upon his appointment as Professor of Economics in Freiburg, asserted that the influx of Polish workers from the east threatened the hegemony of German culture where it had been strongest, among the *Junker* landowners. He called for the immigration to cease and the borders to be secured (Giddens 1972: 11; cf. also the Heidelberg Manifesto 1981).

Until 1905 employers hired workers informally, privately. In 1905 the Deutsche Feldarbeiterzentrale (later the Deutsche Arbeiterzentrale), had emerged, which were agencies in the federal government (Rhoades 1978: 558). The latter were 'the precursor of the present Bundesanstalt für Arbeit, the Federal Labour Office, that still, in conjunction with sending-country agencies, recruits and selects workers' (p. 259).

In the 1910 census 1,259,880 foreigners and 64,935,993 Germans lived in Germany (Krane 1975: 65).[1] The official term by which the foreigners were designated was *Reichsausländer*; they were residents but not citizens. Though there was a significant repatriation of Poles, many did remain and assimilate into the surrounding population. In Germany today it is not uncommon to encounter Polish surnames, particularly in regions that once had major Polish worker populations. This historical precedent is used in revisionist arguments frequently made about the present Turkish migrants. Ignorant of the history, until recently some Germans complained about the high profile of the Turks and the associated

---

1. Compare with 2.2 million foreigners employed in West Germany in 1974.

'foreigner problems' in terms of the Poles: 'Why can't the Turks just settle in and assimilate like the Poles did?' Now, with the new wave of ethnic Polish-'German' immigrants, the xenophobia has become more complex.

Castles tells us that 'as late as 1960 West Germany had no significant number of non-European residents. During the sixties large numbers of Turkish workers were recruited, so that by 1970 469,000 (or 16 per cent) of the nearly 3 million foreign residents were Turks' (1984: 75). With the halt of labour recruitment in 1973 the demographic composition of the migrant community began to change. Male workers, having overstayed their initial short-term residence, started to bring their families. The foreign population rose with the birth rate, so that 'by 1975 there were more non-employed foreigners than employed' (p. 74). In addition the national composition was changing, as Greek and Spanish migrants saw that repatriation was increasingly attractive, as their countries' economies began to develop and the respective military dictatorships collapsed (Spain: 1975; Greece: 1974).

'Foreigners' and Refugees

It should be stressed that a large portion of these 'foreigners' were born in, and have grown up in Germany. The confluence of German laws of citizenship and ideologies of ethnicity, nation and state, have effectively prevented this population from achieving legal and social equality, and civil rights, by denying them crucial access to full citizenship. This must be viewed in the context of the granting of full citizenship – quite literally overnight – to all of the citizens of the former East German state, as well as to the so-called 'ethnic Germans' from East European countries such as Poland, Czechoslovakia and Romania. Proof of a German ancestor who resided within the 1937 boundaries of the German Reich has been sufficient to claim German citizenship today. Perhaps it is not so surprising that acceptable evidence for this is a grandparent's membership card in the Nazi Party. Thus, descendants of card-carrying Nazis, in most cases monolingual Poles, have an automatic 'bloodright' to German citizenship, but *not* necessarily the second- and third-generation descendants of Turkish migrant workers, born and reared in Germany. The irony is glaringly apparent when one looks at Germany's history of Polish immigration.

The disturbing escalation of xenophobic violence, sometimes fatal, aimed at Turks and other foreigners, particularly in the districts of the former East Berlin and a number of regions of the former German Democratic Republic, is indicative of growing tensions that have yet to be resolved. The well-publicized, violent riot organized by (east) German neo-Nazis at the refugee shelters in Saxon Hoyerswerda in the summer of 1992 was seen by many as merely the tip of an iceberg; their fears were later confirmed with the murder of 3 Turks in Molln and 5 Turks in Solingen, all the victims of arson attacks.

Furthermore, not unproblematically, the German government's reaction mildly echoes the radical right – their explicit policy, that 'the boat is full', paves the way for even more restrictive immigration legislation. Germany's new asylum law, a virtual dismantling of Article 16 of the constitution, fundamentally changes the nature and practice of asylum in Europe. Before the recent constitutional changes this spring, Germany served as the country with the most liberal asylum policy in Europe, accepting 60 per cent of all asylum applicants in the EC. This was a remnant of moral reparations or compensation after the Second World War; in some senses, it was a recognition of collective culpability for the ethnic cleansing carried out by the German National Socialist state. Now, one consequence of the political unification of the two German states has been to revoke this liberal stance. In effect, this can be understood as the State's more than symbolic endorsement of, if not capitulation to, the right-extremist agenda of *'Ausländer raus'* – foreigners out.

However, despite what on paper was in fact a liberal asylum policy, most applicants for asylum have been denied. The figures in December 1992 showed that 1,516,000 persons had taken refuge in Germany, of whom 1,286,000 were in that liminal status of being stateless foreigners, *de facto* refugees under threat of being sent away, or asylum applicants. Of the more than one-and-one-half million foreign refugees, only 100,000 or 6.6 per cent had been granted asylum (Federal Government Foreign Affairs Division 1993: 63).

Foreigners of a different sort from the refugees, the status of the nearly two million resident Turkish citizens and other non-German foreign resident migrant workers and their families is becoming ever more precarious. Though they lack the right to become citizens, most are legal residents.[2] Many have lived there since the early 1960s, when Germany recruited them for needed manual labour to fuel the post-war boom economy. Between 1960 and 1973, when the international oil crisis brought recruitment to a grinding halt, over one million workers were brought into Germany. Since that time, the numbers have grown, due to the reproduction of a second and now a third generation, offsetting those who have repatriated.

German unification has rendered many aspects of the lives of the migrants insecure. In addition to the openly hostile environment and violence, there have been major changes in the shape and meaning of living space. For example, the well-known 'Turkish ghetto', Kreuzberg, before unification was located at the periphery of the city, surrounded on three sides by East Berlin and the Wall. The most dilapidated quarter of the Western, American sector, it was little changed since the War. Its rents were kept low, as the cold-water apartments often lacked inside toilets and central heating. Now, Kreuzberg's identity has changed, as it finds itself in the centre of a larger and unified Berlin, vulnerable to encroaching eager real estate speculators, gentrifiers and violent gangs of neo-Nazi youth from the east, now only a few subway train stops away.

Germany has yet to come to terms with this sizeable foreign population within the context of its own new identity. The government, for years having denied that the labour migrants were permanent immigrants, must now account for what seems to be an intractable problem between its disgruntled citizens from the former German Democratic Republic and the resident foreigners.

---

2. As of 1991 the Foreign Residents Act was changed to include the following groups of persons having a right to naturalization: (1) foreigners between the ages 16 and 23 who have lived in Germany on a regular basis for a period of at least eight years and have attended a school in Germany for a period of at least six years; (2) foreigners of 24 years or older who have lived in Germany on a regular basis for a period of at least 15 years and are able to make a living for themselves and their families; (3) spouses and children (minors) of foreigners of 24 years of age or older having lived in Germany on a regular basis for at least 15 years.

The obvious problems with this liberalized naturalization law are first, that a common pattern for the second generation youth has been to be shuffled back and forth between Turkey and Germany throughout their childhood; this could easily exclude a large share of the foreign youth. Second, 'are able to make a living' can be subject to interpretation. Since the recession, three times as many Turks have been made redundant as Germans; to be able to make a living and to be able to find a job are two entirely different things.

Turkey in and out of Europe

Long an affiliate member of the European Community, Turkey has been juggling with its liminal east–west identity since the mid-Ottoman Empire (see e.g. B. Lewis 1961). On such fundamental issues as rights of residence, work and travel, this incomplete affiliation is of critical importance. In this section of the chapter I examine the meanings of this marginality, and compare the different consequences of relative 'European-ness' for labour migrants in Germany.

In Germany the migrant workers from Turkey, who have been known colloquially and collectively as *Gastarbeiter*, guestworkers, are not welcomed by Germans as fellow Europeans. Nor are they welcomed any longer as guests. They are associated with the *Morgenland*, land of the morning, the orient – the implicit opposition is with the [more mature] *Abendland*, the occident, the west. Clearly, the twin concepts are ordered hierarchically.

In Germany the image of the Turk is frequently objectified and essentialized. And, the essentializing generalizations distance them beyond the embrace of Europeanness. This leaves them pushed to the margins, their identity being relegated to that of permanent outsiders. One of the central problems in terms of claiming a legitimate locally-based identity is the seeming absence of a conceptual space (inside the social margins) for a group that might claim to be separate and different but equal.

However, just as clear divisions between segments of the German population can be identified, parallels within the foreign community are found as well. First, reproducing the Germans' perception, the many nationalities place themselves within a hierarchically ordered scheme. Christian European *Gastarbeiter* clearly rank at the top. Italians, Greeks and what were once Yugoslavs compose this group. Spaniards and Portuguese, though less numerous, also would be ranked here. Italians would probably be at the top of the pecking order. The more distant and different from German society – in terms of social, cultural and physical proxemics – the further down a group finds itself. That the Turks occupy the lowest rung is indicated linguistically – as mentioned above, the word 'Turk' has come to be synonymous with *Ausländer*, foreigner, outsider. Among the various migrant groups, internal differentiation is also apparent. For example, urban Turks from Western Turkey often feel little if any kinship with their poorer rural compatriots. Worse yet, from the perspective of some, are the Kurds from Eastern Anatolia, whom they regard as little better than primitive. The self-designated 'Westernized' urban Turks often feel shame and resentment towards their 'backwards, embarrassing' compatriots, who, they say, give *all* Turks, 'even the well-integrated, modern ones' a bad name. Some also blame them for the considerable *yabancî düsmanligi* – *Ausländer-feindlichkeit* (prejudice, ill-will, stereotyping and xenophobia) most migrants claim to experience.

The migrants from Greece stand in a marginally better position in German society. At least in part this is due to the fact that Germans trace their intellectual heritage to Greece (albeit the Greece of 2,500 years ago). Germany produced schools of classical Greek philology, and Goethe was much enamoured with Greece, idealized it and translated modern (nineteenth-century) Greek folk songs. Furthermore, Greece has been for many years an established favourite vacation spot for Germans, growing numbers of whom own property there and return annually. The vacation potential of Turkey, on the other hand, has only more recently been discovered by German tourists; thus, the familiarity of Greece is far greater than that of Turkey to many Germans. Also, Greek music and food are well known and appreciated in West Germany. Moreover, Greece has been an almost-full member of the European Community since January 1981: the economic links symbolize a sense of inclusion into Europe that Turkey lacks.

In Greece the most salient 'other' has nearly always been the Turk, to the extent that Greekness is often conceived of in direct opposition to imagined and feared Turkishness. But in Germany the labels, treatment, and concepts of *Auslander* and 'Turk' are frequently used synonymously and interchangeably, and it is therefore surprising and confusing, if not highly upsetting, for Greeks to be mistaken for and called 'Turks'. The situation elicits novel reactions and responses, from a critical rethinking and re-evaluation of the traditional nationalist, acutely anti-Turkish animosity, to the Greeks' wholesale appropriation of the dominant culture's values and attitudes about Turks (cf. Herzfeld 1987: 107).

Insiders, Outsiders, Citizens

The objectification of the Turks, as mentioned above, contributes to their marginalized status. It also continues to mark them as an unassimilable 'other', by affirming an essential difference between the 'foreigners/Turks' and 'us'. This is clear not only in the rhetoric deployed by the right-wing politicians and neo-Nazis, who are clear in their agenda for Turks to repatriate. The liberal civil-rights-minded groups, as well, use language that serves to separate, and treat as other, the Turks and other non-Germans. This is not unrelated to the twin ideologies of nation and citizen, guided by the native notion of ethnicity.

In a statement by Chancellor Helmut Kohl, given at a cabinet meeting in 1992, he said of the foreign workers, 'We want to live together as friends and neighbours' . . . the coda he implied, by neglecting to add it, was 'but not as citizens'. This is because the German law recognizes the powerful symbol of blood, in the form of German ancestry and ethnicity, as the basic criterion for citizenship.

The pervasiveness of the term *Auslander*, having replaced *Gastarbeiter* in many contexts, reinforces the marginal role of the Turks, be they first, second or third generation in Germany. Another term, *Mitburger*, co- or fellow-citizen, can be heard as well, particularly among well-meaning politicians and in certain sectors of the public. The collocation 'foreign co-/fellow-citizen', marks even more an already marked population in a way that 'real' unmarked citizens – citizens without the *Mit-* prefix – are not. One does not hear of German Protestants or Bavarians singled out as co-citizens. The simple prefix *Mit-*, used to indicate euphemistic inclusion by those to whom *Auslander* sounds too harsh, instead highlights the fact that the foreign *Mitburger* are not true citizens, and, in effect, they are further excluded.[3] It is important to note that the word 'immigrant' is avoided, and the people in question are seen irredeemably as the 'others' among us; the Turks in our midst.

Germany is a nation-state whose identity is becoming ever more problematic as it is threatened by outsiders already inside the 'fortress'. The new asylum law will effectively preclude legal and social admission to many, if not most, of these outsiders. One of the central problems is that the definition of who is a German is

---

3. Interestingly, *Mitburger* is also used to describe German Jews. Again, this term emphatically marks out as different those people to whom it refers.

based on notions of ethnicity and blood – not civil citizenship.[4] Until *jus sanguinis* makes what to many Germans must appear to be the quantum leap to *jus solis*, the future of foreigners of all types in Germany promises still more insecurity.

References

Bade, Klaus. (ed.) (1987). *Population, Labour and Migration in 19th and 20th Century Germany*, Leamington Spa: Berg.

Brubaker, Rogers. (1992). *Citizenship and Nationhood in France and Germany*, Cambridge MA: Harvard.

Castles, Stephen. (1984). *Here for Good: Western Europe's New Ethnic Minorities*, London: Pluto Press.

Castles, Stephen and Godula Kosack. (1973). *Immigrant Workers and Class Structure in Western Europe*, London: Oxford University Press.

Federal Government Foreign Affairs Division. (1993). *Hostility towards foreigners in Germany: Facts, analyses, arguments*. Publication of the Press and Information Office of the Federal Government Foreign Affairs Division.

Forsythe, D. (1989). German Identity and the Problems of History. In *History and Ethnicity* (eds E. Tonkin, M. McDonald and M. Chapman), ASA Monograph 27, 137–56.

Giddens, Anthony. (1972). *Politics and Society in the Thought of Max Weber*, Basingstoke: Macmillan.

Heidelberger Manifest; 17 June 1981.

Herzfeld, Michael. (1987). *Anthropology Through the Looking Glass: Critical Ethnography in the Margins of Europe*, Cambridge: Cambridge University Press.

Krane, Ronald. (ed.) (1975). *Manpower Mobility across Cultural Boundaries*, Leiden: Brill.

Lewis, Bernard. (1961). *The Emergence of Modern Turkey*, Oxford University Press.

Mandel, R. (1990). Shifting Centres and Emergent Identities: Turkey and Germany in the lives of Turkish *Gastarbeiter'*. In *Muslim*

---

4. In Germany there appears to be no categorical or conceptual room for a civil definition of citizenship. This is the reason for the complete absence of any immigration policy, despite the fact that close to six million 'foreigners' reside in Germany, many of them having been there for several decades, and many of them having been born there.

Travellers: Pilgrimage, Migration, and the Religious Imagination (eds
Dale Eickelman and James Piscatori), London: Routledge and
Berkeley University of California Press, 153–71.

Rhoades, R. (1978). Foreign Labour and German Industrial
Capitalism 1871–1978: The Evolution of a Migratory System.
American Ethnologist, **5**, (3), 553–73.

Chapter 6

Nationalism and European Community Integration: The Republic of Ireland

Joseph Ruane

The Maastricht Treaty was the subject of three referenda during 1992. The Danes voted 50.7 per cent against the treaty, the Irish 69.1 per cent in favour, and the French 51 per cent in favour. Most attention has centred on the Danish and French referenda, where the results were close and the survival of the treaty at stake. The Danish rejection was the first blow to a process of accelerated integration which began in the mid-1980s and seemed unstoppable. By September a large NO vote in France was expected; but the close result was disturbing in a country whose support is crucial to the whole process of integration.

In both countries opposition stemmed from concern about the diminution of power to make decisions in the national interest. It pointed to the continued strength of national feeling in the EC, and challenged the assumption that nationalism was in terminal decline. But it also raised the question whether nationalism in the EC should be seen as a legacy of the past, something that will disappear as integration proceeds, or as something more permanent. In fact the view of the EC as a post-nationalist community has always overlooked the extent to which integration is motivated, mediated and underpinned by nationalist concerns.

Nationalism is understood here in a distinctive way, as 'an ideology of the nation', one whose defining characteristic is that it 'places the nation at the centre of its concerns' (Smith 1991: 74). According to this principle the primary concern of each nation is its own well-being. How this is achieved varies with circumstances. It does not necessarily mean a disregard for the well-being of other nations, rule out the possibility of co-operation for the good of all, or insist on absolute sovereignty. Nationalism in this sense is compatible with EC integration; it suffices merely that on balance EC membership advance the well-being of the nation.[1]

I deal with the ways in which nationalism, so defined, is shaping attitudes to EC integration in the Republic of Ireland. The large Irish vote in favour of the Maastricht Treaty has not attracted the same attention as the French or Danish votes, or led commentators to draw lessons for the future. This is in part because its explanation seems clear: Ireland is the largest beneficiary of EC funds per head of population in the EC, and an increase in EC funds was expected to follow the passing of the Treaty. The primacy of economic issues seems confirmed by the issues raised during the campaign. Economic considerations – markets for Irish goods and EC transfers – were most important, followed by concerns about the implications of integration for Irish legislation on abortion and about Irish neutrality. Research since the referendum confirms the importance of these factors in the minds of the voters.[2]

What role did nationalism play in the positions taken on these issues, and how is nationalism mediating and shaping the Irish response to integration? One could play down its role by arguing, for example, that one does not need to be a nationalist to want more money, to dislike armies or to be concerned about abortion or women's rights. But this would detach these issues from current debates about the nature and future of Irish society – debates conducted largely in nationalist terms.

I begin by sketching the goals of Irish nationalism and the extent to which they were realized by the new Irish State. I then look at the different strands of nationalism in the Republic of Ireland today, how they have responded to the intensification of the process of EC integration from the later 1980s, and how they impinge on the integration process. I conclude by drawing out some of the implications for research on EC integration and contemporary nationalism.

---

1. This concept of nationalism contrasts with those which define it in terms of an insistence on the correspondence of cultural and political boundaries. For example, for Gellner nationalism is 'a political principle that holds that the political and the national unit should be congruent' (Gellner 1983: 1).

2. *Irish Times* 16 December, 1992.

The Project of Irish Nationalism

Irish nationalism was a response to Ireland's long-term semi-colonial status within the wider British world, and, more proximately, to the integration of the British Isles during the nineteenth century which left most of the country peripheral. Nationalism crystallized in the early twentieth century as a (largely) Catholic phenomenon. Its goal was Irish political independence, and, through independence, the rebuilding of the economy, the construction of a State that would respond to Irish interests and concerns, and the establishment of a distinctive national culture, linked through the revival of the Irish language to the Gaelic culture of the past. However, Irish nationalism met strong opposition from Ulster Unionism and the British State; only part of the island achieved independence in 1922, and that in the form of Dominion status rather than the republic that was sought.[3]

Post-partition Irish nationalism set itself two goals: the achievement of full independence, and economic, political and cultural development.[4] Two quite different phases can be identified: from the 1920s to the 1950s, and from the 1960s to the present. The first phase was a foundational one, during which the main emphasis was on establishing the framework of a national economy (stressing Irish control over resources and industrialization behind tariff barriers) and political system (achieving full independence) and reGaelicization (concentrating in particular on reviving the Irish language). Pressure was also maintained on Northern Irish unionists and on the British government to end partition.

The second phase began in the late 1950s. The emphasis turned to new policy initiatives to develop the Irish Republic (declared in 1949). Policies became more outward-looking with the reduction in tariff barriers and the encouragement of inward investment. Politically the emphasis was on participation in supra-national bodies as the concrete expression of Irish sovereignty. Culturally Ireland became more outward-looking with the relaxation of the strict censorship laws passed in the 1920s, the intensification of mass communications and foreign travel. Meanwhile pressure to end partition weakened, although the aspiration to unity remained.

3. On the origins of Irish nationalism see Garvin (1987) and Hutchinson (1987).
4. On Ireland since independence see Lyons (1971) and Lee (1990).

Progress toward the twin goals of independence and development has been uneven. Separation from the wider UK economy was gradual. In 1960 the United Kingdom (UK) still took 75 per cent of Irish exports (down from 92 per cent in 1929) and the Irish pound was kept at parity with sterling. The link with sterling was broken in 1979, and export dependence had fallen to 33 per cent by 1985 (Kennedy *et al.* 1988: 83). However, Britain remains the single most important market for Irish goods and the key destination for Irish emigrants, and Irish trade union and business practices draw heavily on British models.

Political independence went farther faster, the major points of rupture being the adoption of a new constitution in 1937 and the decisions to remain neutral during the Second World War and to leave the Commonwealth in 1949. However, close political ties have remained, and new ones have been formed in the recent period. The latter include the Anglo-Irish Agreement of 1985, which gave the Republic a consultative role in the governing of Northern Ireland (NI) and also provided for an Anglo-Irish parliamentary tier. Irish political institutions and much Irish legislation continue to look to British models.

Culturally, too, the degree of secession has been uneven. The public symbols of Britishness were removed and the primary social carriers of British state culture – the anglicized gentry – also disappeared from view. Few in the Republic now feel part of a 'British world'. However, more informally, Britain remains the key point of reference for popular and high culture, as well as for the symbols of status. British newspapers, comics, books, magazines, radio and television form an integral part of everyday life.

Meanwhile, little progress has been made toward Irish reunification. If the Anglo-Irish Agreement gave the Republic a consultative role in the administration of Northern Ireland, it reaffirmed the Republic's acceptance that there would be no reunification without the consent of a majority in Northern Ireland – a consent that is not now forthcoming.

Contrary to nationalist assumptions, independence did not bring rapid economic development. Relative to the UK, Irish total product per capita improved only marginally between 1913 and 1985 (from 61 per cent to 62 per cent); during the same period every other Western European state improved its position relative to the UK, in some cases dramatically (Kennedy *et al.* 1988:14). Ireland's GDP per capita is the third lowest of the 16 major Western

European countries, and there are also serious structural problems: an agriculture overly dependent on the CAP; an industrial sector whose more advanced and competitive sector is almost wholly foreign-owned; an unemployment rate that fluctuates around 18 per cent despite recurring emigration; a high level of public indebtedness, internal and external.

Full independence was achieved and democracy maintained in spite of a bitter civil war and the enduring tensions created by partition. But at an institutional level there are many problems. The political system has shown a limited capacity to address the country's current economic problems, and the political élite a lack of interest in internal reform. There is considerable tension associated with the limited separation of (Catholic) Church and State, and the denial of rights to individuals and minority groups, religious or secular, who dissent from Catholic views on social issues. The result is both anger and cynicism about the political process.

The cultural goals of the nationalist movement have only partially been achieved. The language revival movement was by and large a failure, though other symbols of Irishness proved more resilient. A much clearer sense of Irish identity emerged, but for many (e.g. Fennell 1983; Kirby 1988) the culture on which it is based is a mish-mash, dependent and imitative, without a clear idea what it is or can be – precisely the qualities which turn-of-the-century nationalists sought to overcome.

Contemporary National Projects

In the 1980s the problems of public indebtedness, unemployment, renewed emigration, cultural *malaise* and frustration at the failings of the political system intensified and emerged sharply into public consciousness. There was a sense of crisis, reflection on the limited achievements of independence (although no serious doubts about its necessity or desirability), calls for radically new policies, or for a renewal or redefinition of the national project. In fact the nature of the crisis made consensus on a new national project very difficult. Four distinct ideological positions can be identified in the writings of Irish intellectuals and among the general population since the 1980s.

The first is 'traditional nationalism', so named not because it is identical with the nationalism of the earlier period but because it is closest to it in spirit.[5] It is distinctive in its stress on the continued relevance of principles of national self-determination and independence, and in its fear that they are being abandoned. For many in this category Ireland's present state of crisis is the product of the retreat from nationalism. Examples of this approach may be found in Fennell (1983, 1989, 1992), Coughlan (1985, 1986), O Ceallaigh (1991), and Boland (1988).

For Fennell (1983) the immediate cause of Ireland's problems lies in the abandonment of the goal of national independence from the 1960s on and its replacement by the goal of modernization. The opening up of Irish society from the 1960s to international influence was initially beneficial, but was carried to a destructive extreme. The resulting erosion of national autonomy has led to an incapacity to think about Irish problems – whether in respect of the economy, the political system, or Northern Ireland – in an original and creative way and to find solutions to them. Fennell (1983) conceives of independence primarily in a cultural sense – the capacity to develop one's own thoughts, concepts, world-image, as opposed to borrowing uncritically from outside; the other writers place greater stress on political independence.

The second ideology is 'liberal nationalism'. It dates from the 1960s and is now the dominant ideology of both society and State. The concepts and assumptions of nationalism are as often implicit as explicit; its approach is pragmatic, modernizing and outward-looking. Despite Ireland's current problems, it is optimistic about Ireland's potential and future prospects. It is realistic about the difficulties Ireland faces, but unlike the first ideology, it is self-confident about its own ability to shape events. Examples of this approach include Lee (1990), Tovey *et al.* (1989), de Paor (1990), and Fitzgerald (1972, 1991).

Liberal nationalism is critical of particular policies, but does not dissent from the fundamental project of the State after independence or after 1960. Thus the concern to create an independent Irish nation through the revival of the Irish language was valid, although some of the policies followed were overly rigid and authoritarian. Similarly the adoption of a more liberal, outward-looking and pragmatic approach after 1960 and the

5. The classification and the names I give to the four ideological positions are my own, but they draw on contemporary Irish ideological debate.

emphasis on industrial development were valid, although some policies – for example, over-dependence on multinational industry – were flawed.

Today the solution to current problems lies not in charting a radically new direction, but in a process of renewal that takes account of the circumstances in which Ireland now finds itself. There is need for structural and institutional reform to realize the potential that exists in the society, and for a continued liberal and outward-looking approach. But there is need also for a higher level of cultural autonomy; current problems are due in part to the failure to break with British institutional and policy-making models and to devise imaginative solutions appropriate to the Irish context (e.g. Lee: 627 ff.).

The third ideology is 'revisionism'. Its roots lie in 1930s dissent from Catholic-nationalism, but in its contemporary form it dates from the 1970s and 1980s. Its hostility to any expression of Catholic-nationalism gives it the appearance of anti-nationalism. It has, however, simply redefined the national community as the present Irish Republic; within its own frame of reference its goals are unmistakably nationalist. Examples of this approach may be found in Bolger (1992), Harris (1989, 1991, 1992), Murphy (1989, 1990), O'Brien (1991, 1992), O'Toole (1987, 1990, 1991), and Walsh (1990).

For revisionism the direction the State took in the decades after independence was profoundly misguided. Current problems in the Republic and the conflict in Northern Ireland are the legacy of Catholic-nationalism and of the class that came to power under its mantle. It is that legacy rather than colonialism that is the problem now. For Harris (1989: 20) 'Politics in Ireland today is about the removing the remnants of that trinity [i.e. Catholicism, nationalism and the rural bourgeoisie] from power.' The changes after 1960 were a step in the right direction, but they have to be carried much farther. Irish society and culture have to be rebuilt on radically new foundations: 'start again, make it new, make it better' (O'Toole 1991: 11).

The way forward is the full acceptance of the present Republic as the Irish State and nation for the foreseeable future and its comprehensive modernization. Modernization is defined primarily in continental European terms, and includes social-democratic politics, separation of Church and State, and cultural and religious pluralism. The models are the small-scale European states: Denmark, Norway, Finland, Switzerland.

The fourth ideology is 'de-colonization', a development largely of the 1980s, and distinctive in its stress on the Irish colonial experience and its legacy. It differs from 'traditional nationalism' in its stress on colonialism and on the similarities between Ireland and the Third World, and in its more critical approach to cultural nationalism. Nationalism is seen as a necessary, but transitional, step toward liberation of a more radical kind. For examples, see the writings of Crotty (1985, 1992), Coulter (1990, 1992), Kiberd (1991, 1992a,b), and Kirby (1988).

From a decolonization perspective, Ireland's contemporary problems are symptoms of its unresolved colonial past. The Northern Ireland conflict is also a legacy of colonialism, which has to be addressed rather than consigned to an indefinite future. The failure to deal with these problems arises from the fact that the ruling establishment in Ireland, like post-colonial élites elsewhere, profits from the colonial legacy and has little interest in undoing it. The decolonization approach is critical of the policies followed in the first years of the new state, but ultimately sees the Irish problem as one of structures, not policies.

Nationalist Responses to EC Integration

The four national ideologies had emerged by the mid-1980s, a time when there was little reporting or discussion of EC matters. Irish ratification of the Single European Act (SEA) required a referendum; for the first time in over a decade the EC – what it stood for, what it could achieve – received wide coverage in the speeches of politicians, in the statements of the major pressure groups and in the media generally. This intensified with preparations for '1992' and the lead-up to the Maastricht Treaty. The EC is now part of the political and cultural landscape to a degree scarcely imaginable a decade ago.

All ideological positions have had to take account of this and adopt a position on it. In doing so they have had enormous latitude. The EC is itself a project, its present obscure and its future open, and it can be imagined almost as one pleases and fitted virtually to any ideological purpose. It suffices simply to select one set of asssumptions, aspects or predictions rather than another. Two of the ideologies described have opposed continuing EC integration; the other two favour it, though with different degrees of enthusiasm. At the same time there have also been attempts radically to recast Ireland's national project in a post-nationalist way.

In general traditional nationalism and decolonization have opposed EC integration. Many of their prominent representatives campaigned against the Single European Act (SEA) and the Maastricht Treaty. Some advocate complete Irish withdrawal; others resist further integration. The arguments advanced by both groups are much the same. Some are economic. For Fennell (1992) Ireland's economic and social condition has deteriorated since it joined the EC, and the evidence suggests it will worsen in the future as capital and people move from the periphery to the European core. This is what happened in an earlier union with Great Britain and there is no reason to expect the EC – despite its cash grants – to be any different. By contrast, a wealth of opportunity exists outside the EC. Crotty (1992) makes similar arguments.

Other arguments are political, and centre on the threat the EC poses to Irish political independence and neutrality. The EC is presented as a super-state in the making. Integration into a supra-national union will make democracy impossible (Coughlan 1985). It is also a union composed for the most part of post-imperial powers indifferent to the Third World. Thus Kiberd (1992b) sees the 'resource wars' predicted for the next century by Jacques Delors as wars that will 'pit developed Europe against the undeveloped Third World', 'And in that confrontation, should a post-colonial Ireland not support the poor against the post-imperial nations?'.

In both perspectives, Ireland's past has left it with particular problems – economic underdevelopment, an uncompleted national project, an unresolved colonial legacy – and valuable qualities – a hostility to militarism, a sensitivity to the problems of the Third World. Integration into the EC will at once make these problems more difficult to resolve and undermine Ireland's positive qualities.

By contrast, liberal nationalism strongly favours integration. Its emergence in Ireland in the later 1950s underpinned the new emphasis on outward-looking policies in all spheres, economic, political and cultural. Application for membership of the EC in 1961 was seen as a natural expression of the new approach, as was support for membership in the 1972 campaign, and subsequently for the SEA and the Maastricht Treaty. But behind this new outward-looking approach is a much older aspiration of Irish nationalism, first articulated at the turn of the nineteenth century:

that Ireland would one day 'take her place among the nations of the world'. There is no antithesis between the nationalist struggle for independence and membership of the EC. On the contrary, 'it was, in fact, in Irish membership of the European Community that Ireland's movement for national independence in the early part of the 20th century was to find its ultimate justification' (Fitzgerald 1991).

The central themes of liberal nationalism have been the benefits that integration can bring to Ireland: higher prices for its agricultural produce, markets for its industrial goods, regional funds to develop the Irish economy, the opportunity to participate in a wider political forum, a wider arena for Irish culture, a chance to reduce economic and cultural dependency on Britain, increased economic integration between Northern Ireland and the Republic as an important first step toward Irish reunification. But the benefits will not be all one way: Ireland's potential contribution to Europe is also stressed. A YES vote will be, according to a Government advertisement, a vote for 'a united Europe shaped by a compassionate and tolerant Ireland' (*Irish Times* 16 June 1992); a positive vote for Maastricht after the Danish NO would enable Ireland to play a historic role in the progress toward European union.

Revisionism's response to the process of EC integration is rather more mixed, as befits its darker view of contemporary Ireland and of the world generally. Some in this category are hostile to, or ambivalent about, EC integration (e.g. Murphy 1992); however, most are positive towards it. For supporters and opponents the determining principle is the same: the benefits or disbenefits the EC will bring to Ireland; there is little stress on what Ireland has to offer to the EC. As might be expected, arguments concerning the implications of integration for Irish reunification have little appeal unless further to demonstrate the pointlessness of pursuing it.

The economic benefits or necessity of entry are stressed. But most important of all, the EC is seen as a source of external pressure – and therefore an ally – in the reconstruction and modernization of the Republic of Ireland, particularly in its political and cultural attitudes. One commentator, urging his readers to support the Maastricht treaty, asks them to imagine the consequences of its failure: 'the fate of Irish women in a Little Ireland pushed back to the dark edge of Europe' in which fundamentalists on the abortion issue 'strut our streets with enhanced authority as our self-appointed guardians' (Fanning 1992).

Most of the debate about integration has taken place within the confines of the four ideological positions described. However, there have also been attempts radically to recast Ireland's national project in a post-nationalist way. Two variants have appeared so far: a federalist one (O'Malley 1988) and a postmodern/regionalist one (Kearney 1988, 1989). In the first the EC is conceived as essentially a United States of Europe with a high level of internal economic and political integration and a strong European identity. In the latter the EC is envisaged as a decentred community of regions.

Both writers start from the assumption that a new historical epoch is at hand, and that the era of the nation-state is over. The process is most advanced in Western Europe, and is taking the form of EC integration. Both view nationalism as valid for its time, but a time that is now past. They criticize the 'narrow nationalism' which prevents people from committing themselves to the European ideal. The EC can bring enormous benefits to Ireland, though only if Irish people commit themselves wholeheartedly to the European ideal and see themselves as European or as Irish-European and not merely Irish.

Once this is done many apparently intractable problems will be resolved. For example, the apparently unattainable aspiration to Irish unity will become redundant in a wider EC in which 'all borders are coming down', and in which sovereignty is being pooled. The people of Ireland will be united, making territorial unity irrelevant. Emigration will also cease to be a problem, since Irish emigration to other EC countries will be no more emigration than the migration of a Nebraskan or Arkansan to California, Chicago or New Orleans (Kearney 1988: 141). Again, Ireland's sense of having an anomalous past will cease to matter, since it will be able to identify with the wider European experience.

Some of this discourse, particularly that dealing with emigration and the irrelevance of Irish unity, has achieved wide currency. EC integration offers an opportunity to abandon a project thought dated, onerous or unattainable. But this is not the dominant public or intellectual response. The sense of a national community pursuing (or at least trying to pursue) a national project remains strong, and the concept of national self-determination is still an important if implicit part of the political culture. For most, EC integration does not obviate the need for a national project; it simply changes the context within which it has to be pursued.

Moreover, there is more than an undercurrent of nationalism among post-nationalists as well. Although Kearney's postmodern project is explicitly post-nationalist, his advocacy of it is pervaded by nationalist sentiment, including the suggestion that 'Ireland's postmodern project might well serve as a vanguard movement for the wider world' (1988: 116–17). Similarly O'Malley (1988) advocates a federal EC as the best possible arrangement for dealing with Irish (as well as European and international) problems.

Nationalism and Irish Attitudes to EC Integration

Nationalist ideologies are mediating and shaping the Irish response to EC integration at two levels: political decision-making (particularly in referenda, but also in European elections), and perceptions of the EC and its implications for Ireland.

Nationalism impacts on political decision-making by providing the interpretative frameworks within which EC-related issues are considered. Economic issues attract most attention, sometimes suggesting a very superficial and short-term attitude to integration. For example, much discussion during the Maastricht referendum centred on whether or not Ireland would receive the £6 billion in Structural Funds the government claimed, and whether it should have pressed for far more. Such seemingly crude financial calculations, however, have to be seen beside a widespread fear of Irish economic decline as a periphery of the EC, similar to its decline as a periphery of Britain in the nineteenth century – an interpretation that itself reflects a nationalist understanding of Irish history. Since there seemed little choice but to remain within the EC, the priority became that of maximizing aid to improve Irish competitiveness.

The other issues important in referenda also tap into concerns underpinned by nationalism. For example, the abortion issue in the Maastricht referendum was only in part about the rights of the foetus or of women. It was accepted that Irish women would continue go to Britain for abortions. It was much more a symbolic issue in a struggle between groups advancing very different projects for Irish society. Similarly the question of Irish neutrality was not simply whether young Irish people would die fighting European 'resource wars'. For some it was a question of whether

Ireland would betray its past by allying with the post-imperialist powers against the Third World; for others it was about whether Ireland was to overcome its Anglophobic isolationist past and become a mature modern nation.

The influence of nationalist ideologies on decision-making on the EC is made all the more important by the difficulty in making a decision on the issues themselves. For example, in the Maastricht referendum the debate on the structural funds could reach no conclusion since no decision on the issue had yet been made at EC level. The implications of the treaty for Irish neutrality were also unclear, the sections dealing with foreign policy and security being open to different interpretations. The implications of Ireland's special protocol to the treaty dealing with abortion were also unclear in the wake of an unexpected interpretation by the Supreme Court in early 1992 of the pro-life clause in the Irish constitution. In the absence of a clear basis for decision, voters could not but fall back on ideologically informed intuitions.

The second level at which nationalism is mediating the process of Irish–EC integration is in terms of an adjustment in perceptions of the EC and its implications for Ireland. This adjustment is a continuing one. Periodic referenda play the crucial role in this, but all matters pertaining to the EC change perceptions to some degree: elections to the European Parliament, Irish presidency of the European Council, appointments of Irish Commissioners, newspaper articles and television programmes on the EC, signs indicating the contribution of EC funds to new or improved roads.

The ways in which the EC is imagined vary widely, as we have seen. For some the EC is a future super-state of post-colonial powers indifferent to the needs and concerns of small nations; for others it is a community of nations working together for the good of all, in which even the smallest nation can have a voice; for still others it is a pole of modernization and development which can help Ireland overcome its present backwardness. Such contrasting images cannot be explained by reference to what the EC actually is or to its practical expressions in Ireland at present. More than anything else they reflect the different nationalist ideologies to which Irish people, consciously or unconsciously, adhere. In other words, Irish images of the EC – both 'pro-' and 'anti-European' – are primarily projections of convictions, fears, and aspirations that have their roots in different strands of Irish nationalism.

Implications

It was suggested at the outset that the view of the EC as a post-nationalist community overlooks the role nationalism is playing in the process of EC integration and underestimates its resilience within it. This study makes clear the centrality of nationalism in Irish attitudes to integration. It has two implications.

The first is the need to study the place of nationalism within the EC. The tendency to see nationalism as the legacy of a past condemned soon to disappear is distracting attention from its possible role as an integral and dynamic feature of the EC. Some of the member states, particularly Britain, make clear their view of the EC as an institutional arrangement for advancing national interests, especially their own. Others, for example France, strike a more *communautaire* attitude and support a more rapid rate of integration, but for reasons that appear hardly less nationalist once the economic and geopolitical situation of each country is taken into account. It is possible that nationalism will contribute to the formation of the EC and then dissolve; it is just as likely it will become a permanent feature, and that the EC will develop as an inter-national, rather than a post-national or supra-national, community.[6]

The second is the need to take account of nationalism in its different forms and expressions. There is a tendency to identify only certain positions (for example, concern with absolute sovereignty or irredentist designs on the territories of other states) as nationalist, and to take at face value the claims of groups who say that they are 'not nationalist'. But if nationalism is defined as an ideology which 'places the nation at the centre of its concerns' (Smith 1991: 74), most political discourse today is still permeated by nationalist assumptions. If the Irish case is a guide, the major division is not between nationalists and non-nationalists (who are quite rare), but between different kinds of nationalists. I identified four variants of Irish nationalism and the ways in which each has responded to EC integration. To understand the forces shaping the emerging European community, it is necessary to know more about the nationalisms that are mediating and shaping responses to integration in the other member states.

6. On this issue see Petit (ed.) (1991).

References

Boland, K. (1988). *Under Contract with the Enemy*, Cork: Mercier.

Bolger, D. (1992). Why I don't want a United Ireland, *Sunday Press*, January 26.

Coughlan, A. (1985). *EEC Political Union: Menace to Irish Neutrality and Independence*, Dublin: Irish Sovereignty Movement.

Coughlan, A. (1986). *Fooled Again? The Anglo-Irish Agreement and After*, Cork: Mercier Press.

Coulter, C. (1990). *Ireland Between First and Third Worlds*, Dublin: Attic Press.

Coulter, C. (1992). Where in the world. In *Is Ireland a Third World Country?* (ed. T. Caherty), pp. 3–13, Belfast: Beyond the Pale Publications, 3–13.

Crotty, R. (1985). *Ireland in Crisis: A Study in Capitalist Colonial Undevelopment*, Dingle: Brandon.

Crotty, R. (1992). *Maastricht: Time to Say No!* Dublin: The National Platform for Employment, Democracy, Neutrality.

De Paor, L. (1990). *Unfinished Business: Ireland Today and Tomorrow*, London: Hutchinson Radius.

Fanning, R. (1992). Good Europeans or little Irelanders, *Sunday Independent*, June 14.

Fennell, D. (1983). *The State of the Nation*, Swords: Ward River Press.

Fennell, D. (1989). *The Revision of Irish Nationalism*, Dublin: Open Air.

Fennell, D. (1992). Why the Maastricht Treaty will be a national disaster, *Irish Times*, February 4.

Fitzgerald, G. (1972). *Towards a New Ireland*, London: Charles Knight.

Fitzgerald. (1991). 1916 and Irish independence, *Irish Times*, July 13–18.

Garvin, T. (1987). *Nationalist Revolutionaries in Ireland 1858–1928*, Oxford: Clarendon Press.

Gellner, E. (1983). *Nations and Nationalism*, Oxford: Basil Blackwell.

Harris, E. (1989). Hide and seek, *Making Sense*, January, 20–1.

Harris, E. (1991). The permanence of partition, *Fortnight* No 295.

Harris, E. (1992). The Six County and Western Cabinet, *Sunday Tribune*, February 16.

Hutchinson, J. (1987). *The Dynamics of Irish Cultural Nationalism*, London: Allen & Unwin.

Kearney, R. (1988). Postmodern Ireland. In *The Clash of Ideas; Essays in Honour of Patrick Lynch* (ed. M. Hederman), pp. 112–41, Dublin: Gill and Macmillan.

Kearney, R. (1989). Introduction: Thinking Otherwise. In *Across the Frontiers: Ireland in the 1990s* (ed. R. Kearney), pp. 7–28, Dublin: Wolfhound Press.

Kennedy, K., Giblin, T. and McHugh, D. (1988). *The Economic Development of Ireland in the Twentieth Century*, London: Routledge.

Kiberd, D. (1991). The elephant of revolutionary forgetfulness. In *Revising the Rising* (eds M. Ni Dhonnchadha and T. Dorgan) pp. 1–20, Derry: Field Day, 1–20.

Kiberd, D. (1992a). Tourists in their own country. *Irish Reporter*, 6, 12–3.

Kiberd, D. (1992b). Guns 'n' roses deal for Irish neutrality? *Irish Press*, May 18.

Kirby, P. (1988). *Has Ireland a Future?* Cork: Mercier.

Lee, J. (1990). *Ireland 1912–1985: Politics and Society*, Cambridge: Cambridge University Press.

Lyons, F. S. L. (1971). *Ireland Since the Famine*, London: Weidenfeld and Nicolson.

Murphy, J. (1989). Peace first, *Making Sense*, April, 8–9.

Murphy, J. (1990). The misguided claim, *Sunday Independent*, October 7.

Murphy, J. (1992). The 'No' vision, *Sunday Independent* June 14.

O'Brien, C. C. (1991). Pride in the language, *Irish Independent*, May 11.

O'Brien, C. C. (1992). He's gone – but is it the end of GUBU? *Irish Independent*, February 1.

O Ceallaigh, D. (1991). *Labour, Nationalism and Irish Freedom*, Dublin: Léirmheas.

O'Malley, C. (1988). *'Over in Europe': The Issues Facing Ireland in the European Community*, Dublin: Orchard Press.

O'Toole, F. (1987). *The Southern Question*, Dublin: Raven Arts Press.

O'Toole, F. (1990). Light rain and governments falling: Ireland in the eighties. In *A New Tradition: Irish Art of the Eighties* (ed. Douglas Hyde Gallery), pp. 7–11, Dublin.

O'Toole, F. (1991). Defending and defining Irish nationalism, *Irish Times*, July 6.

Petit, M. (ed.) (1991). *L'Europe Interculturelle: Mythe ou Réalité?* Paris: Les Éditions d'Organisation.

Tovey, H., Abramson, H. and Hannan, D. (1989). *Why Irish? Irish*

Identity and the Irish Language, Dublin: Bord na Gaeilge.

Smith, A. (1991). *National Identity*, London: Penguin.

Walsh, D. (1990). Shuffling slyly into backwoods politics, *Irish Times*, February 17.

Chapter 7

Xenophobia, Fantasy and the Nation: The Logic of Ethnic Violence in Former Yugoslavia

Glen Bowman

The violent ethnic nationalisms which replaced Yugoslavia's communalist ethos of *bratstvo i jedinstvo* ('brotherhood and unity') when, in 1991, the Socialist Federative Republic of Yugoslavia fragmented into its constitutive republics took observers by surprise. The bloody ethnic warfare that has continued to rage in the territories of Former Yugoslavia ever since has substituted trepidation for the enthusiasm with which most Europeans had greeted the collapse of Communist hegemony in Eastern Europe. The character of the nationalisms of Former Yugoslavia furthermore challenges the optimism with which theorists of nationalism such as Eric Hobsbawm heralded the demise of a phenomenon they believed – in the light of the developing global economy – could only be seen as atavistic. Hobsbawm's elegiac *Nations and Nationalism since 1780* closes with an assertion which, after Vukovar and Mostar, resonates with modernism's tragic *hubris*:

> [T]he world history of the late twentieth and early twenty-first centuries ... will see 'nation states' and 'nations' or ethnic/linguistic groups primarily as retreating before, resisting, adapting to, being absorbed or dislocated by, the new supranational restructuring of the globe. ... [T]he very fact that historians are at least beginning to make some progress in the study and analysis of nations and nationalism suggests that, as so often, the phenomenon is past its peak. The owl of Minerva which brings wisdom, said Hegel, flies out at dusk. It is a good sign that it is now circling round nations and nationalism. (Hobsbawm 1990: 182–3)

Contemporary nationalisms and the ethnic identities they mobilize may seem, from a global perspective, to be irrational, since the national states they strive to realize appear inappropriate to the economic structure of today's world. I will argue, however, that such a viewpoint is incapable of comprehending the powerful appeal ethno-nationalist rhetorics can have for people caught up in the day-to-day struggle to sustain, and improve, the ways in which they live. In the local domains in which people live, exclusivist identities and strategies seem to be as powerful and goal-oriented as they were in earlier periods – if not more so. In this paper I will analyse the logic of ethnic antagonism as it is manifested in the new nations which have sprung up on the territories of what was Yugoslavia in order to suggest that ethnic nationalism cannot be understood in the terms of the modernist rationalism of its analysts. Instead, I will argue, it is often constituted within political discourses which link passion and rationality in a manner which modernism – with its image of humankind as intellectively rational – is incapable of explaining or undermining. Former Yugoslavia may be a harbinger of a long period of ethnic wars engulfing not only the territories which were, until very recently, stabilized by Communist rule, but also other regions which had been politically fixed by the global antagonism between Communism and capitalism. An understanding of the processes which led to the bloody collapse of the Yugoslav federation may thus enable social scientists to devise new models for the analysis of identity which may allow comprehension of the 'irrational' resurgence of impassioned exclusivist communalisms and the inter communal wars they promote.

The Return to Democracy: But Who are 'The People'?

The collapse of the Communist federal system's legitimacy, which began in 1988–9, when the Serbian nationalist leader Slobodan Milošević abrogated the autonomy of Kosova and the Vojvodina and deposed the government of Montenegro, inaugurated throughout the republics of what was then Yugoslavia a search for new ways of legitimating power structures which, in all instances, were already in place (the state apparatuses of the respective republics remained operative during the transition from republican to national statuses). The discourse in which this new mode of legitimation took place was, without exception, democratic: Yugoslavs, caught up in the pro-Western ecstasy that swept through Eastern Europe after the fall of the Berlin Wall, accepted the Western panacea of democratic elections as the cure for all ills that had afflicted them under Communism. Elections took place in the republics of Slovenia and Croatia in April 1990, and in Macedonia, Bosnia–Herçegovina, Montenegro, and Serbia in December. The results of these elections differed considerably: Slovenia and Croatia voted in centre-right anti-Communist coalitions; the Macedonian elections produced a hung parliament, and a coalition government encompassing old Communist Party *nomenclatura* as well as reformist communists and nationalists was subsequently negotiated; Bosnia – Herçegovina set up a coalition of Croats, Muslims and Serbs which excluded the Communists; and Montenegro and Serbia reinstalled their Communist leaderships.

The politicians who took power in these elections did so in contests in which they claimed that the programmes they wished to enact were the programmes 'the people' really desired. In a situation in which the people had previously had little if any say in what was enacted by the State, there were no elaborated 'popular platforms' which could be appropriated by political candidates (Gaber 1993); the prevalent sense among the populations of the various republics was simply that the previous system had not worked and had, particularly through the previous decade of unequal economic development and massive foreign debt, led to a substantial decline in their standards of living. Thus the only popular will to evoke was one of gross dissatisfaction, and the most convincing programmes to develop out of that were ones which promised to find, and abolish, the reasons that the system had failed. The sudden collapse of socialist hegemony in Yugoslavia and throughout Eastern Europe, which was for the most part brought about by economic bankruptcy and not by organized internal resistance, gave rise to popular fantasies of transformation which were virtually millennarian; people felt that if they took the magical draught of democracy proffered them by the West they would instantly move into a new, and far better, world. Political platforms were thus not organized around plans for serious and rigorous structural changes in the political and economic domains, but around talismanic pronouncements that if the parties running were elected they would transform the State into something that expressed the real will of the real people and would expunge from the nation all those agents and agencies which had in the past perverted that will. What the elections all had in common, then, was the assumption that legitimacy devolved from 'the people' rather than from the self-ordained mission of the previous Communist leadership, which was that of realizing the 'people's state' Communist ideology saw as the inherent goal of the historical process. The central question then, which was foregrounded in all the elections, was 'Who are the (real) people?'

The answer provided by those politicians who won the elections – which was evidently the answer the majority of the voters wished to hear – was that the real people were the members of the dominant ethnic groupings of the respective republics. In Slovenia, for example, the victorious centre-right DEMOS coalition argued on a nationalist ticket that Slovenians were inherently industrious and productive, and that if they could destroy the influence of the Communists and the other ('Southern') non-Slovene national groupings which interfered with their work Slovenes would become as wealthy as the capitalists of neighbouring Austria whom they emulated. The ticket was effectively 'Slovenia for Slovenians', and this 'programme' was far more attractive to the electorate than the platform of the left reformist coalition which demanded full civil rights for all persons resident in Slovenia, as well as radical, and arduous, changes in social and economic organization. At the other end of the political spectrum the winning argument in the Serbian elections, in which Milošević's national socialist party was returned to power, was that Serbs were true communists who would, were they not impeded by anti-Serbian foreign conspirators (people like the 'Croat' Tito, who Milošević claimed had orchestrated a 'Vatican–Comintern' conspiracy against Serbia), re-establish a 'Greater Serbia' as wealthy and as powerful as the (imagined) one which had ruled over vast areas of Balkans in the period before the Ottoman conquest. The only 'Yugoslav' ticket present in all the republican elections was that of the League of Reform Forces led by Ante Marković, who, as federal prime minister, had instituted radical economic reforms throughout Yugoslavia in 1989 and 1990. Marković's platform called for 'an undivided Yugoslavia with a market economy, political pluralism, democratic rights and freedoms for all citizens' (quoted in Thompson 1992: 104). He was soundly thrashed in all the elections, carrying only Tusla, an industrial town in Bosnia–Herçegovina.

Two specific elements operated within the political discourses of the victorious parties, whether anti-Communist or Communist. The first was an evocation of the essential character and desire of the 'people' being appealed to; the second was a scapegoating of 'the other', who denied the people their true realization and the rewards it would bring about. Each of these elements appealed to a nationalist definition of identity elaborated in ethnic terms. The Yugoslav elections were won by parties which called upon people in terms of their ethnic identities and attributed the problems which afflicted them to persons and groups which had in the past been their neighbours (neighbours not only in the sense of the residents of contiguous republics, but also, in most cases, in the sense of literal neighbours in ethnically mixed communities). The appeal of these platforms served to drive wedges between peoples who had previously lived together or in close proximity (see the Disappearing World documentary, 'We Are All Neighbours' directed by Debbie Christie and based on the work of Tone Bringa). Thus 'ethnic cleansing' was already set out as a political agenda in the 1990 republican elections, in so far as what the victorious political programmes sketched out in theory would subsequently be given body on the ground in Croatia, Bosnia–Herçegovina, and areas within Serbia such as the Sanjak and Kosova. It is important, however, to stress that this project was choreographed by the political leadership. Generating ethnic antagonisms provided a facile means for people in power to hold on to it and persons seeking power to achieve it at a time when previously effective means of grasping and holding power were being undermined and overturned.

It is not, however, sufficient to say simply that this was 'done' to the people by an opportunist and unethical political leadership. We must investigate the enthusiasm with which elements of the Yugoslav populace responded to being 'hailed' (Althusser 1971: 162–3) as ethnic nationalists who had to destroy their neighbours in order to affirm their selves. The brutalities which have characterized ethnic interaction in the succeeding three years could not, I contend, have been foreseen by an observer of the patterns of coexistence which had characterized the post-war years; after the eruption of nationalist fervour, intermarriage, co-residence and economic co-operation were replaced by mutilations such as the gouging out of eyes and hacking off of genitals, as well as by the rape of women and children, the wholesale massacre of ethnic groups within towns and villages, the desecration and destruction of the properties and houses of those viewed by the perpetrators as ethnic 'others', and the collection of men, women and children in concentration camps where torture, murder, and genocidal deprivations of food and water are commonplace. Such activities have been carried out by Serbs, Croats and Bosnians; and, although Slovenia has not seen ethnic warfare because of the relative homogeneity of its population, I have observed brutal harassment by Slovene police of persons who were ethnically non-Slovene whose only 'crime' was being within the borders of Slovenia. The ethnic hatred which has erupted throughout the territories of Former Yugoslavia may have been instigated from above; but the popular response to that fomentation has been enthusiastic. Tomaz Mastnak, a Slovene social philosopher, points out that the volunteer militias, which have carried out the larger part of the atrocities, are not anti-social anomalies, but are expressions of precisely the sort of society which has developed in ex-Yugoslavia: 'The militias are exactly the people in arms – civil society at its most uncivil' (Mastnak 1992: 7). Analysis of the current situation must not only ascertain why ethnic divisiveness has served as a successful means of grasping power, but also determine why the call to arms against former neighbours has been responded to with such passion.

* * *

Redefining Identities and Boundaries: Why 'Neighbours' Became 'Enemies'

When new states separate themselves off from an old state in which their peoples had been consolidated, the problem of how to determine which people belong to which new nation is problematic. In the case of the new states which have sprung up on the territory which was Yugoslavia, the clear-cut boundaries of 'inside' and 'outside' are poorly defined territorially. The modernization processes which affected Yugoslavia and its peoples in the twentieth century further mixed ethnic populations already intermingled by earlier experiences of living under the Ottoman and the Austro-Hungarian empires (see Hammel 1993). Bosnia–Herçegovina, which was 40 per cent Muslim, 33 per cent Serbian, 18 per cent Croatian, and 9 per cent 'others' (a census category which designates other national and ethnic groups, as well as persons who refuse to define themselves in national or ethnic terms) is not a demographic anomaly: Croatia is 75 per cent Croat, 12 per cent Serbian, and 13 per cent 'others'; Serbia, not counting its allegedly autonomous regions of Kosova (10 per cent Serbian and 90 per cent Albanian) and the Vojvodina (56 per cent Serbian, 21 per cent Hungarian, and 23 per cent 'others'), is 65 per cent Serbian, 20 per cent Albanian, 2 per cent Croat and 13 per cent 'others'; and even Slovenia, which considers itself ethnically homogeneous, is 90 per cent Slovene, 3 per cent Croat, 2 per cent Serbian and 5 per cent 'others' (van den Heuvel and Siccama 1992: frontispiece). When substantial populations of persons who do not share the ethnicity of the hegemonizing group reside on the territory of the state that group is attempting to create, the process of legitimating statehood in ethnic terms foregrounds the question of what to do with inhabitants who have no ethnic rights to membership in that political collectivity. When the boundaries between 'us' and 'them' do not run along defensible territorial borders but through the middle of towns and villages and, all too often, through the middle of families, the desired 'national entity' can be discursively presented as penetrated and occupied by 'enemies' who must – at least – be disarmed by disfranchisement (Dimitrijević 1993 and Hayden, forthcoming) and – at best – be neutralized by exile or extermination.

This discursive project of transforming neighbours into enemies opposes the dominant state discourse of the previous 47 years of 'Yugoslav nationality', which naturalized co-operation and consanguinity. The traditions which had constituted identities since the Second World War were designed to efface intercommunal antagonisms and to establish Yugoslav *bratstvo i jedinstvo* as the only viable means of ensuring the survival and well-being of individuals. Yugoslav federation had been posited on the drawing of different borders between the `inside' and the `outside'. The partisan war against the Nazi occupation had forged solidarity between individuals from all of Yugoslavia's ethnic groups in defense of the `homeland', and had simultaneously brought Tito and the Communist Party to power. It had been followed by a brutal purging of the `enemy within' which resulted in the deaths of tens of thousands of Yugoslav `collaborators' and the driving into exile of many more. Subsequently the *Ustaše*, Croats who – with Nazi encouragement – had waged ethnic war against non-Croats during the period of war-time occupation, were defined in state rhetoric as `Nazis' (i.e. quislings of a foreign power) rather than as Croats. 'Communist rule entailed ideological control over the representation of the past, [and] those horrible events that would disrupt the new inter-ethnic cooperation were not to be mentioned, except in the collective categories "victims of fascism", on the one side, and "foreign occupiers and domestic traitors", on the other side' (Denich 1991: 2). A later boost to Yugoslav solidarity was provided by Tito's break with the Soviet Union in 1948, when 'the greater part of the nation rallied behind Tito in the face of the Soviet threat' (Auty 1966: 247). Subsequent developments in state policies kept Yugoslavia `balanced' between `East' and `West', and the interests of the nation – and of the various peoples who constituted it – could thus always be drawn up in opposition to the conspiracies of a labile set of enemies threatening Yugoslavia from beyond its territorial, and ideological, borders.

Thus discourses of ethnic antagonism could not easily call upon hegemonic tradition to justify the division of communities in so far as the hegemonic tradition of the Communist state argued to the contrary that the survival of the Yugoslav peoples depended on defensive co-operation. Agencies wishing to establish exclusively ethnic identities had, therefore, to 'invent' traditions (Hobsbawm and Ranger 1983) of ineluctable antagonisms which could validate radical redefinitions of the field of sociality and co-operation. Such invention did not, however, involve the conjuring up of grounds for antagonism *ex nihilo*; the successive Yugoslav constitutions (there were four, with the latest written in 1974) had kept markers of national identity alive within the federation, and many incidents and episodes in recent and not-so-recent Yugoslav history could be re-remembered and interpreted to provide the basis for arguments that putative neighbours were in fact, because of their different ethnic identities, blood enemies in disguise. It was not so much, therefore, that traditions of intercommunal antagonism were 'invented', but that a discursive shift was effected which allowed peripheralized and muted 'memories' to become the central points of new definitions of identities.

Demographically Yugoslavia is made up of six major national groupings (Slovenes, Croats, Serbs, Montenegrins, Macedonians and Moslems) and twelve minority nationalities (Albanians, Hungarians, Turks, Slovaks, Gypsies, Bulgarians, Rumanians, Ruthenians, Czechs, Italians, Vlachs, and Ukrainians) scattered throughout an area characterized by diverse regional histories and considerable variations of wealth. Under Tito six republics were recognized, five corresponding to the dominance of national groups within them and one (Bosnia–Herçegovina) peopled by three major national communities (Croatian, Serbian and Moslem). Two autonomous regions (Kosova and Vojvodina) were furthermore created in acknowledgement of the majority population of Albanians in Kosova and the large proportion of Hungarians in the Vojvodina. The major nationalities can – for the most part – be differentiated in terms of religion and/or language: thus Slovenes are Catholic and speak Slovenian, Croats are Catholics who speak Serbo-Croatian (the 'Croatian' language is mainly distinguishable from the 'Serbian' by the fact that the former is written in Latin script and the latter in Cyrillic), and Serbs speak Serbo-Croatian and are members of the Serbian Orthodox Church. Not only, however, do persons of one 'national' identity live within the territorial bounds of another 'nation's' republic, but there are also categorical anomalies, such as Serbs who are Catholic. Furthermore, some of the other nationalities appear to be products of Communist state policy rather than of 'natural' cultural distinctions. Thus, for instance, Montenegrins are recognized as a national community but speak Serbo-Croatian and share Orthodox affiliation with neighbouring Serbs. Macedonians, who have a distinct language, only took on a religion nominally distinct from that of the Serbs and Montenegrins in 1967 through the machinations of the Yugoslav state (see Pavlowitch 1988: 105–6). The Muslims, a Serbo-Croatian speaking 'nationality' without a territorial base, were only given national status in 1968 in order 'to remove them from the competition to demonstrate their "real" identity as either Serbs or Croats . . . [so as to] neutralize the territorial aspirations of either with respect to Bosnia' (Allcock 1992: 283).

As is demonstrated by the anomalous Moslem 'nation' – a national group without a national territory – the granting of national status was a discursive ploy, which functioned in certain instances to disenfranchise ethnic claims (as when Serbs and Croats wished to lay ethnic claim to Bosnia–Herçegovina through asserting that Muslims were Serbs or Croats who had converted to Islam during Ottoman rule, or when Serbs wished to assert that Macedonia or Montenegro was 'really' Serbian) and in others to provide a strategic sop to ethnic groups being consolidated within a multi-ethnic state. In the latter instance the Communist state provided a rhetoric within which people wishing to assert identities which were not fully assimilated within and dominated by the Communist state were able to declare ethno-nationalities. State patronage of such supplementary identities, which served as a means of dispersing potential federation-wide anti-statist solidarities, encouraged the subsumption of national identities within the encompassing identity provided by the Yugoslavian state. In so doing it maintained those identities as what Edwin Ardener has referred to as 'blank banners' (Ardener 1971: xliv) – signs of identities which are not linked to specific programmes but which can, when appropriate situations arise, be mobilized as icons and given contents appropriate to those situations. Thus national identities served during the period of state hegemony as means of expressing regional conflicts (mostly economic) which could not be expressed in the rhetoric of a unified Communist federation (Allcock 1992: 281–7). When, however, statist ideology lost both its legitimacy and its power to control regional disputes in the late nineteen-eighties, and issues of unequal economic development among the republics became grounds for the expression of opposition to the old order (Plestina, forthcoming), these national identities provided discursive foundations on which to base political activity. Dissatisfaction with the central government, provoked by perceived injustices affecting all the inhabitants of a region, regardless of their ethnic affiliation, could thus most easily be articulated in 'national' terms, and this ensured that it would be the nationalist road, rather than any other, which would be seen as leading beyond the impasse of Communist politics. With the effective self-destruction of Communism, the source of the disasters of the past and the deprivations of the present had to be sought in terms of national or ethnic antagonism.

Official Discources on Identity: Serb, Croat and Slovene

The process of redefining official discourses on identity and developing the political implications of those transformations began in the early eighties, when Milošević fuelled his ascent to power in Serbia by stirring up popular animosity towards Kosovan Albanians through promulgating the belief that 'Muslims' were, as they had in the fourteenth century, threatening to drive Serbs from their historic homeland of Kosova. The official Serbian press began to run stories telling of instances in Kosova of Albanian 'Muslims' raping Serbian women and desecrating Orthodox monasteries, as well as recounting the allegedly frequent expulsions – authorized by Albanian officials empowered by Kosova's autonomous status – of Serbian families from their houses and lands so that those properties could be taken over either by illegal immigrants from neighbouring Albania or by the children of the profligately breeding Kosovans (Ramet 1992: 200). There was, simultaneously, an official blessing and promotion of old traditions (frowned upon as 'folkloric' during Tito's regime) recounting the heroic struggle of the Serbian nation against the invading Ottoman armies. *Vidovdan*, the annual celebration of the defeat of the armies of Prince Lazar Hrebeljanović by the Ottoman armies on the 'Field of Blackbirds' on 15 June 1389, became an official ceremony in the period leading up to the abrogation of Kosovan autonomy. Prominent members of the Serbian government, including Milošević, would listen to village minstrels lamenting the melancholy fate of the Christian heroes who died six hundred years earlier defending Serbia against foreign invasion before presenting rousing speeches on the theme of 'never again'. On *Vidovdan* 1989, with Kosovan autonomy crushed and a state of siege in effect in the towns and villages of Kosova, the bones of Prince Lazar, which had rested in Serbia since his defeat six centuries before, were ceremonially paraded through the towns and monasteries of Serbia before being 'returned' with great fanfare to the Orthodox monastery of Gračanica at the heart of Kosova.

The articulation of a Serbian discourse, which was grounded on antagonism to Albanians, served to reconstitute 'Serbia' as a locus of identity and 'Serbian interests' as a focus of concern. While this was occurring in Serbia, Croatia too was moving towards a nationalist phase in which the definition of the community and its appropriate concerns were central issues and devices. Partly in response to the perceived threat of Serbian nationalism and partly as a means of gaining power, nationalist politicians called for the separation of Croatia from the Yugoslav federation on the grounds that, under communism, the Croatian people as a whole had been punished for the activities of the *Ustaše* (Dukić 1993: 251) and had, consequently, had their rights as Croats and Yugoslavs suppressed by the 'Serb-dominated' state. Croat nationalist invoked memories of the Titoist government's crushing of the 1971 'Croatian Spring' movement (a large scale political agitation which had demanded a

degree of political decentralization and greater financial autonomy
for the republic of Croatia) in order to illustrate this thesis, and
argued that, as long as the central government was in control, the
Serbs would continue to deny Croats their historic rights as a
people. In 1989 Franjo Tudjman – once a communist partisan, at
that time president of the newly established 'Croatian Democratic
Union' (HDZ), and now president of Croatia – cleansed the Croat
national image (sullied by years of an equation being drawn
between *Ustaše* fascism and Croatian nationalism by announcing
at Jasenovac (site of the most notorious *Ustaše* extermination camp)
that the *Ustaše* depredations were nowhere near as extensive as
state propaganda had claimed and, furthermore, that they were
no different than any of the other brutalities which had been
effected in that period (Tudjman 1990). Subsequently, the press in
both Croatia and Slovenia provided apparent validation of the
latter point by publishing pictures of the bodies of thousands of
victims (those of Slovene and Croat collaborators as well as of
Serbian anti-partisan *Četnici* [Chetniks] – and members of their
respective families – who had fled from Yugoslavia in front of the
victorious partisan forces only to be handed over to the partisans
by British troops) of massacres carried out by the partisans after
the close of the war. Photographs of caves full of stacked bones
flooded the newspapers of both republics, giving rise to campaign
rhetorics in which these persons, previously referred to in non-
national terms as 'Nazis' or 'quislings', became 'Croatian victims'
or 'Slovene victims' of Communist brutality.

The Slovene nationalist ticket was, at base, simply an anti-
Communist ticket, and the positivity of a Slovene identity had to
be invented. In the period leading up to the vote for independence
a number of icons of Slovene identity were mustered, including –
most successfully – the *kozolec*, a device for drying hay particular
to certain regions of Slovenia, and a day before independence was
announced heated discussions were still going on in parliament
about what the new-born country would use for a flag (nearly
every suggested pattern was refused by the parliament because
members could discern traces of the old Yugoslavian flag in it). It
is the absence in the Slovene instance of a mobilizable history of
specific ethnic antagonism towards a neighbouring group which
enabled Slovenia to escape the intercommunal warfare that has
desolated the rest of Former Yugoslavia. This lack contributed to
the downfall of the nationalist right in the period following

independence. A central programme of the elected DEMOS coalition was opposition to abortion on the grounds that 'Slovenia is a small country surrounded by large enemies, and women should not have the right to abort future defenders of the nation.' A substantial number of women felt, however, less threatened by an external antagonist than they did by this attempt to abrogate their powers over their bodies, and this new antagonism engendered numerous pro-abortion groups which joined with other oppositional parties in a coalition which overturned DEMOS's parliamentary majority and returned a liberal coalition in large part concerned with local issues (Salecl 1993). Thus while in Slovenia the drive for independence was fuelled by antipathy towards Communism and the federation which imposed it on Slovenia, once the old order had disintegrated Slovenians were left without the convenient distraction of external enemies and with the difficult task of envisaging and creating a viable national identity for themselves.

In Croatia, to the contrary, the 'blank banners' which the anti-Yugoslav parties raised in opposition to the Yugoslav state soon became inscribed with the emblems of earlier collective struggles. Despite Tudjman's partisan past and his attempts to exorcise the ghosts of the *Ustaše* from Croatian nationalism, he adopted many of the programmes and symbols of the *Ustaše* Independent State of Croatia as soon as he was called upon to articulate a programme for the HDZ. Campaigning for the presidency in the election campaigns of spring 1990, Tudjman and the HDZ called for an independent Croatia which would expand to Croatia's 'historical borders' (thus encompassing most of Bosnia–Herçegovina), would fly a national flag on which the red star of the Yugoslav state would be replaced by the 'chessboard' pattern (*šahovnica*) which had graced the national flag of the 'Independent State of Croatia', and would purify the Croatian language of all 'Serbian' words. He also, according to Denich, announced that the 'World War II Independent State of Croatia was not ... a "quisling" formation, but an "expression of the historical aspirations of the Croatian people (nation) for its own independent state"' (Denich 1991: 6). 'Positivity' was achieved for Croatian identity through the taking on of a previous anti-Yugoslav Croatian identity, and this assumption of the trappings of the 'real' Croatia not surprisingly terrified the Serbs who lived within the borders of Croatia. They saw before them – realized once again – the same nightmare order under which they, or their relatives, had suffered between 1941 and 1945.

Bones once again played a substantive role in the constitution of identity (Salecl 1993: 81 and Bloch 1982 and 1989: 170) as Serbs of the Krjina region of Croatia invited local and Serbian journalists and photographers into caves where the skeletons of Krjina Serbs massacred by *Ustaše* had been cached. Not only did these monuments to the fate of Croatian Serbs under the *Ustaše* serve locally to legitimate Croatian Serb resistance to the new Croatian order (a resistance which led to the Krjina's establishing itself, by force of arms and ethnic cleansing, as an independent – albeit internationally unrecognized – Serbian state), but they also provided a focal point for the articulation of ethnic hatred towards the Croats in Serbia proper. Denich points out that while

> the rebellions of Serbian communities in Croatia were motivated by their own memories of the Ustasha regime, now eerily reincarnated in the declarations and symbols of the new nationalist government ... the inhabitants of Serbia itself had not experienced the Ustasha terror, and their wartime suffering had come at the hands of the Germans and other foreign occupiers, rather than Croats. Accordingly, there was little history of overt anti-Croat feeling throughout Serbia. (Denich 1991: 11)

Nonetheless, the Milošević regime ensured that Serbs in Serbia would recognize their own potential fate at the hands of 'Croats' in that of the Croatian Serbs who had died forty-five years earlier. The state-controlled Serbian media repeatedly presented television and newspaper images of the bodies and, as I witnessed when I was in Belgrade during the opening days of the war, the official publishing houses filled the bookshops with multiple-volumed, profusely illustrated texts recounting the until-then suppressed history of the 'Croatian' attempt to exterminate the 'Serbs'. Serbs in Serbia proper, who had already been convinced by the regime-orchestrated hate campaign against the Kosovans that they – as Serbs – stood to lose their ancestral homeland (not, note, their own homes, but the home of the Serbian people), were now being told that they – as Serbs – stood to lose their lives (see the Ministry of Information pamphlets by M. Bulajic 1991 and S. Kljakic 1991). With the successful promulgation of Milošević's brand of national socialism, which involved the putting into circulation of previously discredited traditions and previously silenced atrocity stories, the Serbs gained the promise of a 'Greater Serbia' – invoked by the threat of its theft – and the brotherhood of a 'Serbian people' – conjured up by images of its extermination. Like those who followed the pan-pipes of ethnic nationalism in other regions of Former Yugoslavia, the Serbian people were promised a utopic future in exchange for a commitment to the protracted struggle to destroy the enemies of that future.

What Milošević, Tudjman and other nationalist politicians have gained by playing the ethnic card in their quest for power seems clear. By transforming the discursive field of the social from one based on cohabitation and co-operation ('unity and brotherhood') to one based on exclusivity and ethnic warfare ('blood and land'), they have been able, first of all, to displace people's self-interest on to a plane where self-interest is defined in essentialist terms as the interest of oneself as a 'Serb', a 'Croat', a 'Slovene', or whatever. When a person is induced to imagine his or her self primarily as a representative of an ethnic collectivity, a threat to that collectivity – like a threat to its power or to the life or property of any of its members who are presented as such – is simultaneously a threat to that person. He or she not only sees the threatened co-national as 'the same as' his or her self, but also imagines that co-national's enemy as simultaneously an enemy to all those (including his or her self) who share identity with the threatened one (cf. Bowman 1993: 446–8). The enemy does not attack people as such; it attacks 'Serbs', 'Croats', or 'Slovenes'.

The second advantage gained by playing the ethnic card is that, while the social problems which had generated the initial dissatisfaction with the Communist regime have remained in place and – in most cases – actually worsened, the conjuring up of an enemy (or a multitude of enemies) enables the politicians to fix the blame for those problems on that visible antagonist. It has not proved necessary, therefore, to take on the difficult task of restructuring society in either Croatia or Serbia; all that needed to be done to convince the majority of people that positive steps were being taken was to wage war against the enemy or enemies. One might argue that it is, in fact, the war which keeps the nationalist regimes in power. If the war were to stop, it would be more and more difficult to attribute the radical and increasing impoverishment of the people of Croatia and Serbia to the actions of their enemies, and the corruption and inefficiency of the ruling cliques would become apparent.

The final advantage gained by the nationalist leadership through the evocation of a world structured around an absolute, wellnigh 'ontological' (Kapferer 1988), antagonism between a 'them' and an 'us' follows from this Manichaeism. In Former Yugoslavia, nationalist leaders lay claim to the need to abrogate the rights of the people they lead on the grounds that absolute power is necessary to destroy the absolute enemy of the people. If the enemy is the source of all evil, and the 'we' that would exist were that evil to be eradicated is inherently good, then the leadership which, in these sullied days, directs the struggle to destroy the evil is itself the personification of the principle of good. The elevation of the nationalist leadership, and particularly of the 'Leader' *per se*, to the status of 'agency of redemption' is evident in the impassioned waving of posters of Milošević in Serbian nationalist demonstrations and, even more saliently, in the placing of statues of Tudjman alongside those of the Virgin Mary in souvenir booths at the Croatian pilgrimage centre, Medjugorje (see Bax 1991 and Bax, forthcoming on the development of the shrine). The leader stands in as the charismatic representation of the 'will of the nation' and, as long as it is believed that he represents that will, any activity that he initiates will be seen as 'necessary' for the redemption of the whole.

Such legitimation of power can be undermined in two ways. One occurs when people lose faith in the existence of the evil which serves to justify the State's violence and repression, as happened in Slovenia. Another occurs when people lose faith in the leader as charismatic representative of the principle of the nation, and the challenge offered Milošević by Vojislav Seselj of the extreme right-wing Serbian Radical Party in the 19 December 1993 parliamentary elections in Serbia were grounded on such a reassessment. Here the leader can be exposed as a 'false messiah', and his place can be usurped by another whose even greater violence and extremism seems better to manifest the violence the nation needs to destroy the violence that would destroy the nation.

The nationalist leaderships' discourses on the enemy, which are widely and powerfully promulgated by the media of communication they control, create, in effect, a world divided between two camps in which there is no neutral place to stand. Thus anyone who does not support the national leadership is necessarily a supporter of the enemy (this logic has justified the extreme repression of anti-nationalists in Serbia and Croatia, as well as the brutal murders by Bosnian Serbs and Croats of co-nationals who refuse to take up arms in support of the national cause); and all elements of the social field have to be interpreted in terms of the side on which they stand. A widely circulated story in Bosnia tells of an exchange of graffiti on the contested border between Serbian and Bosnian sectors of Sarajevo. Someone wrote on a wall of the Central Post Office, which stands on that boundary line, 'THIS IS SERBIA' and someone else soon after painted that message out and replaced it with 'THIS IS BOSNIA'. A third interlocutor crossed out the second message and wrote in its place 'THIS IS A POST OFFICE!' Less humorous are other attempts to lay claim to places and cleanse them of the sullying marks of other presences; I refer here not only to ethnic cleansing *per se* but also to its landscaping correlate, in which volunteer squads from Serbia come into areas of Bosnia which have been taken and purged of Muslims by the Serb militias in order not only to tear down mosques but also to turf the ground on which they stood, plant trees, and install playground equipment. A pragmatic interpretation of this activity – based on the perpetrators' subsequent denials to visitors that a mosque had ever stood in the place of the park – would be that the landscapers are attempting to mask the ethnic cleansing that occurred there. I suspect, however, that, in so far as the visitors are known to know that Muslims had lived there, the remaking of the landscape serves to create, for the Serbs themselves, an image of a new world bearing no signs of the history out of which it was violently born. This elision of the historic process is a necessary element of a discursive legitimation of the violence involved in creating those 'cleansed' communities; the institution of the 'real' Serbia is a 'return' to a state of ontological purity, and such a state must be devoid of markers of the polluted and 'unreal' condition 'Serbia' was in before its redemption. The violence on which this new and pure order is founded is not part of the order itself; what is real is the world to come, in which evil will have no place and all that is in place will be good. This fantasy structure is evident in a story told me by a UN worker who recounted an exchange in which, after he berated a Serbian militiaman for having taken part in the destruction of the 'beautiful and ancient Old City' of one of the Bosnian towns, the man replied 'But we will build a new and more beautiful ancient Old City in its place.'

* * *

Explaining Ethnic Violence: A Lacanian Perspective

In the preceding pages I have proffered an interpretation of the genealogy of this logic. Fantasies of the well-being to be experienced once the old destructive order is overcome are put into circulation by nationalist demagogues. However, once the Communist regime is replaced by the new nationalist orders, the promised wealth and fulfilment fail to materialize, and already-designated scapegoats – members of other national groups seen both to obstruct the national interests from outside and to sabotage their realization from inside – are shown not only to carry the blame for the inequities of the old system, but also to bear responsibility for the failures of the new one. As the new nationalist leaderships attempt to gain firmer grips on state apparatuses, they demonize the nations' others by providing 'proofs' that these antagonists are not only opposed to the well-being of the people but are also dedicated to their absolute destruction. Newspapers and radio stations, controlled by the national governments, circulate fear-inducing stories of murders and mutilations carried out against members of the national community by persons of other nationalities. By promoting widespread fear and distrust, the new leadership validates its call for the mobilization of the nation to wage war against internal and external enemies, thereby securing its hold on repressive state apparatuses. Milos Vasić, writing of the militarization of the Bosnian Serbs, demonstrates that 'first, warmongering chauvinist propaganda is spread by the Serbian-controlled media. Fear takes hold and the idea that "we can't live with *them* any more" becomes dominant' (Vasić 1993: 8). Popular acceptance of such stories of persecution itself engenders murders and mutilations directed against the 'other', which defensively returns like for like, thus giving rise to new rumours and stories of atrocities committed by the antagonist. As Christie and Bringa's 'We Are All Neighbours' shows, a spiral of reciprocal distrust and reciprocated violence is initiated by acceptance of these rumours, and this destroys patterns of sociality and replaces them with antagonisms based on fear and manifested in violent moves to destroy the enemy before it can destroy oneself (cf. Riches 1986 and Loizos 1988). Moves to destroy that enemy follow the logic of what Riches calls 'tactical pre-emption' (Riches 1986: 6–7); murdering children, women and the elderly in order to prevent them from becoming, procreating, or aiding those who will murder you makes good sense once the enemy is recognized as such.

That recognition, however, cannot be explained solely in empirical terms, especially when, as in the village portrayed in the documentary, the evidence of antagonism runs counter to the testimony of daily life. Although it is undoubtedly true that political forces play a significant role in giving shape to and disseminating rumours which generate fear and give rise to intercommunal violence, it is not clear why such rumours should be accepted as true and – perhaps more saliently – why they should be seen as pertinent to situations in which no signs of intercommunal antagonism have previously been evinced. The amount of violence now raging between the communities of Former Yugoslavia was not manifest before nationalist mobilization; as Cornelia Sorabji demonstrates in the Bosnian instance 'for the most part tolerance, good will, and a conscious desire for cooperative and civil relationships filled the joints between the three populations' (Sorabji 1993: 33–4; see also Bringa, forthcoming). If we explain the extreme levels of brutality evident in Former Yugoslavia today as something endemic to 'the Balkans' we not only deny such ethnographic evidence and ignore the recent history of modernization in Yugoslavia, but also effectively cast Yugoslavs out beyond the pale of what we term 'human society' (to act in that manner 'they' must be essentially different from 'us'). If, on the other hand, we accept that the political discourses of the contending leaderships of the former republics have somehow transformed Yugoslavs into something different than they were before, we are still left with the question of 'where has this penchant for extreme violence come from?'. Peter Loizos, faced with analogous instances of genocidal violence in the Cypriot context (Loizos 1988: 651), argued that ethnic violence is focused on a specific set of subjects by antagonistic political rhetorics. He left in abeyance, however, the question of what, in the people such rhetorics were addressed to, called them to answer to its call and to adopt an image of the other as enemy with such passion that the will to efface the presence of that other from the earth overcame the moral scruples that had regulated social interaction before the other came to be recognized as such.

While the 'Balkan mentality' argument manifests intellectual sloth in so far as it mobilizes commonsensical and racialist stereotypes in order to ignore the challenge of understanding other cultures, the political rhetoric argument in turn ignores the challenge offered to modernist conceptions of human nature by situations in which communities which have lived together in peace and co-operation suddenly fragment into warring factions. If, as enlightenment theories of human nature contend, human beings will act rationally and co-operatively when given the choice, then there is no reason why – when the options proffered are between a proven model of cohabitation and a radical paradigm of violent confrontation – the choice should be made for intercommunal antagonism and war. Although I have demonstrated in the preceding pages that the latter option was offered up to the peoples of Yugoslavia by opportunistic political factions, I have not been able to demonstrate any 'rational' reason why the people accepted the logic of intercommunal hatred as more verisimilitudinous than their own experiences of cohabitation and co-operation. If, as Mastnak argues, the current situation is an expression of the will of the people, then it is important to try to discern what in people resonates to a call to rise up with a seemingly primal rage to destroy an enemy before that enemy is able to destroy them. I suggest – and in so doing follow the lead of Jacques Lacan – that we must look beyond the rhetoric of social discourses to those primal fantasies mobilized by those rhetorics. These fantasies, generated by the first encounter of the human infant with the symbolic order, resonate with and impel the subject to answer to the call to inflict absolute violence against an absolute enemy.

The infant's entry into the symbolic order, initiated when the child learns that it must call to another for what it desires, is simultaneously an expulsion from a world in which it subsequently 'remembers' it had had everything it wanted. Freud, in the opening section of *Civilization and its Discontents*, posits that 'the infant at the breast does not as yet distinguish his ego from the external world as the source of the sensations flowing in upon him' and that this experience may give rise to inchoate memories of 'an oceanic feeling' like a 'limitless narcissism' (Freud 1963: 3–4, 9). In this pre-linguistic state the child has no conceptual apparatus with which to distinguish 'inside' from 'outside', and thus perceives itself as both locus and source of sensation and what gives rise to sensation. The child's entry into language expunges that sense of narcissistic omnipotence by reordering the world in terms of a dualism; in separating from the mother the child goes from sensing that the world and itself are coterminous to knowing not only that it is only part of a world but furthermore that it is a small and helpless part which must call upon others who have the power to give it – and deprive it of – what it wants. After the moment in which the world is taken up by language, primal 'enjoyment' (which Lacan terms *jouissance*) remains only as the trace of an absence (Lacan writes 'we must insist that *jouissance* is forbidden to him who speaks as such' [Lacan 1977: 319]). That absence or lack serves as a screen on to which we project fantasies of fulfilment – of full enjoyment – in the form of objects or scenarios of desire. These 'part objects', which fetishistically stand in for the *jouissance* which has been irrecuperably lost, seem to promise access to the fulfilment from which language has banished us. As such they cover the abyss of that primal lack, and enable us to fantasize that 'if we had this thing we would have our happiness (*jouissance)*'. Thus, although that lack can never be anything more this side of language than the wound of an amputation, it nonetheless remains the field on which we inscribe the desires which drive our self-motivated activities. The idea of amputation – of something brutal that has been done to sever us from that part of ourselves which gave us our pleasure – brings up, of course, the question 'Who has done this thing to us?'. In Lacanian terms this violator is that being which makes us know the foundations of language by introducing us as infants to presence and absence (self and not self) through its demand that the mother leave the child and come to it. Although Freud calls this figure 'the Father', it need neither be personified nor gendered – it is something/someone outside the union of the infant's body with that which feeds, comforts and sustains it which the infant, in its initial incursion into signification, recognizes as breaking that union through the assertion of its presence – its 'voice'.

However, once the child comes to recognize the necessity of operating within the symbolic order, it channels its desires into certain patterns of behaviour through learning that certain activities will provide fulfilment (and others punishment). Through its experience of parental reward and deprivation it comes to constitute for itself an image ('the ego ideal') of what it must be to earn the love of those it desires and the things with which those others can provide it. This image of the `good self' serves, through an internalization of what the child perceives the parents desire it to be, to establish the child's identity within normative patterns of motivation and expectation. This apparently rational process of enculturation functions, nonetheless, through a process of temporary displacement whereby the child imagines that it will still be able to fulfil all of its desires despite having to modify its tactics to accommodate the demands of its parents. The narcissistic will to power still underlies the child's relationship with the symbolic order. It is only through negotiating the Oedipal Complex that the child learns that there are limits to its desire which cannot be evaded. The Oedipal Complex is resolved when the child, which until that time continues to demand the body of the mother (the first fetish substitute for *jouissance*) as the object of its desire, is 'convinced' that it must – in its own self-interest – abandon that demand. This occurs, in ways that differ according to the gender of the child, when the child is brought to realize that, if it continues to demand that which neither society nor the parental voice which 'speaks' for society will allow it, it will be deprived of the possibility of any future pleasure through what Freud asserts the child recognizes as 'castration' (Mitchell 1974: 74–100). The threat of castration is consequently internalized in the 'super-ego' which effectively serves to remind the child, and the adult it becomes, that if it is to have pleasure at all certain objects of desire must be abandoned and substituted for by objects society acknowledges as appropriate. The properly socialized person is, in other words, one who recognizes that full satiation – the return to *jouissance* that the Oedipal fantasy evokes before the threat of castration drives it back into the unconscious – is rendered impossible by 'reality'.

Nonetheless, traces of this difficult construction of individual identity remain inscribed in the unconscious. People will always encounter – dispersed through the wide field of their activities – frustrations of their strategies of fulfilment, and such moments frequently evoke the pre-linguistic scenario wherein a generalized antagonist is set in opposition to a fantasy of pleasure and fulfilment. In such instances failures to achieve fulfilment are experienced as a consequence of the activities of the 'demonic' antagonist the infant first encountered when its primal omnipotence was shattered by the 'voice of the Father'. When frustration of desire evokes the fantasy presence of this antagonist – perceived in infantile terms as a being which exists only to steal all it has from the child in order to pleasure itself – persons are likely to respond by directing primal rage and violence against what they perceive as the source of that frustration. In most instances, however, such eruptions of unconscious materials into conscious life are subsequently interpreted (by both the actor and the recipient of his or her violence) as irrational behaviour (i.e., a `temper tantrum') and are forced back into quiescence by the individual's super-ego. However, certain individuals who have failed to internalize the requirements of `reality' dictated by the super-ego impose the logic of a psychic structure polarized between desire and antagonism on to the full field of their relations with society. They thus interpret the world in terms of a dualism dividing all the elements of the social field into friend and foe (self and Other). In most instances such persons are perceived as paranoic and, if their violence proves endemically disruptive, are institutionalized. Certain discursive structures, however, draw upon the psychic opposition of antagonist and ego by establishing as real and normative a world polarized between obdurate enemies and a community threatened by them (Adorno and Horkheimer 1972: 187). The forms of nationalism which have been mobilized in Serbia and Croatia (and which were stripped of verisimilitude in Slovenia because of difficulties in convincingly arguing for the presence of a demonic antagonist) draw upon this unconscious structure, and mobilize the passions caught up in it by setting up the 'real' nation as the part object which covers lack. In these nationalist rhetorics all real fulfilment follows from the realization of the Nation, and the `other' (whether Jew, Croat, Muslim, Serb, Albanian or whatever) is inscribed in that rhetoric as precisely that which has as its only reason for being the desire to deny, steal and destroy the national identity that gives one what one wants and makes one what one really is; it steals land, rapes women, desecrates holy objects and, finally, annihilates the community in which one finds one's identity. These rhetorics not only define the Nation as the `Thing' which recuperates *jouissance* but also set up the Nation's `others' as incarnations of the demonic antagonist threatening pleasure at the very root of its being (cf. Žižek 1990).

The Nationalist Fantasy – After Communism

It is important, however, to recognize that peoples' identification with the structure set out in nationalist discourse is dynamic, and it is the processual character of this interpellation which enables nationalist rhetoric to evoke unconscious psychic structures. Liberation from what it defines as antagonistic repression and the legitimation of desires it posits as both essential and realizable sets up projects for the subjects of nationalist appellation which promise not only to restore the true nation but also to realize their authentic identities for them. During the period of Communist hegemony (a hegemony established by Tito and celebrated, until the fall of Communism, under the omnipresent gaze of his portraits) the 'pleasures' of national identification were explicitly proscribed by the ideology of *bratstvo i jedinstvo*: Yugoslavs were told – and convinced – that they had to give up the fantasy of ethnic nationhood in order to guarantee survival and the construction of a social system which could provide them with well-being. Socialist ideology served, in other words, as a form of social super-ego in so far as it asserted that if people were to continue to demand the fulfilment of nationalist aspirations they would be destroyed by the activities of external antagonists. The collapse of Communist ideology occurred when the supra-national identity promulgated by the Yugoslav state came to be interpreted not as something which functioned for the self-interest of Yugoslavs but as something imposed upon them by 'external enemies' (the 'Croat' Tito or 'Serbian hegemonists'). The Yugoslav State's proscription of ethnic nationalism came to be seen not as a rule one had to follow to survive and prosper in the real world, but as a manifestation of antagonism, and at that moment Tito and the order he represented became 'enemies of the people' and the nationalist fantasy became, not something impossible and self-destructive, but something which could be – and should be – realized. The discursive field was transformed into what Adorno and Horkheimer term a 'paranoic' structure (Adorno and Horkheimer 1972: 179–200) by the popularization of the belief that possession of people's 'real' object of desire (the nation) was possible, and was only prevented by the presence of others whose sole reason for being was denying that object to the people.

This structure was set in place by propaganda, which simultaneously evoked the future 'restored' nation as a fantastic object, promising the utopic recuperation of pleasures lost when, in some hazy past, the people were exiled from their 'homeland', and a demonic antagonist, standing as the corporeal antithesis of all configurations of will and desire. However, while the promised 'motherland' is sketched in these nationalist rhetorics in edenic yet imprecise terms, the evil of the antagonist and the heroic devotion of the national leader to its extirpation are portrayed with graphic realism. In the nationalist fantasy it is the leader and the enemy which are the crucial, and operative, elements. One fights against the enemy under the guidance of the leader in order to 'recover' the nation, but since access to the pure enjoyment of being which the nationalistic rhetoric claims will be afforded by the defeat of the enemy is always already blocked by the limitations of both social and psychic realities, the destruction of the enemy will always prove inadequate. Implicit in the psychic structure on which nationalist rhetoric draws is a spiral of violence which leads the members of the national community to always, at the moment of victory, seek yet another enemy who can be blamed for the 'real' nation's not being in the place they have just recovered from the enemy they have defeated (Žižek 1991: 6). If the Nazis had had the opportunity to exterminate every leftist, Jew, cripple, homosexual, and Gypsy that could be blamed for blocking the advent of the 'Thousand Year Reich' they saw as their true heritage, they would have had to begin exterminating those Germans who, despite fitting all the criteria of 'pure Germans', were nonetheless the causes of the failure of the Millennium to materialize. Vesna Pesić suggests that the same logic operates in the Serbian instance, when she writes that 'after ethnic cleansing we will soon have traitor cleansing' (Pesić 1992: 7).

Conclusion

The nationalist rhetorics which have led to war in Former Yugoslavia function, I contend, by prompting persons of a widely diverse range of social and historical backgrounds to recognize their essential identities as national rather than as based on gender, occupation, class, or place of residence. They succeed in doing so through the discursive construction of enemies of the nation which not only serve as scapegoats to be blamed for everything which goes wrong in both society and the lives of its members, but also function to evoke – through their negativity – a national positivity which people can fantasize would suddenly and paradisiacally emerge if the enemy were to be destroyed. I have suggested, following Freud and Lacan, that this process of creating nationalist fervour succeeds because it echoes – in the social domain – processes of identity-formation individuals negotiate in their earliest encounters with social reality. The violence of the infant's entry into the symbolic order is mirrored in the violent scenarios through which nationalist propaganda presents the antagonism of the nation's other to the ways of life of the national community, and it is – I argue – the resonance between these two 'scenes' which impels individuals – regardless of their adult experiences – to recognize themselves as addressed by calls to join the national struggle.

Psychoanalytic interpretations of social action are perceived by most social anthropologists as profoundly antagonistic to the way of life of the academic community to which they owe allegiance. This is because it appears as though psychoanalysis challenges the axiomatic assumption upon which that community is founded – the *a priori* truth that social reality is a social construct. The interjection I have here attempted to make does not, however, oppose that axiom; it instead suggests that, in so far as humans act within society because they recognize the identities with which society provides them as their own, so we must seek to understand the processes by which persons 'recognize' themselves in the subject positions provided by social discourses. The domain of the 'irrational', which analytic discourses based on Cartesian assumptions of rationality and identity disclaim, is, I contend, what impels persons to desire to take up, and defend, the cultural identities offered in social discourses. The ex-Yugoslav instance is, in some ways, an extreme case; but as I have argued there is both a social logic operating in those political discourses which construct blood-enemies out of previous neighbours and a logic of identification – which draws upon moments inscribed in the human unconscious by the first encounter of the infant with the social order – which impels ex-Yugoslavs passionately to take up the bellicose ethnic identities proffered by those political discourses. Neither that social logic nor the structures of the unconscious it mobilizes could, I suggest, independently create the uncivil societies we see active in Former Yugoslavia, but brought together they engender logical, self-affirming social realities capable of both sustaining and reproducing themselves. Other articulations of the social and the unconscious create other, less 'extreme', social orders where antagonisms are variously dissipated through the numerous social encounters persons have in the course of their daily lives; ex-Yugoslavia is an extreme instance only in so far as its politicians have succeeded in transposing fantasies of ethnic nationalism so effectively on to unconscious structures of antagonism. Such a juxtapositioning is not, however, anomalous, and other ethnic nationalisms active today throughout Eastern Europe and beyond engage in analogous constructions of idealized essential identities and demonic others. The appeal of such discursive articulations is profound, and provides the nationalists who recognize themselves in the identities proffered with powerful and logical models of interpretation and motives for action. To understand such persons, and the communities they constitute, we, as anthropologists, must attend both to the discourses through which their real is constituted and to the processes of identification through which they recognize those social realities as places in which to dwell and act.

References

Adorno, T. and Horkheimer, M. (1972). *Dialectic of Enlightenment*, London: Verso.

Allcock, J. (1992). Rhetorics of nationalism in Yugoslav politics. In *Yugoslavia in Transition: Choices and Constraints* (eds J. Allcock, J. Horton and M. Milivojević), pp. 276–96, Oxford: Berg Press.

Althusser, L. (1971). Ideology and ideological state apparatuses (notes towards an investigation). In *Lenin and Philosophy and Other Essays*, pp. 121–73, London: Verso.

Ardener, E. (1971). Introductory essay: social anthropology and language. In *Social Anthropology and Language: ASA Monograph X* (ed. E. Ardener), pp. ix–cii, London: Tavistock.

Auty, P. (1966). The post-war period. In *A Short History of Yugoslavia from Early Times to 1966* (ed. S. Clissold), pp. 236–66, Cambridge: Cambridge University Press.

Bax, M. (1991). Marian apparitions in Medjugorje; rivalling religious regimes and state formation in Yugoslavia. In *Religious Regimes and State-Formation: Perspectives from European Ethnology* (ed. E. Wolf), pp. 29–54, Albany: State University of New York Press.

Bax, M. (forthcoming). How the mountain became sacred: antagonism and the construction of religious community in a Yugoslav rural parish. In *Antagonism and Identity in the National Idiom: the Case of Former Yugoslavia*, (eds G. Bowman), Oxford: Berg Press.

Bloch, M. (1982). Death, women and power. In *Death and the Regeneration of Life*, (ed. M. Bloch and J. Parry), pp. 211–30, Cambridge: Cambridge University Press.

Bloch, M. (1989). Almost eating the ancestors. In *Ritual, History and Power: Selected Papers in Anthropology*, pp. 166–86, London:

Athlone Press.

Bowman, G. (1993). Nationalizing the sacred: shrines and shifting identities in the Israeli-occupied territories. *Man: The Journal of the Royal Anthropological Institute*, **28**, (3), 431–60.

Bringa, T. (forthcoming). 'We are the way our surroundings are': identity formation in an ethnically mixed village in Bosnia. In *Antagonism and Identity in the National Idiom: the Case of Former Yugoslavia* (ed. G. Bowman), Oxford: Berg Press.

Bulajic, M. (1991). *Never Again: Genocide of the Serbs, Jews and Gypsies in the Ustashi Independent State of Croatia*, Belgrade: Ministry of Information of the Republic of Serbia.

Denich, B. (1991). Unbury the victims: rival exhumations and nationalist revivals in Yugoslavia. *American Anthropological Association Annual Meeting* pp. 1–14, Chicago.

Dimitrijević, V. (1993). Ethnonationalism and the constitutions: the apotheosis of the nation state. *Journal of Area Studies*, **3**, 50–6.

Freud, S. (1963). *Civilization and its Discontents*, London: The Hogarth Press.

Gaber, S. (1993). The limits of democracy: the case of Slovenia. *Journal of Area Studies*, **3**, 57–64.

Hammel, E. A. (1993). Demography and the origins of the Yugoslav civil war. *Anthropology Today*, **9**, (1), 4–9.

Hayden, R. (forthcoming). Constitutional nationalism in the formerly Yugoslav republics. In *Antagonism and Identity in the National Idiom: the Case of Former Yugoslavia* (ed. G. Bowman), Oxford: Berg Press.

Hobsbawm, E. (1990). *Nations and Nationalism since 1780: Programme, Myth, Reality*, Cambridge: Cambridge University Press.

Hobsbawm, E. (1983). 'Introduction'. *The Invention of Tradition*, E. Hobsbawm and T. Ranger, eds. Cambridge: Cambridge University Press pp. 1–14..

Kapferer, B. (1988). *Legends of People/Myths of State: Violence, Intolerance and Political Culture in Sri Lanka and Australia*, Washington, DC: Smithsonian Institution Press.

Kljakic, S. (1991). *A Conspiracy of Silence: Genocide in the Independent State of Croatia and Concentration Camp Jasenovac*, Belgrade: Ministry of Information of the Republic of Serbia.

Lacan, J. (1977). *Écrits: A Selection*, London: Tavistock Publications.

Loizos, P. (1988). Intercommunal killing in Cyprus. *Man: The Journal of the Royal Anthropological Institute*, **23**, (4), 639–53.

Mastnak, T. (1992). Civil society at war, *Yugofax*. **16**, 7.

Mitchell, J. (1974). *Psychoanalysis and Feminism*, Harmondsworth: Penguin Books.

Pavlowitch, S. (1988). *The Improbable Survivor: Yugoslavia and its Problems – 1918–1988*, London: C. Hurst and Co.

Pesić, V. (1992). The problems of minority rights in new nation states. *Yugofax*, **14**, 7.

Plestina, D. (forthcoming). Economic development and nationalism: the Yugoslav lesson. In *Antagonism and Identity in the National Idiom: the Case of Former Yugoslavia* (ed. G. Bowman), Oxford: Berg Press.

Ramet, S. (1992). *Nationalism and Federalism in Yugoslavia: 1962–1991*, (2nd edn), Bloomington: Indiana University Press.

Riches, D. (1986). The Phenomenon of Violence. In *The Anthropology of Violence* (ed. D. Riches), pp. 1–27, Oxford: Basil Blackwell.

Salecl, R. (1993). Nationalism, anti-semitism and anti-feminism in Eastern Europe. *Journal of Area Studies*, **3**, 78–90.

Sorabji, C. (1993). Ethnic war in Bosnia? *Radical Philosophy*, **63**, 33–5.

Thompson, M. (1992). *A Paper House: the Ending of Yugoslavia*, London: Hutchinson-Radius.

Tudjman, F. (1990). *Bespuca Povijesne Zbilnosti*, Zagreb: Matrix Croatica.

Van den Heuvel, M. and Siccama, J. G. (eds) (1992). *The Disintegration of Yugoslavia*, Amsterdam: Rodopi.

Vasić, M. (1993). The pattern of aggression: two against one in Bosnia. In *Balkan War Report*, **18**, 8–9.

Žižek, S. (1990). Eastern Europe's Republics of Gilead, *New Left Review*, **183**, 50–62.

Žižek, S. (1991). *Looking Awry: An Introduction to Jacques Lacan through Popular Culture*, Cambridge, Mass.: MIT Press.

Chapter 8

The Play of Identity: Gibraltar and Its Migrants

Gareth Stanton

Introduction

In this chapter I want to outline some developments in the production and portrayal of Gibraltar; notably the history of the British presence and its relation to the development of the complex Gibraltarian civil population.[1] These may seem esoteric themes, but in the current European situation the construction of identities and their subsequent mobilization is an increasing focus of interest for anthropologists and other scholars. I, however, have made no rigid appeal to theoretical anthropological debate regarding ethnicity,[2] because much of what will be discussed is closely related to these historical developments, and it seems to me that now classic anthropological arguments which emphasize boundaries need to be given far greater historical scope. Therefore, I prefer for the present to simply develop some themes which I regard as necessary preliminaries to an understanding of Gibraltar's complex presence. Hopefully, the paper will also offer insight into what it might mean to become European in the Gibraltar context or, more pointedly, what it might be necessary to leave behind.

---

1. The first detailed investigation was conducted by Howes (1951).
2. Discussions of ethnicity are, of course, voluminous and not simply restricted to anthropology. In American sociological circles the Chicago school did much to put the topic on the academic agenda. Steinberg (1981) provides an interesting critical review of the American literature. In anthropology a classic reference is Barth (1969). Williams (1989) has recently reviewed some of this literature.

Gibraltar's Contradictory Status: The Sun Sets Over The Rock

My starting-point is what I see as a contradiction. Gibraltar has become a metaphor for solidity and permanence; the solidity and permanence which by extension stand in for the British Empire itself – of which Gibraltar is a glorious outpost. The Rock (as Gibraltar is often known) is even equipped with its own myths of apocalypse cast in animal form. The Barbary apes function in a similar fashion to the ravens in the Tower of London. In the febrile imaginings of school history texts, their disappearance would spell some sort of ending: to Empire, to Britain, to England.

At times of national danger such stories become paramount in the national consciousness. During the Second World War it was brought to the attention of those in high office that the ape population had suffered a dire reverse. In a secret telegram, Churchill ordered that the ape numbers be boosted, and maintained in future at higher levels. Britain and her allies emerged victorious in that war, and the telegram was celebrated in fiction on at least two occasions in the years that followed: in Warren Tute's novel, *The Rock* (1957), and in a book by Paul Gallico, *Scruffy* (1962). These apes are part of the myth or fiction of Gibraltar.

The myth of Gibraltar, as I shall choose to call it, would appear to stretch back a long way, back in fact to the fashion in which resistance to certain military sieges in the eighteenth century was perceived by the population at large back in Britain. In 1757, Pitt considered the idea of returning Gibraltar to Spain in return for a pledge of alliance against France. The *Gibraltar Directory* of 1948 records the popular reaction to these political manoeuvrings: 'The gallant defence during the last siege was a military achievement that excited the popular imagination, and Gibraltar became valuable in the eyes of the public when its name was associated with British gallantry and blood' (p. 11).

The story of Gibraltar and Empire is like many of those stories told when much of the map was red, and, while we can now see the hollow centre in many Empire yarns, the tenacious Rock endures. The Empire has all but passed, and the empty space which remains has been sympathetically unravelled in James Morris's *Pax Britannica* trilogy. Let us examine briefly a denuded version of the

Empire myth, stripped down to the glorious bones of popular history and chewed upon, in its time, by the young seeker-after-fortune. *Outposts of Empire*, written by John Lang early this century and part of the 'Romance of Empire Series', makes no attempt 'to write a history of any of the places touched upon; the endeavour rather has been to extract from their history a portion of the Romance with which each is saturated'(p. vii). To set the scene the author admonishes his reader:

> To us in this twentieth century, who are wont to consider no part of the globe as being very far distant; who have, as a general rule, but little knowledge of the sea beyond what may be scantily gleaned from a more or less brief sojourn on some huge steamship, it is hard to realise that one hundred years ago a voyage to Gibraltar probably took longer time than it now does to reach Bombay. (p. 1)

Lang's description of the sieges of Gibraltar is prefaced with the heart-warming story of the 'little English privateer cutter, the Buck, of Folkestone', running the Spanish blockade against all odds in 1779 and delivering much-needed victuals to the beleaguered Rock. The privations of the garrison and the bravery of those who surmounted them then follow, before we depart for other outposts: Malta, the Caribbean and beyond. The exact content of this romance is something I wish to examine in the Gibraltar context. The British Empire was a romance, it was in love with itself. Identity in Gibraltar is still struggling with the weight of this love, and has been deformed and transformed by it, resulting in the formation of a civilian population of complex migrant origins, yet who declare themselves ferociously loyal to the British Crown. The romance that colours Empire and the many myths which surrounded it – all linked, more or less, to concepts of racial superiority and notions of divine providence – have the self-same, singular quality; but what relation do they bare to the reality of its historical existence? Are they simply the megalomania of Empire? In some almost quasi-mystical sense, Gibraltar came to represent for the British the beginning of Empire and its mission of Empire. The Gibraltar Diocese, in the words of Bishop Collins, ranged 'from the Rock of Gibraltar to the Golden Horn and the mountains of Kurdistan'(quoted by Buxton 1954: 2).

Exiles and Empire

Empire had its exiles. It was the romance that drew the British forth from their hive-like island redoubt to swarm round the world bearing images of their Queens. Britishness and Empire are crucially linked, articulated through the notion of monarchy, but time began to change them in the end. At the turn of the century, in the words of James Morris:

> Britishness itself had become a debatable condition. In Victoria's day it had been embodied above all in the Monarchy, the distant, unfailing source of power and justice. The Crown was the gauge by which a man could claim himself to be British. It was the one abstraction that could unite the loyalties of disrespectful Australians, half-American Canadians and distinctly un-English South Africans. It was very, very grand, surrounded by a mystic sheen of tradition: even the Viceroys, Governors, Captains-General and Commanders-in-Chief who represented it in the field were but suggestive reflections of its splendour. (Morris 1978: 319)

A world once in its thrall came to reject Britishness and Empire, turning in their stead to forms of nationalism. Now I want to trace some features of this process in Gibraltar, where we must return in order to unravel its peculiarities, for, as Rose Macaulay once wrote, 'Gibraltar is, in fact, so far as I know, like no other place on this earth' (Macaulay 1949: 184).

Gibraltar *hoy*

Let's take a quick look at Gibraltar in the mid-eighties. The standard definition can be found in innumerable guides and histories of Gibraltar: the British Crown Colony of Gibraltar, with a civilian population of less than 30,000 and an area of only 5.82 square kilometres. Some may be more precise, and state that much of this area is the Rock itself, and that the inhabitable portions are much smaller (*Punch* magazine around this time described it as 'two square miles of underdeveloped limestone, partially covered with tarmac and souvenir shops'); but who are the inhabitants of Gibraltar? I shall answer this question first through the eyes of the visitor – not necessarily a sociologically aware portrait, but still a picture of sorts, and informative in its own way. A visitor from the

UK might first be struck by the military presence on the Rock. The constant coming and going of jeeps, the preponderence of uniforms of one sort or another. Now as before, the traveller might have been struck, as Rose Macaulay was in 1949, by a certain linguistic anomaly: 'The Gibraltar frontier officials (not the La Linea ones) are, like the police, all bilingual; they speak English with a queer, clipped accent, rather like Eurasians' (p. 183).

In 'modern' times a day-tripper from the Costa del Sol would be able to distinguish at a glance the fellow tourists drifting aimlessly up and down Main Street; but the others would appear an indistinguishable mass. Certainly the Hindu traders who have taken over most of the electrical goods shops would appear 'foreign', as would the groups of Moroccans drifting back and forth, to and from work; but the tourist would be hard pressed at first to distinguish the rest: the Gibraltarians proper, the British expatriates. Drifting into a bar for a refreshment, the tourist might strike up a conversation with one of the bar staff who, should they turn out to be British, which is quite likely, might provide some answers and shed light on the 'Gibos', as the 'Brits' call the Gibraltarians. In such a situation the judgement is often very harsh; the 'Gibos' are always 'on the make', childlike, don't do anything for themselves, 'Grab-all-tarians', arrogant, hard-headed, very 'thick'. Gibraltarian skilled workers are often viewed as irredeemably incompetent by their UK counterparts. The chief interest of the Gibraltarian is his or her family and money.

These sorts of remark reflect a dented pride. The ex-pats are often in a structurally weak role; often they are escaping from their own pasts or failure to find work back home. They've come to somewhere which is British, but can find no real place for themselves. Their scorn for the Moroccan workers, or 'Rockies' as they call them, is even greater. They emphasize outright rejection. The Moroccan workers are strange, stupid, untechnical, exceedingly lazy: 'Moroccans and work? Are you joking? I'll tell you what, they work at two speeds, dead slow and stop. . . .' The Spaniards are the 'Spicks'. They live in a dirty country, eat greasy food; but the booze is cheap. Some venture the opinion that the 'Gibos' are little more than English-speaking 'Spicks'. Shorn of the derogatory connotation of the term, this was also Franco's opinion:

> There are no English people in the place except the families of the garrison and the employees of the administration and the warehouses.

The *Llanitos* [Gibraltarians] are entirely Spanish, though they take advantage of their British citizenship, and the rest, the Jews and aliens, can live as well under one flag as under another.' (quoted in W. Jackson 1987: 301–2)

These are not the views of all the Britons in Gibraltar; but they are more likely to be heard than any others. The tourist might conclude that this is not the ideal place to settle. Indeed, the modern tourist, drawn by a vision of Gibraltar, is often as disabused about the place as Macaulay was on her visit:

The Rock bristles with regulations, bayonets and guns, and casual explorations about it are let and hindered. The climate is tiringly hot in summer, often with an exhausting wind, and in winter beaten by the Levanter and by chilly and damp Atlantic gales. 'Gibraltar is with reason called the Montpellier of Spain,' one reads; but with what reason is not clear.[. . .] Could there be, has there ever been (I inquire without dogmatism, pre-judgement or enough information), art, letters or music created in Gibraltar, by any race or any mixture of races? One imagines not. (Macaulay 1949: 193)

Even the modern package tourist fails to flourish. In 1987 worries surfaced over the threat of one of the big tourist carriers to Gibraltar withdrawing their hotel-inclusive holidays. The company, Marshall Sutton, claimed that 50 per cent of their complaints concerned Gibraltar, while the Rock accounted for only 4.4 per cent of their trade. The main problems, a company spokesman told the Gibraltar Chronicle, lay 'in the state of the town and the environment' (*Gibraltar Chronicle*, 21/9/1987).

These negative comments strike us as strange for a place that has such a glorious sense of history. And yet as we look through the accounts of the place written over the last two hundred years they are repeated with an almost dirge-like monotony. Let me briefly list a few.

Here is General Bland, governor from 1749 to 1754: the civilian population, he writes, consists of 'Jews, Genoese, Spaniards, Portuguese, Irish Papists, Scotch peddlers and English bankrupts . . . the riff-raff of various nations and religions ready to commit any fraud in their power' (quoted by Jackson, op. cit.: 143). I'll add just one more contemptuous description at this point. In Gibraltar, wrote the visitor Galt:

> . . . there is a contemptible theatre, where strolling Spanish comedians
> sometimes perform. The Garrison Library is the only place of rational
> amusement for strangers, and there are few towns which have anything
> comparable to it. The inns are mean, but the rate of the charges is
> abundantly magnificent. A dollar here passes under the name of a cob;
> and it is a small matter that a cob can purchase. (Galt 1813: 7)

These voices are those of Empire,[3] and they betray the contempt in
which the rulers of Empire regarded its inhabitants in many
instances. And yet it proved a powerful magnet for the many
Mediterranean peoples who were attracted to Gibraltar's small
shore by the wealth of Empire. The power of the Union Jack is
evoked in an interchange described by a female traveller, Amelia
Perrier, in 1873; a story which highlights the mixed origins of the
Gibraltarian. Anxious to ascertain the nationality of the boy working
in her hotel, she asks young Louis if he is Spanish. His face registers
a mixture of surprise, displeasure and disgust:

> 'No, madame-sare,' he replied coldly, but politely still.
> I hastened to correct myself.
> 'Oh, I beg your pardon; French, of course!,
> 'No sare-madame,' almost angrily, 'I am Ingleesh.'

Proudly elevating his chin the boy goes on to elaborate:

> 'My fader he was Spanish, and my mother she was Maltese; de fader
> of my moder he was Italian, but de moder of my fader, she was Ingleesh:
> and I am Ingleesh too; I was born under the Ingleesh flag . . .' (Perrier
> 1873: 18–19)

Space does not allow me to elaborate here on the detailed origins
of the Gibraltarian; but this last quotation will indicate the complex
variety of backgrounds of those who came to make their homes on
the Rock. One point of importance, however, is that it only became
possible to imagine such a concept as a 'Gibraltarian' in the light of
the decline of the Empire; it would have been an almost unthinkable

---

3. While it might be said that this form of presentation is a frequently used device, especially
within the nineteeth-century travel genre, here there is a particularly virulent feeling of betrayal
stimulated by the Gibraltan 'real' as opposed to the Empire myths of Gibraltar. Evelyn Waugh
(1930), as might be expected, was driven virtually apoplectic by the place. The link between
the Imperial and the travel genre in literature has been evoked in an enterprising fashion by
Mary Louise Pratt in her study *Imperial Eyes* (1992).

term in days of Empire, so vestigial was the civilian population considered by the authorities. Even as late as 1939, G. T. Garratt was to record the political commonplace in Britain that the population of Gibraltar was 'so small, so cosmopolitan, so parasitic that it [could] not develop a real nationalist movement' (quoted by Hills 1974: 407).

La Linea: Gib's ugly sister

Gibraltar is not an island, more an outcrop, and now I want to look at its mirror image: the town which grew up in order to besiege it. This will give us further insight into the nature of the Gibraltarians. In 1833 new military dockyards were constructed in Malta, and Gibraltar's usefulness in this regard was seriously undermined. By this time, however, it had become important as a recoaling stop on the routes to the East. To this end several hundred Spaniards were employed in the carrying of coal, then a simple matter of baskets on the head. The convict labour which had been used in Gibraltar was finally brought to an end in 1875 for economic reasons. Free Spanish labourers were twice as productive as the convicts, and the wages they received amounted to less than the cost of keeping the convicts. This additional Spanish labour force, like the coal carriers, came from the town of La Linea on the other side of the frontier. As historian George Hills points out, 'Gibraltar was not devoid of slum tenements, but La Linea was the working-class district proper of Gibraltar' (Hills, op. cit.: 381). This fact is reflected in the size of the town's population: between 1830 and 1900 it quadrupled, whereas in Gibraltar the corresponding increase amounted to no more than 20 per cent. Labour had also been imported from Malta towards the end of the nineteenth century; but local opposition finally put an end to this source of labour. As a result further Spaniards were recruited. By 1900, 2,200 Spaniards were working on a new dry-dock and the extension of the 'new' mole alone. The wages these men received were roughly one-fifth of corresponding levels in Britain, but were nonetheless good by the standards of the region, being some three times greater than the usual rates for farm labour in Andalusia.

Spaniards came to refer to the Rock as *la piedra gorda*, the fat rock, in tribute to this source of wealth. Over time, however, the actual composition of the town came increasingly to reflect its relationship with Gibraltar. Stewart writing in the fifties comments that: 'Many of the poorer citizens used to live in Spain before the Civil War drove them back to the Rock. Many of them are actually half Spanish. They are as much the products of Spain as the members of the upper classes are products of England' (1967: 70).

Conditions in Gibraltar led naturally to the expansion of La Linea. Overcrowding on the Rock had been a constant feature of life for the civilian population since the earliest days of the settlement. The 1814 census records that there were 1,657 houses, with 5,804 rooms. With 10,136 civilians Stewart estimates about 2,500 families, which gives the average family two rooms; but 'it is assumed that there were many families with one room only'(op. cit.: 159). Even as late as 1955 there were hundreds of families in single rooms on the Rock, with many more housed in two-roomed Nissan huts (a situation exacerbated by the influx caused by the upheavals of the Civil War in Spain). To quote Stewart's views once more, 'The Government has never done more than begin to play with the provision of houses, and the home life of the Gibraltar citizen had always been, typically, one of crowded squalor'(op. cit.: 172). This squalor was exported to La Linea, which only really existed as a satellite of Gibraltar:

> There in La Linea in 1953 the very essences of squalor lay everywhere in the ill-lit streets – broken bottles, nettles, ashes, excrement, the all-pervading odour of urine and rancid oil and rotten fish and cabbage. [. . .] Boot-blacks and little boys pimped at street corners, and there was a district full of formidable harlots leering from their white-tiled dens with paper flowers in their hair. (Stewart, op. cit.: 206)

Indeed, the traffic was not just one-way across the frontier. Already in the early twenties the Gibraltar branch of the National Council for Combating Venereal Disease had been meeting to discuss the advisability of the total closure of brothels in Gibraltar – these, at the time, being confined to Serraya's Lane. Some people were opposed to such moves. Carrara and Huart, local people of radically different political views, at least agreed on this issue. The proposed measures, they suggested, 'would result in driving the civil population to the brothels in Spain with disastrous results to health, and would lead to prostitution and soliciting and to the offers of insults to virtuous women and girls of Gibraltar' (from an issue of the *Gibraltar Chronicle* from 1921). Nevertheless, by the 1930s Gib had become the 'only whoreless port in the Mediterranean'. The women moved to La Linea, where they took over a whole street pointing at the Rock. Some claim this to be the reason for its name, Calle de Gibraltar – others blame nostalgia. The reasons are probably more complex – the street did not receive this name until 1903; but nostalgia may well play a part in the fact that, unlike many other streets in La Linea, its name has never altered since that date. The name Gibraltar, Gómez (1986) suggests, was simply easier to remember for visiting sailors and foreigners. Something of the atmosphere of this part of town is conveyed in Anthony Burgess's neophyte novel, *A Vision of Battlements* (1965).

In many respects, however, La Linea is a mirror image of Gibraltar, and its existence is the result of very similar forces, i.e. the provisioning of a garrison. As Gómez writes, 'the first civilians came in order to supply the fortified lines' (op. cit., 27). In addition, like that of Gibraltar, the nascent civilian population was by no means purely Spanish. Those Spaniards who were chased from the Rock in 1704 had not chosen to stay in the close vicinity but, rather, had set themselves up some kilometres away. People were attracted from deprived regions of Spain, but there were also many foreigners: Genoese, Maltese and Portuguese (who even had a consular agent in La Linea in the latter half of the nineteenth century). The similarity of the two towns can be seen in the similarity of people's surnames and aspects of the local dialect. Historically one is tempted to suggest that ulimately the Genoese and other foreigners who settled on the 'wrong' side of the Lines lost out. Here it is important to consider another aspect of life for the civilian populations of both Gibraltar and the surrounding Campo region, for it is a world linked to Gibraltar in many ways, as can be seen in the matter of smuggling, which is also linked to work and the secret economies of the region.

Smuggling and Religion[4]

Smuggling had long been recognized as a problem in Gibraltar, and for certain of the British witnesses of life there it had coloured their vision of the civilian population of the Rock. Even other European

---

4. Much of this paper, and this section in particular, owes a large debt to Hills' magisterial study *Rock of Contention* (1974).

travellers in the region were infected by the impression. The Marquis de Custin wrote in 1838:

> The dregs of the Mediterranean make up the population of Gibraltar
> . . . riff-raff no state, no family would acknowledge theirs, a gathering
> of bandits . . . in consort with highwaymen and pirates . . . The officers
> of the garrison warned me to tell no one, our innkeeper least of all, when
> I would be leaving, or my route, or the weapons I would be carrying.
> (*L'Espagne sous Ferdinand VII* quoted by Hills, op. cit.: 377)

By the latter half of the century even the British government were beginning to acknowledge the scale of the problem (with frequent Spanish prodding). By 1876 evidence was available that four times as much tobacco was coming illegally into Spain from Gibraltar as was being legally distributed by the Spanish government. It was claimed at the time that the introduction of a tobacco tax in Gibraltar would be an effective means of combating the smugglers. But the tobacco industry generated some 1,450 jobs in Gibraltar at the time, and any measures directed at tobacco smugglers would effectively end the industry itself. The extent of the economic linkages on the two sides of the border are hinted at in a document penned by the then bishop, Dr Scandella. Hindering the small smuggler and his shore supporters, he wrote, 'would cause deep irritation throughout the great neighbouring towns . . . whose inhabitants depend, in a very great measure, on their trade with Gibraltar . . . It is questionable that The Lines, Campamento, San Roque, Algeçiras, Marbella and Estapoena will be almost ruined' (quoted by Stewart, op. cit.: 134–5). More powerful voices, however, were to decide the issue. When, finally, revenue men were sent out from London to impose the tax:

> The Chambers of Commerce of Manchester and Liverpool, Glasgow
> merchants and the British shipowners stepped in: the tobacco trade was
> only part of a whole; if it was inhibited by taxation, they argued,
> Gibraltar's position as a centre for British trade in the Mediterranean
> would be ruined; such taxation was in any case contrary to the
> principles of Free Trade . . . (Hills, op. cit.: 384)

The smuggling continued. There is an interesting aside to this particular episode, one which few writers seem to have picked up. These events surround the replacement of the Bishop on his death, and demonstrate to some extent the nature of class alliances which were exposed by the smuggling issue.

As a result of the Napoleonic wars the Bishop at Cadiz had lost all real contact with his parish in Gibraltar. In 1839 Rome had appointed a Bishop *in partibus* to Gibraltar. The first man to fill the post was Irish; but his successor in 1855, Dr Scandella, was a Gibraltarian of Genoese descent. His intervention on the question of smuggling was essentially a defence of the Rock's poor, who would in large part have lost any form of livelihood if the tax had been imposed. Scandella is also remembered as the founder of schools in which the wealthy parents in effect financed the schooling of poorer members of the community. On Scandella's death in 1880 there were a series of disturbances over the person who was chosen to succeed him.

This man, Dr Canilla, had been closely associated with Scandella. He was an unpopular man with the wealthy of the Rock because of his constant criticism of their lack of generosity. This group, led by a wealthy merchant, Luis Imossi, conducted a press campaign against Canilla. Constituting themselves as a 'Committee of Elders', Imossi and his followers tried to prevent Canilla occupying his post. As wealthy men and employers of labour the 'Elders' had at their disposal a mob, drawn largely from their employees and various anti-clerical groups from La Linea. This mob, on several occasions, prevented the bishop from entering St Mary's church.

Meanwhile the authorities had distanced themselves from the trouble; but finally the time came for them to act. On 3 April 1882 Governor Napier made a move. Soldiers were stationed at the frontier to prevent any trouble from La Linea, and two further companies were mobilized to prevent any threat 'from the upper part of the town from whence the roughest of the crowd came' (from a report by the Attorney-General, quoted by Hills, op. cit.: 396). Police and soldiers took up positions around the church; but they discovered that it had already been occupied by some two hundred men who had barricaded themselves inside. The police forced their entry into the church and 48 arrests were made. Canilla was finally able to enter his church, and resistance to his appointment was broken.

Hills has pointed to the rather anomalous situation here; the Colonial Office had been fairly active in giving support to the Catholic Church at a time when, back in Britain, there were still occasional outbursts against 'papists' (op. cit.: 379). This must have left many ordinary Gibraltarians in somewhat of a dilemma.

Catholicism could not be used as a rallying cry against the British and, indeed, an active clergy was defending the rights and interests of many poor Gibraltarians. Imossi and his renegade Catholics were powerful men who clearly wanted to use the church in Gibraltar to further their own interests – for once the authorities were defending the rights of poor Gibraltarians.

These are perhaps the first germs of the schizophrenia which has marked Gibraltarian politics in later years. Conditioned by respect for both the Catholic Church and the British, many Gibraltarians failed to see the trick played on them by the Rock's merchant classes when they joined the political bandwagon and started playing opportunistically with sentiments of class and religious loyalty. Stewart put it as follows: 'The Gibraltarian worker was conditioned to submission by generations of autocracy; he was misled by his "popular" party, the AACR[5] [the heirs, cynics might say, to Imossi and his cronies]. He was told by his leaders to wait, not to rock the boat, to be patient, to eschew "class hatred", and so forth' (op. cit.: 209).

When Stewart was working in Gibraltar in the fifties he claimed that Gibraltarian labour contractors refused to employ Gibraltarians, and waited until the official employers took them off the lists of unemployed. Then they would employ Spaniards. Earlier in the century, older Gibraltarian informants told him, they had spent the day as navvies on the works and the whole night heaving coal. The coalmen did form a rough association and had struck repeatedly (on one occasion strikebreakers had been imported from Morocco); but, as we have seen, many of the coal-heavers were themselves Spanish. When the Transport and General arrived in Gibraltar in 1919 its members were by no means all Gibraltarian. As a correspondent wrote to the *Gibraltar Chronicle* in 1921: 'Can any of your readers supply me with information as to the exact percentage of Non-British subjects who are members of the local worker's union? If current rumour is correct it appears that Gibraltarians and therefore British subjects form rather less than one-fifth of the total membership of the union, the remainder being Spanish.'

The Empire subsumed within its dominions only one category of non-English, the native. The Gibraltarians were natives too, but

5. The Association for the Advancement of Civil Rights. For further details consult Stewart (1967: 223–6).

they grew into Gibraltarians in their own right as nationalist fervour took hold in the wake of Empire's decay. Ironically, however, the identity they took for themselves was that of British Gibraltarian, thus denying the close historical ties many of their number had with those on the other side of the border: those who as a result of political struggles taking place in another arena were seen to be ranged against them. Empire left its marks.[6]

Scruffy: a way of concluding

Paul Gallico's jaunty amusement *Scruffy* (Gallico 1962)[7] takes its inspiration from a real incident, but from then on it is simply the novelist's fancy. The Scruffy of the title is in fact Harold, one of the Rock apes, a Barbary macaque, *Macaca sylvana*.

As with many of the disclaimers used by novelists, there is an element of disingenuousness here. Captain J. Fitzgerald, MBE, RA, gave up his responsibility for the apes in 1947 and left behind a chronicle of the four years for which they had been his charges. The whimsical treatment that they receive for novelistic purposes from the pen of Gallico belies the surly reality of the beasts. Stewart reports that the officer describes the problems of procreation for the simian population treated in the novel. A young female, Pat, as a last-ditch measure, is confined with an elderly male, once known as Adonis but now called Scruffy, for the aforementioned purpose. The result, rather than twin apelets as in Gallico's story, is related by Fitzgerald as follows: 'Next morning, Scruffy had both arms torn from wrist to elbow, a wound in the centre of his back which exposed his spine for four and a half inches, and his testicles badly

---

6. I have been unable to address the question of the military presence in Gibraltar in this chapter. It is, however, of some considerable importance.

7. The evidence offered up by a reading of an avowedly fictional account of Gibraltar might seem slight to many. My model here is Edward Said and the many authors inspired by his 1978 work *Orientalism*. His recent work *Culture and Imperialism* (1993) expands the general project of the earlier book. 'Post-colonial criticism' or 'colonial discourse theory' are the rubrics under which this work appears in the field of literary studies. A brief overview is provided by Bill Ashcroft, Gareth Griffiths and Helen Tiffin in their book *The Empire Writes Back: Theory and Practice in Post-Colonial Literatures* (Ashcroft *et al.* 1989). Naturally, not everybody believes in this sort of thing. For a controversial appraisal of Said's project consult Ahmad (1992). For a more general critique see Leonard Jackson's witty *The Poverty of Structuralism* (1991).

torn' (quoted by Stewart, op. cit.: 51).[8]

The decline in the ape population is given rather a different gloss from that to which the mythologists of Empire subscribe. Fitzgerald in his report describes the behaviour of some of the rest of the troop faced with a mother in labour. Surrounding her, they snatch away the newborn apelet and run about with it until the rough treatment causes its death. Having been fought over and killed the lifeless corpse no longer holds any interest and is discarded, to be picked up and suckled by the grieving mother.

How long will the Gibraltarian civil population[9] wait to awake from their dream of British Empire, and drop their claims to be more British than the British? Perhaps not very long. Recent years have seen the increasing withdrawal of the British military presence and intense business involvement on the Costa del Sol. The socialist opposition have been voted into power. Now they start to emphasize their Europeanness. Empire too is dead in the Mediterranean. As generation succeeds generation the exact meaning of Empire dims and fades, its reality reduced to a few drab clichés, its meaning and *raison d'être* increasingly unintelligible (it is unusual to discuss the scars of the British Empire within the European context). In some respects historical and anthropological investigation can still call up the 'imperial world view' (MacKenzie 1984: 253) and give a further insight into the contradictory position of Gibraltar in the national psyche. As MacKenzie has written: `A whole range of propagandist imperial bodies, conventionally regarded as failures, in fact succeeded in diffusing their patriotic intentions and their world view, if not their specific and sophisticated plans of action, through almost every institution of British life' (ibid.: 253).

Was Gibraltar only ever this: a mirage projected by the imperial

---

8. Some readers might find this description unwarranted, but the violence of the imagery is important and demonstrates effectively the extent of the repression operating in Gallico's scenario. While this point might be lost on some, the psychoanalytic allusion is deliberate – Frantz Fanon knew his Lacan.

9. In Gallico's novel the only Gibraltarian to be described in any detail is portrayed as a complete buffoon. More interestingly, however, he is also a Nazi collaborator who harbours a deep antipathy for his Empire/Father/Mother. He also wears a toupee which in one scene from the book is stolen by Scruffy, who passes it on to the rest of the apes. They are described as playing with it in a fashion which resembles Fitzgerald's description almost exactly. Indeed, it seems almost certain that his chronicle was the source of Gallico's inspiration on this occasion.

imagination?[10] Napoleon, in exile on St Helena, commented when questioned as to whether he had ever entertained any notion of taking Gibraltar: 'That was far from my thoughts. Things suited us as they were. Gibraltar is of no value to Britain. It defends nothing. It intercepts nothing. It is simply an object of national pride which costs the English a great deal and wounds deeply the Spanish nation' (quoted by Hills, op. cit.: 367).

For all the fictions, the Gibraltarians are still there, and 1992 and its aftermath will require that Spanish wounds are afforded greater attention.

References

Ahmad, A. (1992). *In Theory: Classes, Nations, Literature*, London: Verso.

Ashcroft, B., Griffiths, G. and Tiffin, H. (1989). *The Empire Writes Back: Theory and Practice in Post-Colonial Literatures*, London: Routledge.

Barth, F. (1969). *Ethnic Groups and Boundaries: The Social Organization of Cultural Difference*, London: Allen & Unwin.

Burgess, A. (1965). *A Vision of Battlements*, London: Sidgwick and Jackson.

Buxton, H. J. (1954). *A Mediterranean Window: Fourteen years in the Gibraltar diocese*, Guildford: Biddles.

Gallico, P. (1962). *Scruffy: a diversion*, London: Joseph.

Galt, J. (1813). *Voyages and Travels, in the years 1809, 1810 and 1811;*

10. In response to work detailing the complex hybridity of the colonial subject (the writing of Homi Bhabha in particular) some literary critics are calling for a more nuanced approach to the colonizing subject. David Trotter (1990) provides an interesting case. He gives us the example of C. F. G. Masterman, an Edwardian journalist and Liberal politician, who recognized in the institutions grouped around a London suburb – prison, workhouse, fever hospital, lunatic asylum – a principle which could be identified abroad:

From the turnip fields of Tooting I apprehended the British Empire and something of its meaning; why we always conquered and never assimilated our conquests; why we were so just and so unloved! [. . .] For the spirit of that Empire – clean, efficient, austere, intolerably just – is the spirit which has banished to these forgotten barrack-prisons and behind high walls the helpless young and the helpless old, the maimed, the restless and the dead (quoted by Trotter, p. 6).

At a more general level such concerns are not novel. Apart from the rebirth of interest in Fanon in some quarters (Gates (1991) provides a balanced assessment of this literature) these matters have been the life-long focus of Tunisian writer Albert Memmi. Less well known in this context is the work of Indian writer Ashis Nandy. *The Intimate Enemy: Loss and Recovery of Self Under Colonialism* (1983) is of particular interest.

containing statistical, commercial and miscellaneous observations on *Gibraltar, Sardinia, Sicily, Malta, Serigo, and Turkey*, London: Cadell and Davies.

Gates, L. H. (1991). Critical Fanonism. *Critical Inquiry*, **17**.

Gibraltar Directory and Guide Book (1948), Garrison Library: Gibraltar.

Gómez, J. (1986). *La Línea de la Concepción: Guía critica*, Juan Manuel Ballesta Gómez: La Línea.

Hills, G. (1974). *Rock of Contention*, London: Hale.

Howes, W. H. (1951). *The Gibraltarian: the origin and development of the population of Gibraltar from 1704*, Colombo: City Press.

Jackson, L. (1991). *The Poverty of Structuralism*, London: Longman.

Jackson, W. (1987). *The Rock of the Gibraltarians*, London and Toronto: Associated University Presses.

Lang, J. (n.d.). *Outposts of Empire*, London: Caxton.

Macauley, R. (1949). *Fabled Shore: from the Pyrenees to Portugal*, London: Hamish Hamilton.

MacKenzie, J. (1984). *Propaganda and Empire*, Manchester: Manchester University Press.

Morris, J. (1968). *Pax Britannica: the Climax of an Empire*, London: Faber and Faber.

Morris, J. (1973). *Heaven's Command: an Imperial Progress*, London: Faber and Faber.

Morris, J. (1978). *Farewell the Trumpets: an Imperial Retreat*, London: Faber and Faber.

Nandy, A. (1983). *The Intimate Enemy: Loss and Recovery of Self Under Colonialism*, Oxford: Oxford University Press.

Perrier, A. (1873). *A Winter in Morocco*, London: King.

Pratt, M. (1992). *Imperial Eyes: Travel Writing and Transculturation*, London: Routledge.

Said, E. (1978). *Orientalism*, London: Routledge.

Said, E. (1993). *Culture and Imperialism*, London: Chatto.

Steinberg, S. (1981). *The Ethnic Myth: Race, Ethnicity, and Class in America*, New York: Atheneum.

Stewart, J. D. (1967). *Gibraltar: the Keystone*, London: John Murray.

Trotter, D. (1990). The Colonial Subject. *Critical Quarterly*, **32**, (3).

Tute, W. (1957). *The Rock*, London: Collins.

Waugh, E. (1930). *Labels*, London: Duckworth.

Williams, B. (1989). A Class Act: Anthropology and the Race to Nation Across Ethnic Terrain. *Annual Review of Anthropology*, **18**, 401–44.

Acknowledgments

The fieldwork upon which the background for this paper is based was financed by the ESRC and by a generous provision from the Central Research Fund of the University of London.

Chapter 9

Ethnic Identity, Gender and Life Cycle in North Catalonia

Oonagh O'Brien

In this chapter I shall discuss the mechanisms of the reproduction of ethnic identity in a village in French Catalonia. My thesis is that multiple identities exist in that community. The 'majority' identities are French and Catalan. Gender appears to influence ethnic identity, with men being permitted a constant ethnic identity throughout their life cycle, while women experience a marked shift of ethnic identity, from being French to being Catalan. As women are more influential in reproducing ethnic identity, this shift plays an important part in maintaining the patterns of concurrent and changing ethnic identities in the community.

My argument is based on fieldwork carried out in St Llorenç de Cerdans, in the Vallespir region of Northern Catalonia in France. The community there was, from the mid-nineteenth century until the 1980s, a small but flourishing centre for the textile and soft shoe industry, which attracted migrant workers from Spanish Catalonia and, more recently, from Morocco. The interweaving patterns of ethnic identity, gender and life cycle are closely related to a clear-cut class structure and the socio-economic base of the community.

During my first visit to St Llorenç de Cerdans I was frequently told by people, in the community and outside it, that traditional values were dying out, and in particular that the use of the Catalan language was disappearing. I was informed that young people no longer spoke Catalan, and that shortly it would be a thing of the past. This picture of the relative decline of local languages and dialects is not an uncommon view of life in small communities in Europe during the late twentieth, century and the sentiments seemed both familiar and plausible to me. However, various observations caused me to question this view of the village. I met people who had left St Llorenç de Cerdans in the 1930s, and was told that at that time the young people no longer spoke Catalan. These earlier emigrants presumed that, by the early 1980s, nobody would be speaking Catalan except the very old. This was not in fact the case. One of the reasons St Llorenç de Cerdans had been chosen as a place to do fieldwork was precisely because it was known to have a large population of Catalan-speakers. Those 'non-Catalan-speaking' people who had been young in the 1930s were now the generation who were telling me in the 1980s that young people no longer spoke Catalan. These observations alerted me to the possibility that changes in language use might take place during the life cycle, and indeed perhaps even shifts in ethnic identity. I have found evidence that both of these occur. Evidence for language and ethnic identity shifts has come from talking to different generations in one family about attitudes to the two topics, and also from observations during regular return visits that have taken place over a ten-year period.

From being Catalan to being French

The whole process of language shift and ethnic identity shift in St Llorenç is tied closely to social mobility. Factory workers in particular are ambitious for their children to have improved life chances. Employment opportunities are restricted for the children of migrant factory workers. The most realistic opportunity for employment outside the textile and shoe factories and workshops is to work for the French State as a *fonctionnaire*. In order to become a *fonctionnaire*, the applicant must speak good French, and have completed French state education. In essence, a transition from being Catalan to being French is required in order for the children of migrant factory workers to succeed in the highly competitive business of obtaining employment as a *fonctionnaire*. For various reasons it is women who are charged with the greater share of responsibility for ensuring that the shift in language use and in ethnic identity has already occurred within the home.

Ethnic Identity and Gender: The Life Cycle of Women

Women appear to experience these changes rather than men; and it is also women who are linked more closely to the reproduction of language use and ethnic identity. In the literature on ethnicity and nationalism there is rarely any reference to gender. Despite statements arguing that ethnic groups should not be seen as homogeneous entities, but as heterogeneous groups with interrelating factors affecting the members (see for example J. Cole 1984: 98 and Anthony Cohen 1986: 11), it can be said that most volumes dealing with the theoretical issues of ethnicity and nationalism are gender-blind. This most frequently results in women, rather than men, being invisible. When reference is made to intellectuals, it is made to the intellectual life of men, rather than the contribution women might have made through, for example, their high profile in the teaching profession. F. Barth (1969), A. Cohen (1974), Anthony Cohen (1982) and E. Gellner (1964 and 1983), among other anthropologists who have contributed to the debates on ethnic identity, have made but the briefest, if any, reference to gender as an issue.

The place where some illuminating work *has* been done on gender relations and ethnicity and/or nationalism, is in specific case studies – for example di Leonardo (1984), M. MacDonald (1989) and Rogers (1991) among others. There are also volumes which deal specifically with women and ethnicity, such as *Ethnicity and Women*, edited by W. A. Van Horne (1986), *Caught up in Conflict*, edited by Rudy and Callaway (1986), *Feminism and Nationalism in the Third World* by K. Jayawardena (1986), and *Enterprising Women: Ethnicity, Economy and Gender Relations* (1988), edited by S. Westwood and P. Bhachu. One volume which has summarized some of the current theoretical issues on ethnicity and gender is *Women–Nation–State* edited by N. Yuval Davis and F. Anthias (1989). By drawing together conclusions from the case studies in the book, Yuval-Davis and Anthias set an agenda for further studies of gender, ethnicity and nationalism. They argue that women have tended to participate in what they term ethnic and national processes in the following ways: as biological reproducers of ethnic collectivities;

as reproducers of the boundaries of ethnic/national groups; as central to the ideological reproduction of the collectivity and as transmitters of culture; as signifiers of ethnic/national differences and as a focus and symbol in ideological discourses used in the construction, reproduction and transformation of ethnic/national categories; and lastly as participants in national, economic, political and military struggles (Yuval Davis and Anthias 1989: 7). These five participatory forms are not intended by the authors to be exclusive, and additionally are subject to different historical contexts.

When analysing the life cycle of women in St. Llorenç de Cerdans I will be referring largely to the third category in the list, that is to women as central participants in the ideological reproduction of the collectivity and as transmitters of culture.

As well as searching for answers in the literature on ethnicity and women that might help one to understand the role gender plays in the various changes that take place during the life cycle, I have had the opportunity to return to the area of fieldwork regularly over a period of ten years. During this time I have observed many changes, and have exchanged ideas with people living in the community. Drawing on this information, I would propose the following thesis on the role of women in the reproduction of culture in St Llorenç de Cerdans:

> In St Llorenç de Cerdans mothers reproduce French culture and language and grandmothers reproduce Catalan culture and language. The fact that each woman takes on both roles appears to be contradictory, but is in fact a reflection of the changes women go through during their own life cycles whereby they become progressively incorporated into a Catalan ethnic identity from a French ethnic identity. Men do not experience the same changes during their life cycles.

In order to clarify this statement I will firstly give some background information about St Llorenç de Cerdans, and then discuss the changes in language use and ethnic identity that people experience in the community. While I am particularly interested in the active role played in this process by women, the life cycle of men will be examined simultaneously in order to contrast the position of men and women. The life cycle is divided into the following stages: childhood, youth, parenthood, grandparenthood. Reference to socio-economic position will also be made.

St Llorenç de Cerdans

St Llorenç de Cerdans is situated in the *comarca* of Vallespir which is one of the four *comarques* of Catalonia that were allocated to France from Spain after the Treaty of the Pyrenees in 1659. French Catalonia is generally referred to as Rousillon or North Catalonia. I will use the name North Catalonia throughout this paper. Perpignan is the capital of North Catalonia and the nearest urban centre. The community lies in a valley in the Pyrenean mountains ten kilometres from the French–Spanish border at an altitude of just over 2,000 feet. In the census of 1992 it had population of just over 1,300, and since then the population has continued to decline, as it has done since the 1950s.

From the mid-nineteenth century until the 1980s, St Llorenç de Cerdans was dominated by the industrial manufacture of textiles and *espardenyes* (rope sandals). Before this period *espardenyes* appear to have been produced by family groups for their own consumption or as a cottage industry. As a result of various taxes and import restrictions imposed on cloth at the border, textile smuggling was a major source of income during the nineteenth century. The same legislation made it profitable to start producing tough cotton cloth for making *espardenyes* in St Llorenç de Cerdans, and to export this to villages throughout the region, and eventually throughout France. This was done by the 'big' factory started in 1864 by a family called Sans, who had a similar factory in Barcelona. This factory nurtured the small but growing number of artisans and workshops by giving credit, linking in with export networks and effectively controlling a large part of the local economy. The industry was subject to fluctuations, particularly related to seasonal work, and workers usually had to find alternative employment for the summer months. In the early years of the twentieth century a trade union was established; and by 1923 a worker's co-operative producing textiles and *espardenyes* was competing with the 'big' factory. The first half of the century was a successful period for the factories, including the co-operative, which went from strength to strength. It built a social centre with a bakery, a café, showers, a cinema and a dance hall in the lower part of the village. At the height of this industrial period there were eight *espardenya* factories and one textile factory. The big factory alone employed 300 workers. The population grew to over 3,000. But a series of crises during the 1950s and again in the 1970s led to the closure of some factories and cuts in the number of workers in others. During my first fieldwork visit in 1981–2 St Llorenç de Cerdans had a population of 1,600. It still had four factories and five workshops employing a total of 195 workers. In 1993 there were just 20 workers employed in the industry.

Socio-Economic Stratification

The industrial base of the community resulted in a clear-cut socio-economic stratification which runs through every aspect of community life. This stratification can be said to divide the population into four groups: the workers, the petty bourgeoisie, the industrial bourgeoisie, and the *fonctionnaires*. There is a clear link between changes which occur during the life cycle and social mobility between these groups. These links are most evident in the first-listed socio-economic group: the workers.

Workers

This group includes factory workers and agricultural workers. Most people within this group have migrated from Spain within the last two or three generations. The migrants from Spain did not travel far, but moved here from the textile and shoe-producing towns on the other side of the border in Catalonia. They were skilled workers, and spoke the same language as people in St Llorenç de Cerdans. However, they were officially classed as migrants travelling from one state to another. There has been only a very small proportion of the workers that are engaged in agriculture for the last two centuries. (The 1982 census lists 6 per cent of the population as being economically active in agriculture). The factory workers have formed the largest socio-economic group in the village for the last 150 years. The workers have also been the most unstable group, with a large proportion migrating out, usually to take up employment as *fonctionnaires*. This group is now the most rapidly declining group, although there are many retired factory workers who still live in St Llorenç de Cerdans. Both men and women worked in the factories and agriculture. Additionally women did piece work, sewing the shoes for the factories at home.

The Petty Bourgeoisie

The petty bourgeoisie consists of artisan workers and shopkeepers. It also includes workshops from some other trades, such as woodwork and metal work, that are practised locally. Both men and women are economically active in the *espardenya* workshops and the shops; but women do not appear to be so in other trades. This is the most stable group in the community. The common pattern is for one child to inherit a position or job in the small family concern, and for the others to leave to work elsewhere, either as *fonctionnaires* or in some other employment or profession.

The Industrial Bourgeoisie

This group consists of the factory owners. There are about six families who own or did own factories, and all six families have intermarried. In a number of instances the women inherited the factory, and their marriage partners took over the running of the factories. However, many of the women of these families were actively involved in running the factories, and played an important role in economic affairs and in keeping moral order among the workers, in particular the young women. Some of the women in this group married men from France – that is, from France north of Perpignan. This is very rare for other women in the community. The industrial bourgeoisie own a large proportion of the property, both houses and land, in St Llorenç de Cerdans. At the turn of the century they also owned most of the shops, and dominated the local political positions. This group is declining as the factories close (frequently when the owner retires), and the children are not being encouraged to carry on the family business – perceived to be old-fashioned and doomed to fail.

Fonctionnaires

There is one additional socio-economic group that cannot be called a class, as there are a wide range of different status and economic positions within the group; but certain of its characteristics are shared by all members. This is the *fonctionnaire* group, who are employed by the French State and are an important and expanding group both within the community and outside it, as some locals work as *fonctionnaires* outside the area. *Fonctionnaires* have little choice about where they work, and people from St Llorenç de Cerdans are employed as *fonctionnaires* elsewhere in France. Many return for the holidays during the summer and at other periods and for festivals. *Fonctionnaire* employment is open to both men and women, and there appear to be approximately equal numbers of young men and women leaving the village to take up these posts. However, this information is difficult to assess accurately, as it is not always possible to track down everyone who has left the community to find work elsewhere. The children of those classified both as petty bourgeoisie and as workers become *fonctionnaires*; but many more come from the latter group.

Social Mobility

These four socio-economic groups affect gender roles and ethnic identity. They are not static groups, and the interrelationships between the groups are one of the factors which explain the role of women in reproducing ethnic identity. The workers were the largest group in St Llorenç de Cerdans. The petty bourgeoisie have always been a small and tightly controlled group, achieving social mobility from the working class into this socio-economic group was difficult. I have argued elsewhere (O'Brien 1990) that the workers had a two-pronged approach to achieving enhanced life chances: firstly the development of a strong co-operative and workers' movement, and secondly an improvement in employment prospects for their children. Until the late 1970s there was plenty of work in the factories in St Llorenç de Cerdans, even if the work was insecure and the conditions poor. It was possible for five or six members of one family to obtain work in the factories. The migrant workers that came from Spanish Catalonia were better off in the French State, as wages were higher, workers conditions were better and education was also generally considered as being of a higher quality. They perceived France as a place offering them opportunities, and also, during periods of dictatorship in Spain, political freedom.

The constant stream of migrant workers from Spanish Catalonia reinforced Catalan language and culture in St Llorenç de Cerdans. France is often held up in politics and history as a paradigm of centralizing Jacobin ideology, encouraging and cajoling its citizens into a uniform state structure. In St Llorenç de Cerdans efforts to transform Catalans into French people took place largely through the education system. However, neither the French language nor being in any sense 'French' was necessary for life in the community. The carrot encouraging language- and identity-change for Catalan workers was social mobility. For workers, the only employment open to their children in a community with such a hierarchical socio-economic structure was to become *fonctionnaires* and work for the French State. This required completing the French education system,and in essence required a shift from being Catalan to being French. In the early twentieth century it took approximately two generations before a migrant worker's family could afford to let their child complete secondary education and thereby obtain a high-grade *fonctionnaire* post. In the late 1950s and early 1960s the process happened more quickly, sometimes within one generation, both because workers coming from Spain have been better off financially and educationally and because of improved educational opportunities in France. In recent years migration has stopped, because of the decline in the local textile and shoe industry.

Identity Changes and Life Cycle

Having described the socio-economic structure of the community, and some of the issues affecting social mobility, this section deals with the shifts in ethnic identity and language use at each stage of the life cycle. In each subsection reference is made to each of the various socio-economic groupings within the community.

Childhood

In St Llorenç de Cerdans both boys and girls of all socio-economic groups are spoken to in French by their parents and by most adults. This happens even if the parents speak Catalan between themselves, so that compound bilingualism exists, i.e. parents interchange languages. The only families where this does not happen are families where the parents knowledge of French is so poor that they cannot use it with children. When children go to school, French is further reinforced by the teachers, who are often from elsewhere in

France, and may have little or no knowledge of Catalan. Education has been the major method of socializing the population into being French. It is not only the French language that is taught in schools, but there are also classes in civic obligations and in the meaning of being a French citizen. Because of the enthusiasm with which most of the migrant workers in St Llorenç de Cerdans have come to France, this aspect of school education is reinforced by parents, in particular those who work or worked in the factories. In other socio-economic groups there is also widespread approval of French socialization in schools.

The sole exception to this has been during the 1980s, when a small number of parents have put pressure on the school to teach Catalan. These parents are mostly *fonctionnaires* themselves, or from the petty bourgeoisie group, i.e. families where social mobility is not an issue and where French is not under threat because the parents speak it so well that the children will learn it whether or not they learn Catalan in school. During the 1970s and 1980s more and more schools in North Catalonia have been teaching Catalan. It is interesting, however, that St Llorenç de Cerdans, which is perceived as the most Catalan-speaking community in North Catalonia, is one of the only places where Catalan was not taught in school during this period. Children from the industrial bourgeoisie families are sent to school outside St Llorenç de Cerdans, usually to boarding schools further inland in France, so that language use and French socialization are not an issue for them.

Although the pressure on children to be French affects both boys and girls, it is permissible for boys to joke in Catalan. The jokes made in Catalan are usually crude, and relate to a male world of drinking, camaraderie and hunting. Hunting takes place on Sundays; and a very large proportion of men from the village, from all socio-economic groups, hunt boar and other wild game. It is a social activity, often accompanied by eating together afterwards, and very central to the life of the men in the community. It was one aspect of village life that a female anthropologist had no opportunity to participate in or observe! Young boys are sometimes taken hunting by the men, and in these situations, I have been told, they are sometimes spoken to in Catalan by older men – something that would not happen to girls of the same age. This happens with all socio-economic groups, including the factory-owning families. While there is no clear explanation of why this is so, it could be seen as a form of marking boundaries between women's worlds and men's worlds. It is complementary to a further socialization that occurs with girls: that it is not 'nice' to speak Catalan, because Catalan is a rough male language; for children and young girls should be 'genteel' and 'ladylike' and speak French. Additionally, girls from the workers' families are not generally encouraged to expect to work in the factories. It is said that young girls should be saved from 'dirty factory work if possible, and have a 'clean' occupation. As well as this, the hope is often expressed that a woman may marry into a better class of family if she has good spoken French, and will then be able to afford not to work at all. This is an aspiration, and, as far as I could find out, one which was rarely fulfilled, as marriage patterns were closely related to socio-economic position in the community.

Youth

The emphasis on being French and speaking French continues for young women throughout the latter years of school and while they are starting to have their first serious relationships with young men. Young men are also encouraged to speak French, and, if from workers' families, to aim for a *fonctionnaire* post. However, a young man that is lined up to inherit a small business from a family in the petty bourgeoisie group has to be familiar with Catalan language and Catalan ways if he is to deal well with customers, who will be local. A brother or sister who will not inherit, but will have to look for work outside the community, may have a completely different language use despite being close in age. Since the early 1980s young men from factory-owning families have not been encouraged to consider taking over the factories, which are no longer seen as having a viable future. However, in the past they too needed to have a good knowledge of Catalan in order to communicate with workers.

All young men are permitted to speak Catalan in cafés and when hunting, particularly when making crude jokes, or generally larking about. These situations are not accessible to young women. During the festival of Carnival, which is an important festival in St Llorenç de Cerdans, Catalan is spoken by the young when they are dressed up and masked, and so is associated with the burlesque, the life that is forbidden everyday. While young women are permitted to speak Catalan at this time, they are often self-conscious about doing so even in costume, because they have had little opportunity to speak it.

When young people start to have serious relationships they socialize in a world of other young people. Until the late 1960s this socializing took place within St Llorenç de Cerdans, which had for a number of years an active social scene, with two cinemas, two dance halls and up to thirteen cafés, most of which had live music and in some cases dancing. The whole community was divided between left-wing and centre–right political allegiances, and the workers' co-operative ran one of the dance halls and one cinema, while the factory owners set up a group to run the competition. Rivalry was fierce between the two dance halls, and young people did not circulate between the two social centres unless they were looking for trouble. Since the 1970s young people go to discos and nightclubs in neighbouring towns and villages. There are some discos serving the rural areas in quite isolated areas in the Pyrenees. People travel by car and motorbike, and access to transport is essential for a successful social life. In general the factory-owning families do not participate much in this social life, and relationships in these families are formed with young men and women outside the village, usually from a similar socio-economic background, and often from other parts of France.

This is the stage at which young men leave the community to carry out their military service. In the past this had an important impact on men s level of French language use and identity. In recent years the impact is not so great, as boys are brought up in an overwhelmingly French world.

Although both young men and young women have close friendships with members of the same sex, open romantic relationships are always with members of the opposite sex. Only veiled references are made to young people not choosing to be in a heterosexual relationship, and these references are usually either joking or judgemental. Where this is the case the people concerned either successfully hide their sexual orientation or leave the community.

For all socio-economic groups in the village, this is the stage of the life cycle when they are most linked in to a national and international culture. The social life of discos and nightclubs is definitely categorized as French, with modern French and international music being played. This social life continues through the serious relationships that are earmarked for marriage to the early years of marriage. It is understood, and more or less tolerated, that at this stage young people are having sexual relationships with each other. Older women discuss this a great deal, and make comparisons with their own periods of courting. They often expressed the opinion to me that young women are being duped into giving the men what they want (i.e. a sexual relationship) without demanding that the men pay the price of marriage and commitment. The pill is perceived as the mechanism by which men have managed to 'have their cake and eat it'.

For young women the 'Catalan' world is a million miles away, a backward world that is a cause for mimicry and humour. There are some small restaurants run by farmers in farmhouses in the mountains, with Catalan food and rather primitive décor. While groups of young men might go there, particularly after a day's hunting, young women would call them dirty, and only want to go to smarter, more sophisticated places. During this phase young people who have successfully obtained *fonctionnaire* posts leave the community, and the region if their post demands it. Most *fonctionnaire* posts except those specifically based in St Llorenç de Cerdans require the person to go to Paris for a period of about ten years. I have argued elsewhere (O'Brien 1993) that it is this group of departed *fonctionnaires* who become the most nationalistic about their Catalan identity.

Parenthood

When women have children their world changes dramatically. They no longer participate in the group of young couples whose social life takes place outside the village. They are often forced to leave employment outside the community and take up work in the factories or, if they have married into petty bourgeoisie families, to work in the family shop or other business. Women who have become *fonctionnaires* are usually in protected employment, and can keep their jobs. (Most of these live outside St Llorenç de Cerdans and return in the holidays.) Women from the industrial bourgeoisie probably mostly stop work when they have children; but the group is too small to make any generalizations. They do not appear to socialize with older women from the community.

Other women who remain in St Llorenç de Cerdans when they have children enter a world of older women who speak and identify as Catalan. They become dependent on older women for advice and help with child care and domestic tasks if they are to carry on working. The social life of older women and mothers takes place in shops and on the street, around the public benches, which become the spot for a chat, in homes and in the factories. Social life becomes gender-specific; although there are mixed trips and events, and husbands and wives do socialize together, women do not socialize with men as much after having children, but spend more time with other women. While this is happening the woman herself is under pressure to socialize her child as French, in order to ensure that the child will 'have a better life than she has'. It is not uncommon to see a group of women on the street who are speaking Catalan turn to a recently born baby, far too young to understand either French or Catalan, and talk to it in French. The women then revert to Catalan among themselves.

Mothers socialize their children into being French, even though at that stage of the life cycle the mothers themselves are being increasingly brought into a Catalan world. In St Llorenç de Cerdans both women and men often comment on the fierce ambition women have for their children. Encouraging their children to be successful French citizens is perceived as the only way mothers have to ensure that their children will have employment with economic security when they are older.

Grandparent-hood

Grandparents are an important part of the family in St Llorenç de Cerdans. If they do not live in the same house, or in another flat in the same building, they live nearby and visit often. The grandfather's vegetable plot is usually an important supplement to the family s diet, and the grandmothers retain the majority of domestic tasks in a household where the mother is working in the factories. Grandmothers appear to have no further need for French. Although older women do speak in French with each other at times, they speak more Catalan, and when speaking French they constantly drop words of Catalan into the French. This mixing of the two languages is seen as a source for humour and mimicry among the young. I have found it difficult to assess whether the move towards greater use of Catalan is simply the result of relaxing into being an older woman, or a decision, either conscious or unconscious, taken in order to preserve Catalan culture and language. Certainly young people confirmed to me that their grandparents, and particularly their grandmothers, were a source of knowledge about language, customs, cooking, music and the past. Those same grandmothers often told me that they had only spoken French as young women. Clearly the fact that grandmothers are seen as reservoirs of Catalan culture and customs can only happen as a result of the changes a woman herself goes through during her life cycle – changes which men do not appear to experience.

The obvious question arising here is how the women learn Catalan in order to be able use it when they have children. Girls and young women in St Llorenç de Cerdans hear Catalan all the time, and do in fact have a knowledge of it, through a process of absorption, although they do not use it. They also learn it from their grandmothers, who constitute a reservoir of culture for boys and girls. But the change of language use does not happen overnight, and young mothers are often embarrassed at their accent when they speak Catalan.

Conclusion

While the socialization of children as French can be explained through ambition for social mobility and the positive values attributed to being French, it is still not clear why women appear to move toward a more Catalan identity as they get older. One explanation could be that, as they have patently not achieved the sought-after *fonctionnaire* post, and are not going to leave the community to work elsewhere, being French is no longer of paramount importance. It could also be that the Catalan identity of the community is still so strong that unless there are strong reasons for being French, members revert to a community norm of being Catalan. An alternative explanation might be due to the demographic pattern of the community. St Llorenç de Cerdans, like many rural villages in the region, has a large proportion of older people in its population, and among them are many first-generation migrants. These may still tip the community balance toward the side of being Catalan. However, none of these suggestions explains the gender difference: men do not go through a similar shift in identity and language use during their life cycle. Throughout their life they have been permitted a wider ethnic and language choice than women, and that pattern appears to be consistent, so that they neither become more French nor more Catalan as they get older. Women, however, move from a position of being strongly discouraged to participate in Catalan language use or identity, to a position where they are expected to adopt Catalan language use and identity.

Women in St Llorenç de Cerdans play a central role in the ideological reproduction of the collective identity of the community. They are acknowledged to be an important cultural and linguistic resource. They are central to the changes and contradictions that are evident in the plural ethnic identities of the community.

Acknowledgements

The research in Catalonia was supported by grants from the SSRC and the University of London Central Research fund, which I gratefully acknowledge.

References

Barth, F. (1969). *Ethnic Groups and Boundaries. The Social Organisation of Culture Difference*, London: Allen & Unwin.

Cohen, A. (1974). *Two Dimensional Man: An Essay on the Anthropology of Power and Symbolism in Complex Society*, London: Routledge and Kegan Paul.

Cohen, A. (ed.) (1982). *Belonging: Identity and Social Organisation in British Rural Cultures*, Manchester: Manchester University Press.

Cohen, A. (ed.) (1986). *Symbolising Boundaries, Identity and Diversity in British Culture*, Manchester: Manchester University Press.

Cole, J. (1984). Reflections on the Political Economy of Ethnicity. In *Ethnic Challenge: The Politics of Ethnicity in Europe* (eds Vermeulen and Boissivain), Gottingen: Herodot.

di Leonardo, M. (1984). *The Varieties of Ethnic Experience: Kinship, Class and Gender among California Italian Americans*, Ithaca NY: Cornell University Press.

Gellner, E. (1964). *Thought and Change*, London: Weidenfeld and Nicolson.

Gellner, E. (1983). *Nations and Nationalism*, Oxford: Blackwell.

Jayawardena, K. (1986). *Feminism and Nationalism in the Third World*, London: Zed Books.

MacDonald, M. (1989). Brittany: Politics and Women in a Minority World. In *Caught up in Conflict: Women's Responses to Political Strife* (eds R. Rudy and H. Callaway), London: Macmillan.

O'Brien, O. (1990). Perceptions of Identity in North Catalonia. In *Family, Class and Nation in Catalonia* (ed. J. Llobera), Special Issue of *Critique of Anthropology*, **10**, (2) and (3).

O'Brien, O. (1992). Sisters, Parents, Neighbours, Friends; Reflections on Fieldwork in North Catalonia (France). In *Gendered Fields* (ed. D. Bell, P. Caplan and W. J. Karim), London: Routledge.

O'Brien, O. (1993). Good to be French? Conflicts of Identity in North Catalonia. In *Inside European Identities* (ed. S. Macdonald), Oxford: Berg.

Rogers, S. C. (1991). *Shaping Modern Times in Rural France*, New Jersey: Princeton University Press.

Rudy and Callaway (eds) (1986). *Caught up in Conflict: Women's Responses to Political Strife*, London: Macmillan.

Westwood, S. and Bhachu, P. (eds) (1988). *Enterprising Women: Ethnicity, Economy and Gender Relations*, London: Routledge.

Van Horne, W. A. (1986). *Ethnicity and Women*, Madison WI University of Wisconsin System American Studies Co-ordinating Committee/Urban Corridor Consortium.

Yuval-Davis, N. and Anthias, F. (eds) (1989). *Women–Nation–State*, London: Macmillan.

Chapter 10

Gender Relations and Social Change in Europe: On Support and Care[1]

Dolors Comas d'Argemir

Gender relations, and the social changes which influence them, have been analysed most frequently in the context of the division of labour. In this article, I will refer to a specific aspect of the division of labour, that is, forms of support and care, since their cultural expression and their forms of institutionalization offer interesting insights into our understanding of the relationship between the division of labour, gender and kinship in different social contexts.

In European anthropology, much attention has focused on the study of the division of labour between men and women, but the treatment has been uneven because different points have been emphasized depending on the ethnographic area under consideration or on the type of society analysed. In the case of the Mediterranean, for example, the honour and shame complex has become a consolidated stereotype. In Northern Europe, by contrast, the main emphasis has been on the dichotomy between work and family. The fact that these studies produce such different emphases suggests that they tend to reproduce the dominant *models of representation* and *language* through which social relations are expressed. It is therefore necessary to find an alternative focus of comparison which will encourage the exploration of new dimensions of gender and thereby contribute toward shifting the anthropology of the Mediterranean to an anthropology of Europe. One way to do this, I suggest, is through an analysis centred on support and care.

1. My thanks to Liz Russell for her help with the translation of this paper and to Victoria Goddard for her comments and suggestions.

Support and care have received relatively little attention in social research. This is probably due to their 'invisibility', their conceptual ambiguity, and to the fact that they both tend to become diluted within different kinds of social relationships. They deal with activities which seem to be very restricted (many of them are provided in the context of the family), and which are associated with `natural' behaviour (is it not `natural' and `instinctive' that a mother should care for her child?), and are imbued with a deeply emotive duty (don't parents care for their children because they 'love' them?). These connotations have made it difficult to perceive the *cultural* character of these activities as well as their *economic value* and their *social importance*. For the same reasons, it has been difficult to identify the full range of such activities and their crucial role in *social reproduction*. It is important, therefore, to uncover these hidden dimensions of support and care. Their analysis may help us revise certain basic theoretical presuppositions and facilitate a more comparative approach.

Indeed, the analysis of support and care obliges us to transcend the well-worn dichotomies current in the social sciences, such as public–private, work–family, structure–emotions, dependency–individualism, production–reproduction. It also allows us to compare the institutional contexts and the role of the State in the organization of welfare activities. In Great Britain, for example, there are a great number of articles and books which deal with these matters, reflecting a deep social preoccupation. In contrast, this subject has barely been dealt with in Spain. This may be due to the different historical contexts of the two countries. In Britain, the Welfare State became the backbone of numerous institutions related to health, the care of the old and social policy in general. Significantly, those writings came at a time of crisis in the Welfare State, and simultaneously there emerged an ideological discourse which defended community care (that is, care by family, friends, neighbours, or voluntary groups).[2] Feminists criticized the fact that such responsibilities fell basically to women, placing them at a difficult crossroads. Cultural values rooted in individualism and privacy contrasted with the moral and emotive duties involved in caring for dependent persons. In Spain, on the other hand, family ties and friendship networks seem to be stronger than in Britain, and

2. See Allan (1983), Finch (1990), Finch and Groves (1983), Rodger (1991), Thane (1978), and Ungerson (1990).

it is through them that duties related to support and care have been channelled. The institutional framework of welfare is less developed, and consequently support and care are provided mainly through interpersonal relationships. This is not only due to the presence of specific cultural characteristics, but also to historical trends which have led to a different model of the State, one which had little to do with the resolution of welfare problems.

Support and Care as Activities

Support and care include a number of activities which are directed towards the physical, psychic and emotional well-being of people. It is difficult to separate the two concepts, which are situated in a kind of continuum that includes different forms of help. According to Finch (1989), support and care may be composed of the following aspects: economic support, accommodation, personal care, practical support and child care, and emotional and moral support. This set of activities is variable and unequal, and can be carried out continuously or at specific moments; they can overlap with daily activities or be required only sporadically. These variations are related to the life cycle of individuals or to critical moments in people's lives. Their common goal is to solve problems that make people temporarily or permanently dependent.

As noted, the diversity of these activities, their inclusion in different kinds of social relations and their conceptual ambiguity make it difficult to delimit them and perceive them. This is due to the fact that *in support and care there is no separation between person and activity*, as is the case with activities incorporated into the labour market (Strathern 1985). This, in turn, is as much due to the characteristics that generate situations of personal dependency as to the fact that the activities they include function basically through kinship ties.

Although both support and care are considered to be integrated into the division of labour by sex and age, the ambiguity regarding their conceptualization is of interest here. On the one hand, support and care may be considered to constitute 'work' in that they involve the provision of goods and services, hours of dedication and the deployment of knowledge and skills. But because such activities are seen as overlapping with ties of affection, of 'instinctive' behaviour, or moral obligation, it may be that socially they are not conceived as 'work' but as part of the repertoire of biologically determined human behaviour or as a consequence of social forms of reciprocity. Both considerations influence the division of tasks between men and women as much as does the tasks' social value.

Support and care combine principles of a material nature with those of an affective nature, and these two sets of principles appear to be mutually contradictory, and, again, make for difficulties when attempting to locate these activities within the division of labour. The material aspects of these activities are expressed through the evaluation of the time, expenditure and dedication which they imply. On the other hand, and again in apparent contradiction, support and care rely on emotions that, like love, affection, or duty, imply attitudes of generosity, unselfishness and morality. Significantly, it is these emotions that do much to constitute and define such activities and give meaning to people's actions. Interest and emotion are thus inseparably combined, although each society will lay greater or less emphasis on each of these factors (Medick and Sabean 1984).

Support and care are, for example, a vehicle for the transmission of goods, particularly in the case of peasants, where access to inheritance is closely linked to the obligation of kin to work and care for fellow kin. In peasant societies sentiment is subsumed by material interest. The language of interest and the language of love create metaphors through which social relationships are structured. A significant transformation in the institutions of marriage and inheritance in Catalonia is a case in point (Narotzky 1991). Marriage was based on a contractual agreement which had a muted but acknowledged content involving the exchange of property (from the side of the male heir or *hereu*) for services (caring services of the bride in relation to her in-laws). This was the language in which the relationships between people on the one hand and people and property on the other were expressed. An alternative contract now tends to underscore love as the basis of interpersonal relations, thus placing emotion at the centre of the work of caring and support that women continue to provide.

Support and care have popularly been considered as a labour of love or as a form of help based on moral obligation. The ethnographic encounter should permit the deconstruction of such categories in order to establish their specific contents in particular societies and within given historical conditions. Post-structuralist approaches have stressed the need for a methodological distinction between analytical tools and folk concepts. In this case, there is no analytical category to express what we have defined as 'support and care' (and which have often been complemented by other concepts such as 'help' and 'welfare'). In Great Britain the term 'care' is more narrowly defined than in Spain, being limited to the care of dependants, while excluding other aspects of welfare which are less organized and more informal.[3] It is, however, important to retrieve the more general content of what we call 'support and care' in order to consider it in relation to human and social reproduction.

Thus, care demands love as much as work, emotion as much as activity. On the one hand it is linked to the construction of personhood and to the person's social relationships (the *production of identities*). On the other hand, it is an integral part of the process through which society reproduces itself and maintains the mental and physical health of its workforce (*social reproduction*). Support and care are particularly relevant to the construction of women's identities and the definition of their activities, being fundamental elements of the social construction of gender.

Support and Care as System of Meanings

Support and care can also be understood as a system of meanings, involving symbols and contents which vary cross-culturally. This means that on the one hand they contribute to the social construction of gender and of identity and, on the other, that they cannot be considered as an *a priori*, as given facts. Instead, they are cultural products, and, as such, are variable, and important objects of study.

Gender is of crucial importance here, for men and women become differentially involved in systems of support and care. Research carried out in some European countries shows that women usually give more support and care than men and receive less help in exchange (Duran 1988; Finch 1989; Finch and Groves 1983; Ungerson 1990; Waerness 1987). This is as much due to social representations regarding the division of work as to the kind of relationships in which they are inscribed. Sexuality and kinship are essential elements when analysing the link between care and gender.

3. In Great Britain the term 'care' has a rather restricted meaning, as it only refers to helping dependent people (usually adults), and is associated with organized welfare policies. Sometimes, the term 'informal care' is used to denote the private and spontaneous dimensions of care (Ungerson 1990). In Spain, however, these concepts have a wider meaning.

Sexuality provides the language of biology to explain the differences between men and women; *kinship provides the language of genealogy* to situate people in a differentiated set of positions and functions.

The connection between gender and care is established through the conceptual link with biology and its association with the division of labour.[4] Indeed, the category of work itself has a strong biological referent as regards both production and care. Support and care are activities necessary for the individual's survival, on which his/her well-being depends, and they demand the organized deployment of energy and skills. Yet it is not the activities themselves which constitute work or care, but their perception as such and their inclusion within specific relationships. Their cultural and social dimensions do not prevent them, however, from being perceived as rooted in biology, as is the case with gender. It is precisely women's involvement in human reproduction that becomes the decisive argument in justifying the existing division of labour (Rosaldo 1974), and in attributing to women a greater capacity and disposition to offer support and care. As Ortner (1974) points out, the perception of men and women as physiologically different beings contributes to the assignation to them of different qualities and skills that predispose them for different functions and roles. These social representations are internalized by individuals and are integral to the constitution of different psychic structures, which consequently shape the construction of different identities.

Care has specific consequences for the identity and activities of women. Because women are thought to be more intuitive, patient and emotional, they are also considered to be more 'capable' of caring. These assumptions are supported by the fact that the wide range of knowledge and skills required for care activities are learned informally, during the process of socialization, and are thus invisible (Gullestad 1988). The most visible dimensions of support and care are to be found in the feelings involved in support and care – in devotion, self-sacrifice and affection. This explains why many women define their own identity through their services to others rather than through themselves (Comas d'Argemir *et al.* 1990; del Valle 1985). Different qualities are attributed to activities carried out by men. Here, the most visible dimensions of care are of a material nature, relating to the supply of goods, which, being more tangible,

---

4. For reflections on the links between gender and sexuality see Caplan (1987), Ortner and Whitehead (1981), and Ross and Rapp (1989).

become more visible. This has important consequences for the identity of men; moreover, it is the men who are considered to be the representatives of the domestic group.

Kinship is another factor that links gender to care. Yanagisako and Collier (1987) identified kinship as a central factor in gender analysis. Their main argument is that kinship is the social relationship through which human reproduction is regulated, distributing people within a genealogical network which is the basis for conferring attributes, rights and roles. These same principles regulate the division of labour within the family and the forms in which help is given and received. As kinship is also a system of cultural meanings (Schneider 1968), it becomes a paradigm through which certain genealogical relations are linked to moral obligation and affection – sentiments so vital to those practices related to support and care.

The fact that both support and care are basically produced through kinship also contributes to linking these activities with women. This is as much due to women's roles in human reproduction as to their centrality within kinship networks (Yanagisako 1977). In urban contexts, women play an important part in disseminating information, in maintaining links, and in organizing ritual practices (Bott 1975; Young and Willmott 1957). In rural contexts their role is just as important, although its content varies according to different patterns of inheritance and residence. In all cases, women's importance as 'kinkeepers' and as trustees of family memory is recognized (Le Witta 1985). This situates women in the position of mediators, representing fundamental elements in the definition of 'us' as opposed to the external context (Goddard 1987). Women, therefore, not only engage in help and care activities, but also mark out the symbolic and social boundaries of their operation.

Age and generation are other important dimensions in the organization of support and care. Age cuts across gender, involving the process of construction of gender identities and of the assumption of different roles. According to the specific point in a person's life cycle, s/he will give or receive more help and care, and this defines the differences in power between generations and the different forms of participation in social life. As with gender, the social construction of age categories is based on biological and genealogical referents.

The division of labour is thus firmly established as an expression of age and sexual difference and in genealogical positions which are seen as 'natural' and 'inevitable' differences (Stolcke 1981; Collier and Yanagisako 1987). It is important to note that this connection is a product of the cultural system of meanings and not, therefore, a universal fact. As Yanagisako and Collier (1987) point out, it is not sufficient to simply ask how men and women are distributed in different activities, thus assuming intrinsic differences. Instead, we ought to address the question of how each society constructs its particular representations of the sexes, and how activities are distributed according to the recognition of different capacities and skills.

On the other hand, the consideration that support and care represent not only a set of activities but also a system of meanings obliges us to consider their variations in different areas of Europe, and to reconstruct the cultural representations relevant to these activities and to gender and generation. Thus, we ought to start by outlining the conceptual content in each case of what can be considered 'support and care', linking them to the relationships and to the social contexts in which they operate. It is essential, therefore, to analyse support and care in relation to specific ethnographic contexts, which shape the forms and meanings variously attributed to such activities.

Support and Care as Social Reproduction

Harris and Young (1981) proposed a distinction between social or systemic reproduction, the reproduction of labour and human or biological reproduction. These three meanings of 'reproduction' represent different levels of abstraction and generality, each one of them having different implications for the analysis of gender relations. It is true that there is a risk here of consolidating the production–reproduction dichotomy, which has strictly economic connotations that tend to link men and women separately with each of these spheres (Comaroff 1987; Collier and Yanagisako 1987). But if we incorporate these criticisms constructively, Harris and Young's conceptualization still remains valid. Therefore it is important to point out the advances that have been made in the past few years in overcoming the dichotomy between production and reproduction by integrating both notions within a unified concept. The work–family dichotomy has also been questioned, as it deals with a specific model of representation which reflects the economic and social logic of capitalism (Rapp 1978).

Care and assistance are intrinsic to *human reproduction* since they enable the maintenance of life, the support of dependent individuals, and the flow of generations. Support and care are not only given from parents to their children, but also upward (from children to parents in their old age) or collaterally (between brothers and sisters, relatives, and friends or neighbours). The patterns of relationships that hold between generations (and some collateral links) are directly related to the transmission of goods and knowledge and, therefore, to the production of socialized individuals in specific work-roles and in specific social classes. Thus, since support and care recreate and regenerate workers, they contribute to the *reproduction of work*.

From a strictly economic or material point of view, therefore, support and care are subsumed in the logic that articulates production and reproduction. The distinction which Marx proposed between labour and labour-power reflects the disassociation which is produced between person and activity with the emergence of waged production. The family and the work sphere are seen as separate entities. While the different work components (such as tools, machinery, raw materials, installations) are reproduced within the work process as a substantial part of the activities which define it, the work-force is reproduced outside it, within institutions such as the family, local or national communities, religious groups, and so on. This contributes to separating the concept of 'work' from that of 'support and care'. This conceptual and institutional separation reveals that people are not only factors of production whose work possesses a specific *value*, but are also social factors whose reproduction generates a *cost*.[5] It is important to establish the specific form of articulation of production and reproduction in different social, economic and cultural contexts (Mingione 1985), as this provides the institutional framework within which roles are allocated to different individuals and in which the social constructions of different types of labour division are expressed. Consequently 'work' and 'care' are organized in different social

5. It is not necessary here to enter into the polemic as to whether wages really pay the value of work or rather the costs of its reproduction. In any case the *value* of work gains its importance in the process of production and is expressed in the market, whereas the *cost* is determined within the institutions responsible for the constitution, physical upkeep and reproduction of the workers.

institutions, according to the logic of *systemic reproduction.*

The family has been the main focus for the explanation of the social division of labour and, in particular, of women's roles (Hartmann 1981). This presents certain methodological problems, as it contributes to considering the family as a natural unit and as a homogeneous group (Harris 1981). The critique of these assumptions has enabled the family to be recontextualized, contesting its apparent autonomy, and disclosing conflicts and negotiations within it. The family is, certainly, the main institution in which support and care are provided; but the family is only one of the contexts in which reproduction is organized. The analysis of support and care discloses the articulation of the family and other institutions which play important roles in social reproduction.

Kinship, friendship and local community are other relational contexts which provide support and care and which delimit other kinds of resources and power for men and women and for different generations. Among these relationships, relatives have the most important role. Kinship is a strategic arena where individuals try to solve general contradictions (in economic, social and ideological practices) generated by specific social processes. This is especially relevant in cases where individual problems are not solved through institutional means. It is significant that kinship ties are strengthened in situations where the individual faces unprecedented difficulties in his or her own experiences, such as those caused by an economic crisis, migration, maintaining a high social status or the upheaval associated with important social and political changes. The persistence of family is due to its adaptability and flexibility, which are based on the multifunctionality of the institution, and on its ability to mobilize individuals through highly emotive and moral symbols (Wolf 1966: 7). These same characteristics give to kinship a crucial role in social reproduction. The practices of support and care, which kinship transmits, exceed the individual value they may possess. Kinship produces a relational basis on which individuals establish reciprocities and alliances that help to perpetuate their conditions of existence. Kinship thus participates in the reproduction of social groups and, thereby, in the social logic on which they are based.[6]

6. Some empirical studies on these subjects show the importance of kinship and friendship in the reproduction of living conditions. See, for example, Buechler and Buechler (1987), Caplan and Bujra (1978), Finch (1989), McDonogh (1986), Pujadas (1988), Segalen and Bekus (1990), and Strathern (1981).

Another context relevant to the organization of reproduction is the set of welfare institutions that attend to those in need of either social or physical care. These vary from long-stay institutions that entail the isolation of individuals (such as old people's homes, hospitals, poorhouses and orphanages) to the recent type of organized institution that is termed 'community care' and provides at-home services from the family, friends, neighbours or volunteers. This implies the delegation of functions that are currently taken on by the State.[7]

Only those countries that have Welfare States have a dense institutional network that provides for aid and care. Even there, however, only a small fraction of support and care is provided for through such institutions. Of far greater importance are the family, kinship networks and personal relationships. The balance between family and specific institutions shows once again the importance of the economic dimensions of support and care, because family services are free and are based on moral obligation. The *cost* is hidden and the activities become invisible. Thus care and support are not measured in terms of value but in terms of cost. What then becomes the contestable issue is how costs are to be distributed between different institutions: family, kinship, community or the State. Each of these entails different relationships and gender identities.

According to the OECD (1988), the highest rates of social and public expenditure as a proportion of GDP (Gross Domestic Product) were found in France (62.6 per cent), Sweden (58.3), Denmark (58.0), the Netherlands (56.6), and Germany (49.9). Norway (44.0 per cent), Finland (42.2), and Britain (39.6) are in a midway position. Spain (33.9 per cent) and Portugal (31.3) show the lowest rates and, together with Greece, have a lower GDP than the other countries. These rates illustrate differences in social and economic trends that are deeply rooted in history. North European countries show the highest rates of female participation in the work sphere, and, moreover, have a more developed Welfare State. Social policies address themselves basically to women, involving direct action within the family and marriage, and they are also concerned with assuring the autonomy of the old. By contrast, Southern European countries have not established Welfare States, but have

---

7. Some centuries ago these responsibilities were adopted by the Church in its activities of charitable welfare.

instead organized social reproduction around kinship links and the high value there attributed to 'familism'. This has had immediate repercussions on women's activities. In Britain the recently developed policy of 'community care' seems to have arisen not only because it is cheap and morally more satisfactory than institutional care, but also because of government attempts to revive 'traditional family values'.

Considerable differences exist, therefore, between European countries in the forms and extent of the institutionalization of the social reproduction of individuals and households, and in relation to the care of children, the sick, the old and the disabled). In all cases, social policies are based on what is seen as a traditional division of gender roles, relegating the responsibility for support and care to women. Because of this, the existence of a welfare state facilitates the participation of women in the public arena. In periods of recession, when unemployment is on the increase and wages are decreased, there is a tendency to reduce expenditure in social and personal services. This has repercussions on the family, and most especially on women.

The values of individualism and privacy, which constitute an important part of capitalist ideology, seem to contradict what has generally been confirmed as the most common of social situations: the situation of dependency. All of us need support and care at some time in our lives, and the extent of this need has tended to increase as the population ages and the young are dependent for longer. The need for financial, residential or even emotional support is quite common and widespread. Dependency is not an 'exceptional' situation. In fact, it might be more effective to consider dependency rather than autonomy as the 'normal' state. People depend on each other, and the family – far from having the functional autonomy which Parsons claimed for it – is an institution that depends on economic and political structures (McIntosh 1979).

Conclusion

Roles linked to activities defined as 'work' or 'care' become the basis on which men and women negotiate their entry into wider relationships and structures such as the economy, the community and the State. This gives men and women different types of power and authority, centred in different spheres. Power has usually been associated with control over property or with participation in public or work activities. However, through the control of support and care, women acquire a capacity for negotiation and considerable power which, although expressed in the domestic sphere, also transcends it.

However, it is one thing to recognize different spheres of power with their different forms of expression, and quite another to recognize the social value attributed to them. To do this, it is necessary to refer to the social logic that structurally integrates all these dimensions. In this sense it seems relevant to question how discourses regarding gender are linked to forms of hierarchy and power that transcend sexual difference (Roldan 1985; Stolcke 1993). The relations established in the division of social labour not only offer a key to understanding gender and age relations but also provide insights into their articulation within other social divisions. This is due to the fact that relations of production and reproduction not only integrate inequalities between men and women and between generations, but also encompass racial or ethnic and class inequalities. The categories of gender and age, together with other criteria of social segmentation, not only give form to the relations which are established in production, but also contribute to the reproduction of social hierarchies more generally. It is necessary, therefore, to identify the separate structure that is the basis of the different forms of social divisions or – what comes to be the same thing – to identify the bases by which the *social construct of difference* is organized.

We have been considering support and care as components of the division of labour. This may be debatable, given the ambiguity involved in defining these activities and the emotional aspects underpinning many of them. If, however, we consider the social relationships in which they are embedded, it becomes very significant that men are linked to activities that imply material transactions, characterized by 'doing', whereas women are more closely associated with activities that imply emotional transactions, characterized by 'caring' (Finch 1989). Age distinctions are also important, because support and care runs principally between generations, shaping the links between them, and having important consequences for the transmission of goods and social attributes. To reject the material aspects of support and care would imply stressing solely their physical and biological dimensions, as if these were a simple reflection of the different psychic natures and needs of men and women. By contrast, I have pointed out that the analysis of care must be understood in a wider context, as part of political and economic relations. Moreover, it is also a cultural system of meanings that is articulated with these relationships.

The institutional contexts in which support and care are located show a convergence of different kinds of relations. Kinship constitutes the main network for the provision of support and care, whereas the economy constitutes the general framework in which the division of labour takes place. The active role of the State in the organization of welfare institutions obliges us to consider the domain of politics. This implies not only that support and care are structured around gender and age, but that they are also deeply embedded in social reproduction. The emphasis of this chapter is thus on a challenge to the commonly accepted divisions and a reassessment of the place of sentiment as a constitutive element of gender identity and of the political and sociological terrain. By looking at care and support it is possible to analyse how difference is socially constructed and the purposes that this construction serves. Therefore, because of the particular ways in which support and care are organized and conceptualized, we might be able to recognize the key elements by which social systems function and change. This is why it may be interesting to take support and care as a point of departure for the comparative study of the societies of Europe.

References

Allan, G. (1983). Informal Networks of Care: Issues Raised by Barclay. *British Journal of Social Work*, **13**, 417–33.

Bott, E. (1975). *Family and Social Networks*, London: Tavistock.

Buechler, H. C. and Buechler, J. M. (eds) (1987). *Migrants in Europe. The Role of Family, Labor, and Politics*, New York: Greenwood Press.

Caplan, P. (ed.) (1987). *The Cultural Construction of Sexuality*, London and New York: Tavistock.

Caplan, P. and Bujra, J. M. (eds) (1978). *Women united, women divided. Cross-cultural perspectives of female solidarity*, London: Tavistock.

Collier, J. and Yanagisako, S. (1987). Introduction in *Gender and Kinship. Essays toward a unified analysis* (ed. J. Collier and S. Yanagisako), pp. 1–13, Stanford: Stanford University Press.

Comaroff, J. L. (1987). Sui genderis: Feminism, Kinship Theory and Structural Domains. In *Gender and Kinship. Essays toward a unified analysis* (ed. J. Collier and S. Yanagisako), pp. 53–85, Stanford: Stanford University Press.

Comas D'Argemir, D. *et al.* (1990). *Vides de dona. Treball. família i sociabilitat entre les dones de clases populars a Catalunya (1900–1960)*, Barcelona: Fundació Serveis de Cultura Popular/Alta fulla.

Del Valle, T. *et al.* (1985). *Mujer vasca. Imagen y realidad*, Barcelona: Anthropos.

Duran, A. (1988). *De puertas adentro*, Madrid: Ministerio de Cultura, Instituto de la Mujer.

Finch, J. (1989). *Family Obligations and Social Change*, Cambridge: Polity Press.

Finch, J. (1990). The politics of community care in Britain. In *Gender Caring. Work and Welfare in Britain and Scandinavia* (ed. C. Ungerson), pp 34–59, New York: Harvester Wheatsheaf.

Finch, J. and Groves, D. (eds) (1983). *A Labour of Love. Women, Work and Caring*, London: Routledge and Kegan Paul.

Goddard, V. (1987). Honour and shame: the control of women's sexuality and group identity in Naples. In *The Cultural construction of sexuality* (ed. P. Caplan), pp. 166–92, London: Tavistock.

Gullestad, M. (1988). Agents of Modernity: Children's care for children in urban Norway. *Social Analysis*, **25**, 38–52.

Harris, O. (1981). Households as Natural Units. In *Of Marriage and the Market* (eds F. Young, C. Wolkowitz and R. McCullagh), pp. 136–55, London: Routledge and Kegan Paul.

Harris, O. and Young, K. (1981) Engendered Structures: Some Problems in the Analysis of Reproduction. In *The Anthropology of Pre-Capitalist Societies* (eds J. S. Kahn and J. R. Llobera), pp. 107–47, London: Macmillan.

Hartmann, H. I. (1981). The Family as the Locus of Gender, Class, and Political Struggle: The Example of Housework. *Signs*, **6**, 366–94.

Le Witta, B. (1985). Mémoire: l'avenir du présent. *Terrain*, **4**, 15–26.

McDonogh, W. (1986). *Good Families of Barcelona: A Social History of Power in the Industrial Era*, Princeton, NJ: Princeton University Press.

McIntosh, M. (1979). The Welfare State and the needs of the dependent family. In *Fit Work for Women* (ed. S. Burman), pp. 153–71, London: Croom Helm.

Medick, H. and Sabean, D.W. (eds) (1984). *Interest and Emotion. Essays on the Study of Family and Kinship,* Cambridge: Cambridge University Press/Maison des Sciences de l'Homme.

Mingione, E. (1985). Social reproduction and the surplus labour force: the case of Southern Italy. In *Beyond Employment* (eds N. Redclift and E. Mingione), Oxford: Basil Blackwell.

Narotzky, S. (1991). La renta del afecto: ideología y reproducción social en el cuidado de los viejos. In *Antropología de los Pueblos de España* (eds J. Prat *et al.*), pp. 464–74, Madrid: Taurus.

OECD (organization for economic co-operation and development) (1988). *Economic Surveys,* Paris: OECD.

Ortner, S. B. (1974). Is Female to Male as Nature Is to Culture? In *Women, Culture and Society* (eds M. Z. Rosaldo and L. Lamphere), pp. 17–42, Stanford: Stanford University Press.

Ortner, S. B. and Whitehead, H. (eds) (1981). *Sexual Meanings. The Cultural Construction of Gender and Sexuality,* Cambridge: Cambridge University Press.

Pujadas, J. J. (1988). Forms of subsistence and social reproduction amongst the urban proletariat of Tarragona. *Social Science Information,* **27**, (4), 583–605.

Rapp, R. (1978). Family and Class in Contemporary America: Notes Toward an Understanding of Ideology. *Science and Society,* **42**, (3), 278–300.

Rodger, J. J. (1991). Family structures and the moral politics of caring. *The Sociological Review,* **39**, (4), 799–822.

Roldan, M. (1985). Industrial outworking, struggles for the reproduction of working-class families and gender subordination. In *Beyond Employment* (eds N. Redclift and E. Mingione), pp. 248–85, Oxford: Basil Blackwell.

Rosaldo, M. Z. (1974). Woman, Culture and Society: a Theoretical Overview. In *Women, Culture and Society* (ed. M. Z. Rosaldo and L. Lamphere), pp. 17–42, Stanford: Stanford University Press.

Ross, E. and Rapp, R. (1989). Sex and Society: A Research note from Social History and Anthropology. In *Desire: The Politics of Sexuality* (eds A. Snitow, C. Stansell and S. Thompson), pp. 105–26, London: Virago.

Schneider, D. M. (1968). *American Kinship. A Cultural Account,* Chicago: Chicago University Press.

Segalen, M. and Bekus, F. (1990). *Nanterriens. Les familles dans la ville,* Toulouse: Presses Universitaires du Mirail.

Stolcke, V. (1981). Women's labours: the naturalisation of social inequality on women's subordination. In *Of Marriage and the Market* (eds F. Young, C. Wolkowitz and R. McCullagh), pp. 159–77, London: Routledge and Kegan Paul.

Stolcke, V. (1993). Is Sex to Gender as Race Is to Ethnicity? In *Gendered Anthropology* (ed. T. Del Valle), pp. 17–37, London: Routledge.

Strathern, M. (1981). *Kinship in the Core*, Cambridge: Cambridge University Press.

Strathern, M. (1985). Kinship and Economy: Constitutive Orders of a Provisional Kind. *American Anthropologist*, **12**, 191–210.

Thane, P. (ed.) (1978). *The Origins of British Social Policy*, London: Croom Helm.

Ungerson, C. (1990). The language of care: Crossing the boundaries. In *Gender Caring. Work and Welfare in Britain and Scandinavia* (ed. C. Ungerson), pp. 8–33, New York: Harvester Wheatsheaf.

Waerness, K. (1987). On the rationality of caring. In *Women and the State* (ed. A. S. Sassoon), pp. 207–34, London: Hutchinson.

Wolf, E. (1966). Kinship, Friendship and Patron–Client Relations in Complex Societies. In *The Social Anthropology of Complex Societies* (ed. M. Banton), pp. 1–22, London: Tavistock.

Yanagisako, S. (1977). Women-Centred Kin Networks in Urban Bilateral Kinship. *American Ethnologist*, **5**, 207–26.

Yanagisako, S. J. and Collier, J. F. (1987). Toward a Unified Analysis of Gender and Kinship. In *Gender and Kinship. Essays toward a unified analysis* (ed. J. Collier and S. Yanagisako), pp. 14–50, Stanford: Stanford University Press.

Young, M. and Willmott, P. (1957). *Family and Kinship in East London*, London: Routledge and Kegan Paul.

Chapter 11

The Commercial Realization of the Community Boundary

Malcolm Chapman

Introduction

This chapter is a revised version of a paper presented to the conference of which this book is a result in June 1992, and '1992' was supposed to be the year at the end of which the 'Single European Market' would be achieved. It was a great year for publishers and media events; a deadline year, rather like the end of a millennium – a visible fault in time, where past became future. That, at least, was how it seemed in prospect. In retrospect, of course, this feature turned out to be less palpable: 31 December 1992 and 1 January 1993 turned out to be much more like, say, a publisher's deadline than like the time of sunrise – the first endlessly negotiable, the second ineluctable. Human deadlines are often like that. The process of the creation of the single market has, in various ways, been going on for years, and will take years more to complete, if indeed it ever can be regarded as ended. Media-hyped as it was, however, 1992 did at least provide an excuse for a great deal of discussion about what Europe was, or ought to be.

This chapter attempts to deal with some trade and business-related aspects of the European Community, and its relationship to non-Community Europe and to the rest of the world. The author is a social anthropologist, whose previous work has been primarily about the Celtic fringe (see Chapman 1978, 1992). Subsequently to this, I have now been working in the field of business studies for several years; I have a particular interest in Poland, and in how European events are perceived from that country. Some of this interest is conveyed below. The study of international business necessarily involves study of events beyond and outside the structure of nation-states, and raises issues of nationality and ethnicity; literature in international business studies, however, rarely meets literature in social anthropology: the conventions of research and reporting are greatly different. What follows is an attempt, unusual though far from unique, to bridge this gap.[1]

In looking at the boundaries of the European Community, as realized (or not) through trade and business, some major trends in the world economy need to be noted. These are discussed below under the headings: (1) Free Trade, regionalism and trade blocs; (2) International trade, investment, and the multinational corporation; and (3) Corporate 'nationality'. Following this, is a short discussion of the implications of such trends for the nation-state, particularly in relation to the frontier between Poland and the European Community.

Free Trade, Regionalism, and Trade Blocs

It has long been broadly accepted that free trade between nations, without government intervention or regulation, leads to lower prices and greater efficiency *overall*. The removal of trade barriers between (say) two countries will always lead to local disadvantage, as this or that group of protected producers or consumers is exposed; the overall level of welfare, however, in both countries will rise. Much political debate around these issues concerns the balancing of the well-organized special pleading of groups of producers against the almost absent voice of the disadvantaged consumers – the Common Agricultural Policy being a particularly pointed example.

The General Agreement on Tariffs and Trade, usually known as GATT, is one of the international monetary institutions established after the Bretton Woods Conference in 1944. It has had free trade in

---

1. There is in fact a lively area of research within business studies, and international business studies, which is perceived by the local discourse to be 'anthropological'. This centres upon the figure of Geert Hofstede, who has published some highly influential work, and set the agenda for hundreds of research workers (see Hofstede 1980, 1991). Hofstede's own background is in social psychology, however, and his work is not of a kind that would be recognized as 'social anthropology' by most British practitioners of the subject (the great majority of whom, as far as I have been able to judge, have not even heard of him). Hofstede's work is based upon questionnaire and large-scale statistical analysis, which is enough to put off most anthropologists from the start. He does, however, supplement this with a most eclectic range of material, and the results are of considerable interest.

the world system as its objective, and through successive rounds of negotiation it has succeeded in achieving very large multilateral reductions in tariff barriers. Some attribute the unprecedented world economic growth in the 1950s and 1960s to these reductions.

GATT was originally conceived to prevent protectionism in the trade of manufactured, tangible goods. It has only latterly, in the recently completed Uruguay Round of talks, turned its attention to the now pre-eminently important questions of trade in services, and of rules relating to cross-national investment. It has also been unable to prevent the growth of covertly protectionist measures in the form of non-tariff barriers of various kinds. Nevertheless, it has set an international free-trade ethic, against which the infractions (still the rule rather than the exception, overall) can be judged.

If all the world were run according to GATT principles, then there would be little need for trade blocs. If there were, internationally, no quotas, no trade restrictions, and if there were free movement of capital, then membership of a trading bloc would offer no advantages. There would still be grounds for national or regional rules concerning the free movement of people (something on which GATT has never sought to rule); but much of the force behind regional economic groupings would be lost.

There is a strong trend in the world, however, towards the formation of regional groupings, in the form of trade blocs. The creation and existence of these groups runs counter, in many respects, to the ambitions of GATT – ambitions which many of the countries involved also share, in that they are all a party to GATT negotiations. The European Community is the most striking and advanced example of a regional grouping of this kind, and it has long provoked attempts at retaliation; COMECON (otherwise known as CMEA, Council for Mutual Economic Aid) was an explicit attempt to provide a socialist response, and more recent groupings, such as NAFTA (North American Free Trade Association) and ASEAN (Association of South East Asian Nations) have, as part of their rationale, a preparedness for a regional trade war, should one ever arise. The Uruguay Round of GATT negotiations went all the way to the wire, but came to a successful conclusion on 15 December 1993, with an agreement to establish a World Trade Organisation, WTO, to replace GATT (this WTO being the much-delayed third pillar of the international organizations envisaged at the Bretton Woods conference in 1944, the other two being the IMF and the World Bank). The danger of a regional trade war is accordingly diminished (see *Focus, GATT Newsletter* no. 104, December 1993).

The GATT (and now the WTO) and emergent regional groupings have important, though rather diverse, consequences for pre-existing nation-states. The trend of GATT activity is to lessen the importance of the nation-state as an entity which sets trade barriers round itself in idiosyncratic ways. The nation-states are the parties to GATT negotiations, to be sure; but they are there to negotiate themselves away. Regional groupings have a similar effect, within themselves; the European Community has a clear tendency to lessen the importance of the traditional nation-states within it, by taking away barriers between them (to the alarm of many, of course). The barriers are taken away at national level, however, only to be reimposed at supranational level; here, the frontiers of the regional grouping, usually congruent with a previous national boundary, assume more importance than ever. The boundary between, say, Germany and Poland, or between Greece and Turkey, is not now only a boundary between two countries: it has become supercharged – a boundary between the European Community and all the rest.

In the 1960s we became used to calling the EEC 'the Common Market'. It is necessary to look at this terminology, for the technical aspects of the vocabulary are of considerable importance. Economists and policy-makers typically distinguish between three different levels of unification in matters of trade and finance:

(1) a Free Trade Area;

(2) a Customs Union; and

(3) a Common Market.

1. In a *Free Trade Area*, a number of countries will agree to eliminate all trade barriers between themselves – trade barriers usually taking the form of tariffs, quotas, idiosyncratic customs requirements relating to health and safety, subsidies and so on. At the same time, they maintain their own existing national barriers against trade with the rest of the world, barriers which may vary greatly from one country to another within the Free Trade Area. There is often a great deal of squabbling about details, and exceptions made for this or that sensitive case, so much as to vitiate the original intention in large degree. The European Free Trade area

is one example of such an association.

2. *Customs Union*. In a Customs Union, barriers to trade within the Union are removed, as for a Free Trade Area. A Customs Union takes the further step, however, of harmonizing trade barriers to the rest of the world outside the Union; all participating countries adopt the same regulations governing trade with the rest of the world, in particular a common external tariff. By about 1968, the EEC was well advanced towards this state.

3. *Common Market*. A common market has no internal trade barriers, like a Free Trade Area, and common external barriers, like a Customs Union. It also, however, takes the further step of allowing the free movement of labour and capital across national boundaries within itself.

It was disagreement in the 1950s about the appropriateness of the two approaches, the Free Trade Area and the Customs Union, that led to the separation of much of Europe into two groups, EFTA and the embryonic EEC. A Customs Union enjoins upon its members a common approach to trade with the rest of the world. Since trade restrictions have traditionally been such an important weapon in the political armoury, a Customs Union also necessarily seemed to imply a degree of political harmonization. EFTA contained countries that were worried, for different reasons, about the political and sovereignty implications of the Customs Union approach: Sweden and Switzerland, for example, because they feared it would encroach on their neutrality; Austria because its neutrality was demanded by treaty; and the UK because it wished to safeguard its special trading relationships with the Commonwealth. The Customs Union path was taken by those countries that formed the original 'six' of the EEC – France, Germany, Belgium, Holland, Luxembourg and Italy. The implications of loss of sovereignty were less important to these countries than other possible gains, in particular that of avoiding having a war every generation. It was a correct analysis, however, that a Customs Union would have a political dynamic towards unification, in a way that a Free Trade Association did not, as we are now discovering.

It was, in my recollection, sometime in 1991 that British newsreaders first started to call the 'EEC' (which we knew to be short for 'European Economic Community') the 'EC'. This truncation was not explained or announced, but we soon came to learn that 'EC' was short for 'European Community'. The implication was that the Community had gone beyond 'economics', into other areas. Not long after this, it rapidly became conventional that the real name was the 'European Union', 'EU', with all that this implies. These uninvited conceptual expansions had many sources, among them, no doubt, the self-aggrandizing nature of the European bureaucracies which we had already allowed to come into being. Another major source, however, was the thrust towards European monetary union. Since the value of money moved from weight of metal to confidence in paper, money has tended to be nationally defined; cross-national transactions have required exchange rates. Money has been at the centre of government policy-making, whether through Keynesian attempts at demand management, or through Monetarist attempts at controlling the money supply – the entire web of macroeconomic cause and effect has strings of money running through it. A tug on one can change the structure in many ways, and this will ultimately have an effect upon the value of money both internally and, crucially, externally: if a national government wants to change its macroeconomic policies (to devalue, say, in order to boost its exports, or to increase public spending in order to bring down unemployment) then it accepts that its actions will have consequences on the exchange rate with other currencies.

If there is no exchange rate, however, and no currencies, the scope for 'national' macroeconomic policies is very much reduced – even completely removed. 'Regional' policies can be employed, much as they are today within the UK, involving transfers of revenue from rich areas to poor areas. The traditional area of operations of national government, however, is much limited (and a good thing too, some might think); its freedom of action, its independence from the activities of the greater unit (whoever controls that), is gone. That is why 'monetary union', innocent enough in sound, threatens to transform the EEC into an EU, whether we like it or not. Monetary union and political union will, it seems to many observers, either come together, or not come at all.

International Trade, Investment, and the Multinational Corporation (MNC)

The world economy since the Second World War has been characterized by remarkable growth, and by increasing internationalization of trade and investment. A major agent of this has been what is often called 'the multinational corporation'.[2] In the immediate post-war period the US economy had many advantages over the rest of the world (it was not indebted, it had not been bombed, it was ripe with the rich technological stimulus that the war had provided), and it was US companies that first made MNCs into striking and major actors on the world stage. There had been MNCs before this, notably British, Dutch, German and North American (not to mention the Italian banks of the Renaissance, or the Dutch and British East India Companies); but the growth of MNCs in the post-war period was on an entirely new scale.[3]

In the 1950s and 1960s, US companies made the running in the internationalization of the world economy. They invested abroad to secure raw material supplies, to employ cheap labour, and to gain access to markets. They invested particularly in Europe, East Asia, and the rest of the Americas. Their rate of growth was so phenomenal that it began to seem as though the end-result of their activities would be a world-economy dominated by US MNCs. The French journalist and politician, Servan-Schreiber, worried by the implications of this for the sovereignty of other countries (and particularly, of course, for France), made an early and famous contribution to the long-running debate about the MNC, in *Le Défi Americain* (1967; translated into English in 1969 as *The American Challenge*). He argued, in effect, that national sovereignty was being sold away to US companies, and made the famous prediction that, by the early 1980s, there would be three major industrial powers in the world – the US, Russia, and American Industry in Europe (Servan-Schreiber, 1969: 3). We know now that he was wrong in two out of the three elements in his prediction, which tends to be the case when short-term trends are extrapolated too far. His point that foreign direct investment has some potentially undesirable effects upon national sovereignty has, however, since been much discussed, and is still a burning issue.

The three major economic powers in the world in 1990 were, in fact, Japan, the US, and the EC/Germany. European companies,

2. This is often shortened to MNC; or called 'multinational enterprise', shortened to MNE; or 'transnational corporation', shortened to TNC; or 'global corporation'. There are diverse moral and politico-academic investments in these different formulations.

3. Compared, at least, to the inter-war period; the pre-1914 situation in some ways merits separate discussion, for a degree of 'internationalization' of the world economy existed at this time which was in some respects not achieved again until the 1960s (see, in general, Dunning 1983, 1993; Teichova *et al.* 1986).

recovering from the war (often with considerable help from US companies), began to make major foreign investments themselves. British companies built on existing positions of strength in the Commonwealth, made tentative forays into Europe, and by the late 1970s were becoming major investors in the USA. Companies from continental Europe invested cross-nationally, although they tended at first to invest in immediately neighbouring countries. And Japanese companies, having limited themselves to trading on a massive scale with the rest of the world, began in the late 1970s and through the 1980s to invest on a massive scale as well. They moved to the newly industrializing countries of south-east Asia for cheap labour, and they moved to the USA and the EC for access to markets – markets which their aggressive trading success seemed to have put at risk, as talk of trade protection increased. The UK was a favourite destination for Japanese capital in Europe: it was relatively open to foreign investment, without excessive regulation or restriction; it posed no greater linguistic difficulties than North America; and it had a relatively favourable cost–skills ratio among the potential workforce. Many elsewhere in the EC, particularly in France, came to see Japanese investment in the UK as a kind of trading fifth column, allowing Japanese companies to circumvent the protective rules of the EC. The French and British views on what precisely the EC was for clashed repeatedly over this issue – the French tending to regard the EC as a way of providing supranational protection for European industry champions (ideally French ones), and the British regarding it primarily as a way of opening up markets on a continental scale, breaking down old regimes of national protection (it is both of these things, of course, by its nature; different aspects were uppermost in different minds, however).

The trend of Japanese investment in the US started a flutter of spirits very like that which US investments in Europe had caused twenty years earlier. For a few years the apparently inexorable rise of Japanese investment in the US, coupled with the persistent trade deficit between the US and Japan, led to fears of domination and colonization, and loss of indigenous industry, just as Servan-Schreiber had expressed them in the earlier context (see, for example, Prestowitz 1988).

Short-term trends extrapolated to eternity usually produce absurdity; but the post-war economic performance of Japan had been so consistently good, that there seemed no reason to suppose, during the surge of Japanese foreign investment in the 1980s, that it would not continue. When the Japanese stockmarket bubble burst in 1990, however, the Nikkei index fell by nearly 60 per cent in the following two years; Japanese property values, on the basis of which much of the investment was carried out, tumbled accordingly; Japanese companies, accustomed to investing for market share rather than profit, found themselves in the novel position of making losses; and the Japanese 'threat' has, accordingly, receded somewhat. Indeed, the Japanese are having, as of writing, a 'recession'. The economy has great underlying power, no doubt; it has at least begun to seem, however, that the Japanese live according to something rather like the same economic rules as everybody else, rather than, as had sometimes appeared, in a different economic universe.[4]

The gradual consolidation of the European Community, and the increased internationalization of the world economy, have together led many major non-EC companies to make investments inside the EC. This has primarily been motivated by a wish to get access to EC markets; and also to secure continued access to these markets,

---

4. The debate about Japanese success, within economics and management studies, brought to the fore some questions which might be of interest to social anthropologists. Much of the debate turned upon the possibility that the Japanese might have a different 'culture', which explained their preternatural industrial success – they were 'collectivist', which explained their loyalty to their organizations, their willingness to work, their reluctance to engage in industrial disputes; they had a different view of time, prepared to sacrifice present reward for future reward, which made them 'long-termist' in their investments, by comparison with the 'short-termist' west, where companies were forced to sacrifice long-term investment for immediate dividend pay-out to shareholders; and so on. Many of these arguments were an attempt to explain why Japanese industrial relations seemed to be so good, and why Japanese companies could apparently get away with paying their shareholders so little in the way of dividends, which made their cost of capital so much lower than that of their competitors. Some of these issues turn upon rather technical financial questions, and are beginning to receive rather technical financial answers, which demystify the phenomena – 'evaporate the inscrutability', as Joy Hendry has put it (1987: 202). Even when the answers are provided, however, the reality of the perception of 'inscrutability' will remain; I have tried elsewhere to argue that perceptions of others are an important, real, irreducible aspect of the way societies react to one another, an aspect that cannot be tidied away into some notion of 'subjective perception', apart from hard reality (social anthropologists do not, in general, have difficulty accepting this; positivist social science, however, has no adequate way of dealing with the problem). In the coming together of mighty economies, in the biggest of big business deals, even the most trivial 'mistakes' of cross-cultural perception can have major consequences; where there is a whole web of intricate misinterpretation, as when Japan meets Europe (say), then anthropological insight into the problem becomes, so I believe, essential. Again, this might seem self-evident to social anthropologists; it is a fact, however, that the great bulk of debate (and bulky it is) occurs with little or no anthropological input.

The debate about 'cultural' factors in development continues, not just in relation to the development of Japan, but to that of other areas of east and south-east Asia. Similar debate surrounds the apparent failures as well: some countries of South America, notably Argentina and Brazil, have been developing countries poised for the leap to industrial stardom for over a hundred years; the leap has never quite occurred, however, and again 'cultural' factors are often invoked to explain this.

when, if ever, the EC gates are closed, either to trade or to further investment. Japanese and US companies in particular have made major investments in the EC, in order to secure access to the EC market.[5]

There are variations in the extent to which the major economies invest in one another, but most of the leading industrial nations have very large investments in one another (in the form of direct investments in production and service subsidiaries; I am not, for the moment, considering portfolio investments). A significant exception is Japan, which now has large outward investments, but still rather small inward investment (much as with the UK in 1913, or the USA in 1965). It seems likely that the Japanese economy will eventually be laid open to foreign direct investment, just as Europe and the United States have been; and indeed there is a significant trend towards inward investment.

The result of all this is a world economy that is dominated by international companies – companies that have major investments

As noted, those involved in this debate have not drawn upon social anthropological work. They have looked, instead, to forms of positivist social psychology. The result is that much of the work is, from a social anthropological point of view, both clumsy and naïve. The first and enduring instinct of those involved is to take a dictionary, look for a definition of 'culture', and then try to find a way of measuring it, so that its 'influence on behaviour' can be assessed, in statistical comparison with other 'influences' that are *not* 'cultural' – those of, say, law, society, language, business, economics, religion and so on (and *sic*; for typical texts in this vein, see Neghandi 1983; Roberts and Boyacigiller 1984; Sekaran 1983). This is not caricature; positivist psychological behaviourism is overwhelmingly the dominant (sometimes tacit or unthought) approach. For a social anthropologist, living in a world of social anthropologists, it would be easy to laugh this off. The philosophical issues were, one might suppose, fully argued as long ago as the 1960s. So they were; nevertheless, outside social anthropology, in many areas of social scientific academia, the debate has scarcely begun: this is certainly true for, say, business and management studies, for some areas of organization studies, and for social psychology. It might be possible to ignore this (as most social anthropologists do). One should note, however, that these subjects dwarf social anthropology in the numbers of people involved, in the number of journals and books published and sold, and in the amount of influence wielded in policy and practice. Any publisher's catalogue will demonstrate this clearly enough. This is deplorable, perhaps, but it is also a great opportunity. In the case of cross-cultural analysis, for example, in the area of business and organization studies, there are important issues at stake, in areas where social anthropologists have considerable relevant experience. The field is wide open, and the possibilities of research funding are at least better than derisory.

5. As of writing, the EC is in large part mired in recession, and its economic and political future look a great deal more uncertain than they did in June 1992 when the paper that preceded this chapter was first given. Nevertheless, the EC, taken in its present form, is still the largest (single) market in the world (considerably larger than the US or Japan). Prospects for the efficiency gains arising from '1992' (see Cecchini 1988), and possible future enlargements of the Community, mean that the European Community cannot be ignored by Japan and the US; the possibility of being shut out of its markets is a frightening one. Foreign direct investment of almost all kinds has reduced dramatically during the last year or so of recession, including inward investment into the EC by companies from the US and Japan; as noted elsewhere, however, many companies have already made their move.

in many different parts of the world, and that organize themselves on a global scale to make global profits. As long ago as 1969 this led one prominent analyst of MNCs to argue that 'the nation state is just about through as an economic unit' (Kindleberger 1969: 207). The major multinational companies have an economic size (measured in turnover, say) in excess of all but the largest developing countries (measured in, say, gross domestic product);[6] their activities cross national borders, carried on electronic media of communication, in a way that defies national regulation or national definition. They are 'global firms' (see Barnet and Mueller 1975; Bartlett *et al*. 1990).

The nation-state is, at least for most people in the developed world, important in self-identification. The education systems of the nation-states have worked in many areas to produce homogeneous populations, sharing language and culture – the education system, the nation-state, and the modern industrial world coming together, out of mutual necessity (Gellner 1983). Historiography has been predominantly national, even to the extent of playing a significant part in the construction of nationhood; we all tend to see the past through a particular set of national lenses. Statistics, too, tend to be gathered and appreciated at the national level; any particular national will regard national statistics as, in some sense, about him- or herself, to the extent that happiness or gloom can follow the otherwise entirely irrelevant announcement of figures concerning, say, the economy, population size, or sporting performance: the nation-state is 'the ideal type of the modern society, documented to the eyebrows, its own adaptations including adaptations to its own statistical data about itself' (Ardener 1989: 117).

The nation-state, then, for better or worse, is important to people, to their understanding of the world. Any threat to its integrity is an accordingly serious matter; the stridency of debate about the activities of multinational companies has demonstrated this convincingly enough (see Fieldhouse 1986). If the world economy is increasingly moving into the hands of stateless and nationless

6. There are only about twenty countries in the world with an annual GDP in excess of the annual turnover of the largest corporations – General Motors, Royal Dutch–Shell, Exxon, and Ford. There are 18 companies whose turnover is bigger than the GDP of Pakistan. There are between 30 and 40 countries whose GDP is smaller than the turnover of the 500th ranking company, Rothmans. And so on (see *Fortune International*, 29/7/1991; *International Business Week*, 15/7/1991; *World Vital Statistics*, Economist Publications, 1990).

multinational corporations, then much of our knowledge of the world might seem to need revision.

No doubt it does. Nevertheless, we can look back to Kindleberger's obituary on the nation-state, in 1969, and see that he was wrong; the nation-state is still a major player in economic affairs, setting a regulatory environment that is binding in many respects upon any corporation, however big. The context of the homogeneous regulatory environment is moving, in the EC, from the national to the community level, but the importance of the regulatory environment remains; in this sense, the EC presents the MNC with the same old problem in a new guise.

Corporate 'Nationality'

The question of the 'nationality' of a firm is an interesting one. For most of us, observers of the world-economy rather than its prime movers, many companies have a self-evident 'nationality'. At the European level, we all know that Nestlé is Swiss, Renault French, Bayer German, ICI British. At the global level, too, the nationality of most of the major players seems to be in little doubt: Exxon, General Motors, IBM, Microsoft, are all from the United States; Toyota, Honda, Sony, are all Japanese.

Our knowledge of this is based to some degree upon the fact that these companies produce goods that we all consume. They are players in the game of international brand names – cars, petrol, sweets, consumer electronics and (latterly) computers and computer software. Outside this sphere of immediate consumption, in industries of great magnitude that do not impinge upon our daily consumption (in, say, engineering, construction, chemicals, paper, mining) we are perhaps less likely to be clear about the nationality of the companies involved – even less likely to have heard of them at all. This does not make them less important as players in the world economy, although it does mean that their activities are less likely to attract popular attention.

The largest companies now aspire to be 'global' in their operations – indeed, the adjective 'global' has become a part of corporate machismo, as witness the advertising in any business journal. The reality is rather complex, however.

The nationality of a corporation once seemed unproblematic. Until relatively recently, it was often the case that a public company's management, workers and shareholders all shared the same nationality; the company carried out all its production and marketing within the confines of one nation-state; the consumers of the products were of the same nationality as well. In such a case, the company was unambiguously 'national'.

When such a firm began exporting to foreign countries, its nationality remained unimpaired. Exporting companies could, indeed, generate a trading surplus, and the wealth generated thereby could give to an entire nation a sense of shared virtue – a sense which Japan luxuriates in at the moment, and which both the US and the UK had once, and would like to recapture.

A company that is clearly national, and that nevertheless engages in international trading on a massive scale, is a potentially great affront to nationalist sentiment in other countries, particularly if it produces consumer products which are readily recognizable, and in which consumers invest their understanding and identity – the confusion of economic rationality and affronted pride with which North American buyers approach 'Japanese' or 'Korean' cars demonstrates this very clearly.

When companies start to invest in foreign countries, particularly when they start to make large-scale investments in production plants, then the question of their nationality becomes more troubled. Many companies, however widespread their activities, tend to have one country which is clearly still home, where corporate headquarters are located, where major decisions are made, where the most value-added and high-tech business activities are carried out (particularly R&D, research and development), and from which the majority of senior executives come. In such a case, the host country, where the company has its manufacturing subsidiaries, can clearly regard the company as a foreigner on its soil, one of doubtful loyalty. There is a large and sophisticated literature on the costs and benefits, to both home and host country, of foreign investment of this kind, and there are no clear or unequivocal statements to be made. At the extreme, MNCs can produce very large-scale movement of wealth from the host to the home country. This was noted by Vaitsos, documenting the transfer-pricing practices of US pharmaceuticals companies in South America (Vaitsos 1974). The issue surfaced not long ago in relation to profit repatriation by Sony and Hitachi from their UK operations to Japan (*Sunday Times*, 22/3/1992). MNCs are also in a position to exercise political influence, often way beyond their commercial remit or their responsibility to shareholders; their interest in securing an environment friendly to big business has unquestionably had a major influence on the domestic politics of many countries (by no means necessarily a malign influence); at the extreme, foreign subsidiaries can become an agent of home-country politics, as ITT's South American operations notoriously allowed themselves to become in the period preceding the overthrow of the Allende government in Chile. Many governments in the developing world have viewed foreign MNCs as undesirable agents of foreign influence, and attempted to exclude them, seeking planned or autarkic economic solutions, which have rarely been successful. Current wisdom in the matter, weary of ideology, is perhaps well summed up by the aphorism – 'there is only one thing worse than being exploited by foreign multinationals, and that is not being exploited by foreign multinationals' (see, in general, UNCTC 1989, 1992).

Extremes of resource transfer and political manipulation illustrate the potential problems, but they are not typical. Many corporations are anxious to be seen to be 'good citizens' of the countries in which they operate, and local credibility is important to their operations. Nevertheless, they have a strong interest in profit, and will usually only pursue host-country interests where these are congruent with their own. In many areas of activity, such congruence exists, so that conflict is not inevitable: indeed, mutual benefit is commonly achieved – what international management consultants, in their egregious dialect, might call 'a win–win situation'.

A multinational is not only of suspect loyalty to host countries, but also to the home country. In its home operations just as much as in its foreign operations, a company is interested in profit, and will not necessarily take decisions of benefit to the home country. Many critics have regarded home-country companies as ripe for political manipulation by the home government, but this is an over-simple view: they will collude with government if they see self-interest in such collusion, but they will actively and often successfully resist policies or pressures that are to their disadvantage (Lego and Bang & Olufsen, for example, as Danish as pastries, were quick to threaten disinvestment in Denmark, when the Danish government seemed ready to accede to the anti-Maastricht vote in the Danish referendum of 3/6/1992; see the *Financial Times*, 4/6/1992, p. 5). The threat was repeated in the debate preceding the second referendum of May 1993, when the Danes were prevailed upon to change their minds.

On the whole, however 'global' a company has become, it has tended to retain strong links with its first home. For many of today's multinationals, however, the bulk of their operations and strategy lie away from this home base, and there has been a long-running debate about whether this means that they will stop being 'national' in any sense. Ohmae, for example, has argued that a future company will not need a 'nationality' (Ohmae 1990); Porter, by contrast, argues that no company can be successful globally without a secure 'home' base (1990).

Some major companies have attempted to decentralize the most sensitive of their wealth-creating assets – decision-making and R&D – in pursuit of global ambitions. IBM is a leader in this. Most companies, however, while anxious to pursue global strategies, pursue global markets, and anticipate global tastes, remain 'national' in some sense; after all, if a company is centralized in its decision-making (as most are), and if it has only one R&D centre (usually the most cost-efficient arrangement), then these have to be located *somewhere*; why not near the golf-course?

The physical location of productive assets is, of course, only one possible measure of 'nationality' for a company. There are others:

Management. Senior management in major MNCs has tended to be dominated by nationals of the original home country; this carries with it suggestions of 'nationality', of loyalty and cultural predisposition, that are not necessarily related to, or compatible with, a truly 'global' approach (nor, indeed, with economic rationality).

Workers. Workers have a nationality, of course; the workers in a multinational tend to have a variety of nationalities, according to the geographical location of productive assets. Their nationality is, perhaps, the least ambiguous of all the elements of nationality related to MNCs: you can globalize capital, globalize strategy, globalize brands, globalize management, but people *en masse*, the masses of unskilled, semi-skilled and skilled labour, are very far from being globalized. Indeed, one of the main functions of wealthy nation-states in the modern world is to keep out would-be migrant workers from poorer countries; the EC has inherited this as an important *raison d'être*. The nationality of the workforce, often clear enough in itself, is not as important a determinant in the nationality of an MNC as it might seem, since the requirements of strategic capital movements can leave the workforce abandoned by the corporation, jobless, while their jobs move elsewhere, to another country or continent. Management that shares a nationality with its workforce can find itself conscience-stricken in this matter (as, for example, Pilkington, when faced with the need to move major investments away from the home base in St Helens). Subsidiaries move with less loyalty, less guilt (see, for example, Hood and Young 1982, on movement out of Scotland by MNCs whose home base was elsewhere, primarily in the USA).

Shareholders. As world capital markets become increasingly homogeneous, the nationality of shareholders is of diminishing importance. There are, however, still major differences in corporate ownership, and in the exercise of the privileges of ownership, between the major capital markets; Germany and Japan, for example, have corporate ownership models which tend to be less open to shareholder control (and foreign takeover) than the US and the UK. As long as differences in this lead to differences in corporate responsibility and control, then the 'nationality' of shareholders will be of some importance.

Capital. The issue of the 'nationality' of capital is related to that of the nationality of shareholders. If securities are traded internationally within a homogeneous legislative environment, then nationality of shareholders will probably cease to be an issue. Where, however, there are barriers to trading, and perhaps associated differentials in the cost of capital, and in the rewards accruing to shareholders (as between, say, the UK and Japan), then capital will continue to have a 'national' profile.

Products. Brand names will continue to have a strong 'national' feel, however multinational the company that wields them; 'nationality', indeed, is part of their power to persuade: Coca-Cola made in a new plant in Poland remains an 'American' product, in the eyes of most Poles that buy it; Nissan cars made in north-east England continue to strike the European consumer as 'Japanese' cars; and so on.

Of course, the perception that capital has a nationality, depends to a great extent upon the sense that a company has a nationality. A company might be seen to be, say, a US company, and its activities abroad resented on nationalist grounds (in the Servan-Schreiber tradition), even though its shareholders, the ultimate beneficiaries of its activities, might be genuinely cosmopolitan, with a majority of non-US shareholders.

Capital, the Community Frontier, and Poland

1992 was the year in which, ideally, barriers to capital movements between the different countries of the community were removed. There will doubtless, however, be a residual sense of the 'nationality' of European companies: Volkswagen will still look German, Bodyshop still British, Pirelli still Italian, Rhone-Poulenc still French. What consequences this will have, in post-1992 Europe, is debatable. Perhaps the effect will dwindle.

The different countries of the European Union vary greatly in the extent to which they are home and host country to foreign investment, and in the direction and source of these investments. The UK and the Netherlands, for example, are, in this sense, international and intercontinental economies; Germany, by contrast, has a much lower level of both inward and outward investment. In general, EU countries (the UK and the Netherlands excepted) have tended to target their foreign investments at neighbouring countries (for example, Germany in France, France in Italy, Spain in Portugal). If the EU starts to consider itself as truly a single economic unit, then all of this intra-EU investment might see itself reclassified as 'domestic' rather than 'foreign', which would radically change the appearance of international investment flows. The EU, taken as a whole, would remain a major source of investment to those countries outside it; it remains to be seen whether capital deriving from the EU will continue to have a separate national profile depending on its country of origin, or whether the EU, in its role as a unified economic power, will be perceived *en bloc* by countries hosting its investments. There are trends moving in different directions here: attempts by the OECD countries to build multilateral rules on investment measures into the Uruguay round of GATT negotiations might suggest a weakening of 'financial nationality'; the failure (at least in the short term) of attempts to move towards European monetary union, on the other hand, suggests that European money is going to have various 'nationalities' for longer than some might have expected.

As far as capital coming into the EU is concerned, it seems likely that the major 'identity' issue, in the short term, will continue to be Japanese investment. Few of the immediate geographical neighbours of the EC are of sufficient economic stature to engage in substantial outward investment. US investment in Europe has been naturalized to a great degree, at least in perceptual terms (and most particularly in the UK); it has also come to be balanced by large-scale European investment in the USA (most particularly by the UK). Very-large-scale investment by the newly industrialized countries of South-East Asia may be a problem for the future, but is for the moment of a scale unlikely to attract popular attention. Latin America, seen as a potentially major source of outward investment in the late 1970s, has so many internal economic problems that it is unlikely, in the short term, to figure in the equations.

For outgoing capital, the problems are somewhat different. Europe has long been a major source of outward investment, and will probably continue to be so. Some of the most acute 'identity' issues will probably occur in relation to investment in Eastern and Central Europe. The confrontation of German and Slav has had a long and sometimes bitter history (see Czubinski and Pajewski 1987; Burleigh 1988; Sugar and Lederer, 1969); it is a confrontation which has been strongly economically marked for most of the last two hundred years – by relative prosperity, through differential political rights, by occupational differences, by the Capitalist–Communist divide, and now by the frontier of the European Community, with its tacit line between the 'haves' and the 'have-nots'.

Parts of Poland and Czechoslovakia were, industrially, areas of economic conflict, as the victors of the 1914–18 war attempted to consolidate their positions, and Germany attempted to rebuild its strength (see, in general, Teichova and Cottrell 1983; Overy 1983). The post-war frontiers of 1918 and thereafter had left large numbers of 'ethnic' Germans in Poland and Czechoslovakia, and there was sometimes conflict between these and the Slav majorities (see, for example, Chalasinski 1935 on Polish–German conflict in Silesia).

Poland in the inter-war period had within it high levels of foreign capital.[7] Poland's debts to foreign countries at this time were also large, and principally owed to the USA and France. It was the active participation of foreign capital which figured most large in the imagination, and here Germany was an important, and of course geographically immediate, player. The level of German capital fell in the years immediately before the outbreak of war in 1939. It rose,

7. Wellisz gave the following figures, for 1 January 1933 (in millions of zlotys; only the five major capital providers are cited): France, 428; Germany, 411; USA., 384; Belgium, 176; Great Britain, 103.

however, during the war years, through expropriation and new investment, to dominant proportions. Major German 'multinationals', including IG Farben, came to dominate industry in German-occupied Poland. The 'Reichswerke Herman-Goering' behaved, indeed, during this period, like the exploitative multinational of radical nightmares (see Overy 1983). It is perhaps not surprising, in view of this, that when post-war Polish historians have looked back to the inter-war period, they have tended to stress the level of German investment, and its malign effects:[8]

> One of the highest levels of participation of German capital in the Polish economy was in joint-stock companies; on the 1st January 1935 it was at 19.8% of the total (compared with France, 25.6%; USA, 21.9%), [. . .] while on 1st January 1938 it was 13.2% (French, 26.1%, USA, 18.6%). Admittedly this level fell in the years before the outbreak of war, as did the U.S. level, but Germany retained its third position amongst contributors of capital to Polish joint-stock companies. The high level of German capital in the Polish inter-war economy made possible the fulfilment of important tasks – economic, but also political. (Luczak 1988: 232)

Wellisz referred to 'insufficient capitalization: the main cause of Poland's delayed economic development' (Wellisz 1938: 19), and this is echoed by Teichova and Cottrell, referring to: 'the constant scarcity of capital in this region during the inter-war period. The largest companies in the mostly highly concentrated industries of East–Central Europe were generally either wholly or partially owned subsiduaries of Western European multi-national enterprises' (Teichova and Cottrell 1983: 45).

The importance of Silesia to the Central European economy, its importance to Poland, the importance of German capital within Silesia, and the constantly vexed question of international boundaries within Silesia, perhaps together explain why German capital, above all, seemed intrusive. US, French and British capital was in Central Europe to make a profit; it was not without links to foreign policy, but it was not primarily an instrument of this. Under the Third Reich, however, German economic and political aims were pursued with the same instruments, and became indivisible (Overy 1983: 269). The German ownership of capital not only permitted the

---

8. Translations from the Polish, here and throughout, are my own.

pursuit of essentially geopolitical ends; it also permitted discrimination against Polish and in favour of German workers (see Chalasinski 1935; also Makowski 1987).

A major work on the Polish economy written during the Communist period gave a lengthy diagnosis of Poland's inter-war economic problems.[9] Of all these, however, two are picked out as being of particular consequence in explaining:

> why Poland, as one of the largest capitalist countries in the European continent for 20 years, did not experience growth, by contrast to other developing countries whose economies met objective difficulties that were no less important. It is clear, that from among many reasons, the most important are the failure to realize radical reform of agriculture, and the dependence of the Polish economy on foreign capital. (Kostrowicka *et al*. 1975: 376)

The stress on the malign effects of foreign capital is made even stronger in a further passage:

> Foreign capital exerted an exceptionally negative influence on the life of the Polish economy. Not believing in the permanence of the Polish state, it aimed to make profits, and to remove as much of these as possible from the Polish territory where they were made. In other countries foreign capital left behind accumulated profits, to build new industries, to provide banks with cheap credit, and so on; in Poland, a large part of profits went abroad. In this way the national economy was deprived of the means to develop its industry, to intensify agricultural production, and of cheap credit. Foreign capital exported from Poland a large part of the national income, which normally would have gone into productive investment. (ibid.: 377)

The argument about foreign capital is echoed by Kolankiewicz: 'Foreign domination of share capital amounted to 40% and the export of earnings from this investment was calculated to be equivalent to the total state investment budget during these years'

9. The full list of reasons, according to Kostrowicka *et al*. 1975: 376, runs as follows: 'Among objective reasons for this [Polish economic] situation, are: the comparatively low level of development of productive forces in the country which went to the making up of the Polish nation after the First World War; the exclusion of a large industrial part of the Silesian coal-field; Polish separation from the sea in consequence of the transformation of Gdansk into a free-port. Further undoubted objective reasons were: maladaptation of the production profile in relation to the needs of the new nation; the financial weakness of the Polish middle-class; close dependence on foreign capital; and difficulties related to the union in one economic system of various previously completely separate territories.'

(Kolankiewicz and Lewis 1988: 20, citing Landau 1985).

The war brought death and destruction to Poland, much of it firmly related to German activities. In the Communist period which followed, foreign capital was not permitted. Its prior malign effects were interpreted within the communist and socialist discourse, within which it was axiomatic that 'international capital' was a force of oppression.

In the period following the collapse of Communist authority in Poland, however, it has become clear that if pro-capitalist economic reforms are to succeed, if large-scale privatization is to be made to work, there is a grave need of capital, and of Western expertise; the likely sources of this are outside Poland; the most likely source is Germany. The initial expectations of a large-scale movement of capital into a 'reformed' Eastern Europe have not so far been fulfilled. The euphoria and optimism of December 1989 have evaporated. In as much as there have been capital movements, however, German capital has been predominant.[10] The detail would

10. Major sources of official statistics, such as the IMF *Balance of Payments Statistics Yearbook*, gives currently available data up to the end of 1992. These statistics show inflows for each country, and outflows for each country, but they do not break down inflows into country of origin. For that, other sources must be used, and I have relied particularly on Boudier-Bensebaa, F. 1993, herself using statistics from (*inter alia*) the Bundesbank and the Banque de France. Direct comparison of country-to-country flows is complicated by the fact that a single major investment (for example VW in Czechoslovakia, Ford and General Motors in Hungary) can dominate the overall figures, while obscuring other important trends. The sectoral distribution of foreign investment shows important differences as between different pairs of home and host countries. The size and type of investing companies varies from country to country (with companies of German 'Mittelstand' prominent as German sources, compared to the large MNEs investing from the USA, France or the UK). The rhythm of the economic cycle, and particularly recession in the investing countries, has a major effect from one year to the next, such that figures for one year cannot be relied upon to represent the general trends. The backing and filling of the governments of Poland, Hungary and the Czech Republic, over their attitudes to foreign investment and economic reform, provides other variable. The pre-eminence of Germany, however, by the end of 1992, as a source of investment for the three fast-reforming economies of Eastern Europe, was in no doubt. This was most evident for the two counties with which Germany has been most closely linked historically, Poland and Czechoslovakia, and less evident for Hungary. In Czechoslovakia, German capital represented over 73 per cent of incoming capital by the end of 1991, and in Poland German capital, representing about a third of incoming capital, was almost three times larger than that of the second major source, France. The statistics also need to be interpreted according to relative expectations. In world terms, and considering the size and strength of its economy, Germany has not engaged in foreign investment to the same extent as other major economies (particularly the UK and the Netherlands) (see UNCTC 1989, p. 24, table 1.2). For comparative purposes, in the years 1986 to 1992, if we regard the total of German foreign investment over this period as 100, then UK FI totalled 145, France 118, Japan 117 and Netherlands 64. If we factor into this the relative size of the economies, and then the relative hesitancy of Germany in foreign investment becomes rather striking (figures derived from *Balance of Payments Statistics Yearbook*, 1993, pp. 66–7). Germany has been a trader rather than an investor. Its predominance in investment in Eastern Europe needs to be interpreted in the light of this; by investing in Poland and Czechoslovakia, Germany is not doing as it does world-wide, but is following old and to some extent familiar patterns of activity. It is for this reason that Germany's investment in Eastern Europe must be considered in the light of the history of the region, and not merely as a set of rational and profit-seeking activities.

require lengthy discussion, and trends and expectations have changed considerably since this paper was first given; they will doubtless change considerably again before it is published. The favoured targets for inward investment among the erstwhile communist countries of Europe have been Hungary and Czechoslovakia (this last now two countries, the Czech republic and Slovakia: the former having the greater attraction to foreign investors). Poland is often spoken of in the same breath as these countries, and it certainly has more attractions than, say, Rumania, Bulgaria, or the CIS; the figures have suggested, however, that among these three 'fast-reformers', Hungary, Czechoslovakia and Poland, it is Poland which very much takes third place. There are many reasons for this, too much so for discussion here (see, in general, UN 1992; UNCTC 1992, ch. 1). Conflicting trends are continually arising: at a time in September 1993 when Poland seemed to be genuinely reaping the benefits of its austere bout of 'economic shock therapy', the electorate put the 'reformed communists' back into power, replacing the committed 'free marketers' of Hanna Suchocka's government. Eight months later much the same thing happened in Hungary. As for the source of incoming investment into the reforming economics of Central and Eastern Europe, the strains of German reunification have considerably slowed the flow of German investment, and recent figures show flows from certain other European countries approaching or overtaking those from Germany.

The question of capital movement into Eastern Europe from Western Europe poses many interesting questions. Two, perhaps, are relevant to this paper: (1) Why Eastern Europe?; and (2) What nationality will European capital have?

Why Eastern Europe? In the early months of reform it seemed self-evident to many commentators that Western Europe would step in to provide the capital that Eastern Europe needed. Both East and West were European; the great rift was healed: capital would doubtless come from Japan and the USA, but this would be primarily a European family affair. This has happened to some extent, and is some measure of the status of Europe as a folk concept – people believe in it; they invest money in it; it forms, as it were, a symbolic horizon, beyond which it is more difficult to see. As time goes on, however, it becomes clear that there are important forces working counter to this. Self-interested protectionist forces in the European Community are important among these. So, too, are the many investment opportunities that the rest of the world offers. Many in developing countries have voiced the fear that, in a world of capital shortage, Eastern Europe would attract capital that would otherwise have come their way. This has probably happened to some extent. At the same time, however, Eastern Europe must compete with the rest of the world for incoming capital, and the special relationship with 'Europe' will only protect it to a limited degree from this competition.

What nationality will European capital have? It is in the spirit of 1992 that capital from European nations will go where in Europe it likes, and will lose its nationality. It is in keeping with some trends in the overall world economy that capital in general will lose its 'national' stamp. There are conservative and opposing forces to both these novelties, however, as we have seen. What will 'German' capital look like in Poland? Given the history, and the foreknowledge that the two peoples bring to the problem, it will almost certainly look 'German' rather than 'European'. If it looks German, how will it be viewed? Not, perhaps, without disquiet, given the history: 'The prospect of German economic domination is still viewed with horror in many quarters, especially in Poland' (Goodhart 1990); '"Our people are afraid of foreign investment, particularly German," says [Andrzej] Zawislak, who chaired Poland's privatization committee in parliament' (Celarier 1990).

If the Communist period is to be sloughed off, a bad dream, then the models of the inter-war and war periods leap to mind as models. From a Polish point of view, looking once again to the west, the memory is far from satisfactory. Much investment in Poland has come from German companies, clearly identifiable as such; the trend is likely to continue. Poland is a natural location for investment in manufacturing subsidiaries that can benefit from Poland's workforce, at the moment both highly skilled and cheap. The argument about whether the employment of low-cost labour constitutes 'exploitation', or simply the best use of comparative advantage, will inevitably surface.[11] However global the capital or global the firm, the north-eastern commercial frontier of the European Community is going to look like an engagement of Germany and Poland, with the latter once again getting the worst

---

11. The engagement of German companies in Poland has been compared to that of US companies in Mexico, where the low-wage *maquiladoras* have caused such controversy. The analogy is interesting and the issue potentially inflammatory (see *Eastern European Business Handbook*, 1993, p. 9).

of it. The possibility of German claims on expropriated property in the once-German lands of western Poland, the claims of the residual German minority in Poland, and German acquisition of property in Poland, all threaten to vex the question further. On the Polish side, the question of 'reparations' for wartime activities has been put aside, as part of an agreement related to German confirmation of the present borders. Nevertheless, there is general low-level Polish outrage that Germany, having caused Poland so much suffering in the war, should now be so wealthy and powerful; history has not, in this popular view, afforded Poland much justice.

All these problems are exacerbated by Poland's position in relation to the IMF and the EU. The IMF has imposed upon Poland, as a condition of economic help, its standard recipe for economies in trouble – control of public spending, realistic exchange rates, deflation, belt-tightening and the like. This is necessary, but painful, as a majority of Poles still probably recognize. Along with this has come an openness to trade, and to capital investment; the Polish economy now has very few barriers to incoming investment (by contrast to its almost complete closure to such investment in the Communist period).

Poland has very little to bargain with: it badly needs trade, it badly needs foreign capital, it badly needed debt-forgiveness; it was in no position to argue with the IMF about the need to open its economy to trade and investment. In an ideal world, the IMF's proposals would in any case have been entirely to Poland's benefit. Perhaps they will be, to a great degree. Nevertheless, Poland has as its major potential trading partner (after the collapse of Comecon) the European Union. The EU is not beholden to the IMF. As individuals, its member nations support IMF activities, among which is encouraging economic openness and liberalization in struggling economies like that of Poland. As a Community, however, the EU operates, for its own perceived benefit, trade practices deeply inimical to liberalization. In particular, it operates a highly protectionist agricultural policy. It also, of course, forbids large-scale entry of non-EU labour migrants. Thus, the two aspects of its own economy which Poland would be best placed to exploit, its agriculture and its skilled labour, are disallowed by EU rules; Poland is only allowed to compete where it cannot compete. In that sense, the combination of IMF liberalization and EU protectionism, neither of which it has the negotiating power to resist, give it pain without pleasure. Again, the local perception of this is likely to take a

German–Polish form. At the time of writing, the Polish governing coalition has broken up over the question of speed of reform; adherence to IMF rules on the one hand, conservative forces in parliament on the other, and a mêlée of small parties, have made government impossible without a further election, held under stricter rules concerning the minimum vote required to secure representation in parliament. The reform process is still supported, so it seems, by a majority in Poland; but reform has been far more painful, and far more lengthy, than many once hoped: this will be reflected at the polls.[12]

The discourse of 'economic nationalism', with a stress on the virtues of protectionism, has been argued to have been of benefit to Poland in the inter-war period (Kofman 1992). There have already been clear signs of anti-foreign-capital right-wing politics in Poland, and this is a theme which will probably continue to have force.

Conclusion

Capital movements, trade barriers, protectionism, the 'nationality' of companies and capital: these are not commonly considered in anthropological reflections on identity. The many elements that constitute Europeanness in the minds of those that think themselves European – culture, religion, civilization, development, wealth, tradition, language, whatever – are not the stuff of trade agreements. The EC frontier, however, is made out of elements from both of these areas of action and perception. It would be futile to try to argue which was the more important, for they interact, forming a particularly potent combination of technicality and sentiment – a combination which is the current frontier of the EC, life-enhancing for those inside it, forbidding and perhaps damaging for those not so privileged.

In relation to the activities of MNCs, and their place in the EU, it might be noted that many MNCs, not only European but also from the US and Japan, have already made their dispositions in Europe. There have been innumerable mergers, acquisitions, and new investments, in anticipation of the single market. The *Financial Times*

---

12. The question of the accession of Poland, and other countries, to the EU, needs to be considered. If Poland were *inside* rather than *outside*, as many in Poland wish (see, for example, Gronkiewicz-Waltz, H. 1994), then issues of foreign investment, and relative prosperity, might come to be both truly different, and differently perceived.

recently quoted a German chief executive as follows: 'However, Mr Heinz Schimmelbusch, chief executive of Metallgesellschaft, the large German mining and industrial group, who said big European companies were already acting as if the Maastricht treaty had been implemented, stated: "This strategy has created a reality in European corporate life which will not be changed by Danish voters"' (*Financial Times*, 4/6/1992, p. 5). Much of the recent British concern about loss of sovereignty arising from the Maastricht agreement, for example, might be regarded as already too late; major companies are involved in a web of investment and strategic alliance which has already, to a great degree, discounted the importance of national frontiers.

References

Ardener, E. (1989). *The Voice of Prophecy, and other essays*, Oxford: Blackwell.

Barnet, R. and Mueller, R. (1975). *Global reach: the power of the multinational corporation*, London: Cape.

Bartlett, C., Doz, Y. and Hedlund, G. (1990). *Managing the global firm*, London: Routledge.

Boudier-Bensebaa, F. (1993). Analyse statistique comparee des investissements directs français et allemands en Hongrie, Tchécoslovaquie et Pologne', Document de travail, Université de Paris I.

Burleigh, M. (1988). *Germany turns Eastwards – a study of Ostforschung in the Third Reich*, Cambridge: Cambridge University Press.

Casson, M. (ed.) (1983). *The Growth of International Business*, London: Allen & Unwin.

Cecchini, P. (1988). *1992 – the European Challenge, the benefits of a single market (The Cecchini Report – official facts and figures*, Aldershot: Wildwood House.

Celarier, M. (1990). Comes the Revolution, *Global Finance*, August 1990, 55–60.

Chalasinski, J. (1935). *Antagonizm polsko-niemecki w osadzie fabrycznej 'Kopalnia' na Gornym Slasku – studium socjologiczne*, Warsaw.

Chapman, M. (1978). *The Gaelic Vision in Scottish Culture*, London: Croom Helm.

Chapman, M. (1992). *The Celts – the construction of a myth*, London:

Macmillan.

Czubinski, A. and Pajewski, J. (eds) (1987). *Polacy i Niemcy: Dziesiec Wiekow Sasiedztwa*, Warsaw: Wydawnictwo Naukowe.

Dunning, J. (1983). Changes in the level and structure of international production: the last one hundred years. In *The Growth of international Buisness* (ed. M. Casson), London: Allen & Unwin.

Dunning, J. (1993). *Multinational Enterprises and the Global Economy*, Addison-Wesley.

East European Business Handbook, 1993, London: Euromonitor.

Fieldhouse, D. (1986). The multinational: a critique of the concept. In *Multinational enterprise in historical perspective* (eds A. Teichova, M. Levy-Leboyer, and H. Nussbaum), Cambridge: Cambridge University Press.

Focus, GATT Newsletter, no. 104, December 1993, Geneva: GATT.

Gellner, E. (1983). *Nations and Nationalism*, Oxford: Blackwell.

Goodhart, D. (1990). German help for Eastern Europe, *Financial Times*, 16 March 1990, 23.

Gronkiewicz-Waltz, H. (1994). Poland: towards a united Europe. *Bulletin – the Credit Suisse Magazine*, 3, 7–9.

Hendry, J. (1987). *Understanding Japanese Society*, London: Croom Helm.

Hofstede, G. (1980). *Culture's consequences*, Beverly Hills, CA: Sage.

Hofstede, G. (1991). *Cultures and organizations*, Maidenhead: McGraw-Hill.

Hood, N. and Young, S. (1982). *Multinationals in retreat: the Scottish experience*, Edinburgh: Edinburgh University Press.

Kindleberger, C. (1969). *American business abroad*, New Haven: Yale University Press.

Kofman, J. (1992). *Nacjonalizm gospodarczy – szansa czy bariera rozwoju*, Warsaw: Wydawnictwo Naukowe PWN.

Kolankiewicz, G. and Lewis, P. (1988). *Poland*, London: Pinter.

Kostrowicka, I., Landau, Z. and Tomaszewski, J. (1975). *Historia Gospodarczi Polski XIX i XX wieku*, Warsaw: Ksiazka i Wiedza.

Landau, Z. and Tomaszewski, J. (1964). *Kapitaly obce w Polsce 1918–1939*, Warsaw.

Landau, Z. and Tomaszewski, J. (1985). *The Polish Economy in the Twentieth Century*, London: Croom Helm.

Luczak, C. (1988). *Od Bismarcka do Hitlera: Polsko-niemieckie stosunki gospodarcze*, Wydawnictwo Poznanskie: Poznan.

Makowski, E. (1987). Tajne zabiegi niemiec o utrzymanie kolonistow w zachodniej Polsce (1919–1929). In *Polacy i Niemcy: Dziesiec Wiekow Sasiedztwa* (eds A. Czubinski and J. Pajewski), Warsaw: Wydawnictwo Naukowe.

Mulligan, T. (1987). The two cultures in business education. *Academy of Management Review*, **12**, (4), 593–9.

Neghandi, A. (1983). Cross-cultural management research: trend and future directions. *Journal of International Business Studies*, **14**.

Ohmae, K. (1990). *The borderless world*, London: Harper.

Overy, R. (1983). Goring's 'Multinational Empire'. In *International Business and Central Europe* (eds A. Teichova and P. Cottrell), Leicester: Leicester University Press.

Porter, M. (1990). *The competitive advantage of nations*, London: Macmillan.

Prestowitz, C. (1988). *Trading places — how we are giving our future to Japan and how to reclaim it*, New York: Basic Books.

Roberts, K. and Boyacigiller, N. (1984). Cross-national organizational research – the grasp of the blind men. *Research in Organizational Behaviour*, **6**, 423–75.

Sekaran, U. (1983). Methodological and theoretical issues and advancements in cross-cultural research, *Journal of International Business Studies*, **14**.

Sugar, P. and Lederer, I. (eds) (1969). *Nationalism in Eastern Europe*, Seattle and London: University of Washington Press.

Teichova, A. and Cottrell, P. (eds) (1983). *International business and Central Europe 1918 –1939*, Leicester: Leicester University Press.

Teichova, A., Levy-Leboyer, M. and Nussbaum, H. (eds) (1986). *Multinational enterprise in historical perspective*, Cambridge: Cambridge University Press.

UN (1992). *World Investment Directory 1992, Central and Eastern Europe*, New York: United Nations.

UNCTC (United Nations Commission on Transnational Corporations), (1989). *Transnational corporations in world development, trends and prospects*, New York: United Nations.

UNCTC (United Nations Commission on Transnational Corporations), (1992). *Transnational corporations as engines of growth*, New York: United Nations.

Vaitsos, C. (1974). *Inter-country income distribution and transnational enterprises*, Oxford: Clarendon.

Wellisz, L. (1938). *Foreign capital in Poland*, London: Allen & Unwin.

Chapter 12

The Spanish Experience and Its Implications for a Citizen's Europe*

Soledad Garcia

Citizens – said Aristotle – 'are all who share in the civic life of ruling and being ruled in turn'. Since the old Greek republican experience of city democracy, the effects of two Revolutions and a declaration of human rights by the United Nations have modified considerably our conception of what a modern citizen should be. Today we think of citizenship in relation to 'national identity', 'sovereignty', 'community', 'participation', 'entitlements' and to some extent 'equality'. The common denominator of these issues is that they all refer to the experiences of 'exclusion' and 'inclusion'.

If we consider the exercise of citizenship as a process and not as a final aim we may see that, throughout history, citizenship has been an arena for discussing who has the right to be 'in' and who does not. We may agree with the view that in modern societies the proportion of those who are 'in' has increased, but that there is still uneasiness and potential conflict caused by those who remain 'out' of their several institutional social arrangements.

Citizenship has gained momentum in particular historical periods. In modern Europe we can recall 1789, the 1880s and 1890s, the 1950s and 1989 as significant years. The current expansion of citizens' rights is particularly interesting because it occurs in a situation of the convergence of several previously disparate historical experiences. On the one hand, modern welfare societies are experiencing what has been characterized as a 'retrenchment' of welfare policies and principles, generating different classes of citizens and bringing back the question of entitlements. On the other

* This paper was written while I was a fellow at St. Antony's College, Oxford.

hand, there are societies in which a redefinition of citizenship involves the key concept of civil society as crucial to the transformation of their economic and political life after the revolution of 1989. Moreover, there are also societies cohabiting in Europe today that, having formally entered the group of modern industrial societies, are still redefining both citizenship and civil society to harmonize with their partners.

In Western Europe the concept of citizenship evolved historically from the city to the nation-state, widening the circles of social inclusion. Today in the modern world citizenship constitutes legal, economic, political and social practices which define social membership and which counteract social cleavages. In this sense the practice of citizenship gives people who differ in age, sex, beliefs or colour of skin the same basic entitlements. It is this aspect of citizenship that has contributed to the legitimacy of the modern state.

There are several definitions and ways of understanding citizenship; but a basic distinction can be made between its formal and its substantive meanings. Formally, citizenship is associated with membership of a political community (state), that is with 'nationality'; substantively, it relates to the possession of specific rights and the obligation to comply with certain duties within the state or political community.[1] Decisions about who becomes a citizen are taken by the state itself, but the quality of citizenship (rights and duties) is often the result of conflict and negotiation between the social and political structural forces in a country.

Recently, within the European Community, the principle of a citizen's Europe has been formally stated in the Maastricht treaty. Thus the introduction of citizenship of the Union in the treaty gives to those nationalized in any of the member states the following rights: to move and reside freely within the territory of the Community; to vote and be eligible in local and European Parliamentary elections, and to formulate a petition to the European Parliament; to apply to a Union Ombudsman; and to have access to diplomatic and consular representation in certain non-member states. Moreover, other social and economic rights (for all but the UK) and cultural rights will be introduced. With the ratification of the Maastricht treaty by all member states, the implications of the status of European citizens are bound to evolve in such a way that

1. This distinction has been stressed by T. Hammar (1990).

rights and duties will be more clearly defined, while the external frontiers for non-citizens are likely to be strengthened.[2] Thus within the EC countries the imminent abolition of internal frontiers has encouraged states to strengthen external controls; in the near future a common and more co-ordinated policy is expected to develop to regulate migration, although some problems may arise from the fact that the definition of who is a citizen varies according to the immigration laws of each country.

This chapter addresses the themes of citizenship and civil society from the experience of Spain as a southern European country. The key questions appraised are: (a) the role of citizens in public decision-making and the context in which relations between citizens and state structures are such that citizens can participate in decisions affecting their lives; (b) and the role of the grass-roots in putting on pressure for institutional changes when such a democratic context is lacking. The case of Spain and other southern European countries, where democratic institutions are still in the process of construction, can be seen as parallel examples to the European Community, where the limited mechanisms for citizens' participation have created a 'democratic deficit'. This deficit can be seen in relation to the difficulties the Community is facing in creating political cohesion and identity.[3]

The challenge of building a European citizenship forces us to consider the diverse paths towards modernity experienced by different West European societies – here experience diverges mainly along the north–south axis – as well as more recent trends towards convergence. Thus important differences have emerged as a result of the particular social and political histories of individual European States, and these variations are more marked between north and south European countries. The development of citizenship in the south has been much more uneven, especially in the 'younger' democracies, where people's civil and political rights were ignored for long periods. In this sense the illustration of the Spanish experience has a particular interest. Moreover, the future reality of a European citizenship has to be in relation not only to a further

2. Denmark will be an exception after it was agreed in the 1992 Edinburgh Summit that this country could pull out of the citizenship of the Union. This decision was taken in order to favour a yes vote in the second referendum to be held in Spring 1993 on the ratification of the Maastricht treaty.
3. This question has been analysed from different intellectual and geographical perspectives in the multi-author volume edited by S. Garcia (1993).

social and economic cohesion (the Spanish official position) but also to the existence of a political community.

The argument stressed in the following pages is that citizenship can only be realized when its political dimension has been developed, that is, when political rights have been granted. As Raymond Aron has pointed out, other rights such as civic or social rights can become very fragile in the absence of political citizenship.[4]

There has been a general view that the levels of participation and open ways 'in' of most advanced democratic societies will be followed by other societies at a different speed. However, this view has wrongly assumed that evolution is unilineal. The evolutionist interpretation has been rightly criticized by M. Mann,[5] who has shown the importance of taking into consideration the different 'strategies' adopted by actors involved in social conflict (mainly class conflict) when analysing the ways in which citizenship has developed in Europe. Departing from Mann's analysis, I intend to show that the paths followed by southern European societies do not represent simply a slow and somehow more chaotic version of the same process, but a different version altogether. Taking the British classical model, brilliantly explained by T. H. Marshall, we can see that it is only partially relevant to understanding citizenship in Spain. Spanish society, like the Greek and Portuguese societies, has confronted modern participatory culture with a variety of strategies which differ from those of northern Europe.

One of the assumptions of T. H. Marshall's analysis[6] is that full citizenship involves the achievement of civil, political, economic and social rights in that sequence. In Britain, political and civil citizenship was strengthened by the consolidation of liberalism and reformism, while social citizenship was granted with the development of the welfare state. An important characteristic that accompanied this process was the shift from local to national institutions, giving more relevance to the national political community. Compulsory education, for example, meant for the citizen not only the right to be educated, but a reciprocal duty to become a trained worker and useful to the national economic requirements. Thus cultural and social incorporation created loyalties to the nation-state.

4. See R. Aron (1974).
5. See M. Mann (1987).
6. See T. H. Marshall (1950).

This model was not reproduced in southern European countries (mainly Greece, Spain and Portugal, although in some aspects Italy may be included). Whereas in Britain the lower classes were incorporated into the 'rules of the game', in the south the confrontations between liberal reformers and reactionaries were often won by the latter. Authoritarian rule brought repression and excluded large sectors of the population, weakened the sense of belonging to a political community and generally curtailed the possibilities of development for civil society. This, however, does not imply that social welfare had to wait for civic and political rights to be introduced. Although civil and political citizenship were denied to a large part of the population, minimal social rights were granted. Alternative social strategies based on family and community solidarity compensated for defective state support. Thus the path towards modernity could be followed, but the landscape formed by constraints on entitlements and the limitation of participation and fractured collective cultural identities (mainly in Spain) left distinctive traits in these societies.

There are several important issues to be considered on the general theme of citizenship and on its specific development in a southern European country such as Spain. One such issue, which is of particular relevance here in ascertaining the extent to which conditions were favourable for the expansion of citizens' rights, is the degree of protection offered by the state to the population at different moments in time. We can assume that the ideal conditions would arise from economic growth in largely urbanized societies with scope for social and political organization. But we may find that different paths reach similar objectives. When referring to citizens' rights I include civil, political and social rights, although I am going to concentrate my analysis on the social dimension of citizenship (particularly if the extension of social rights changes the relation between individuals and the state) and on the nature and extent of the civil society.[7]

7. The concept of civil society here means a realm of social organizations and non-governmental institutions made possible by a degree of social autonomy. However their agency capacity makes it difficult to exclude any connection to the state. Thus civil society is seen here neither as a private sphere independent from the public sphere (state), since Western European societies have been modernized with strong participation of the state, nor as being in an antagonistic relationship with the state.

The Spanish Experience

If we hold Kant's view that 'one must already have citizens before one can have subjects of the state' we can explain not only why the Francoist despotic regime and previous governments in Spain failed to develop a complete nation-state identity or gain more widespread loyalty from the population, but also why national integration was more difficult to achieve in Spain than in more egalitarian and culturally homogeneous democratic societies such as the Scandinavian countries.

Having said that, I would like to argue that to view developments in contemporary Spain as a radical transformation from the total absence of citizens' rights and political organizations to full citizenship and the return of civil society 'from above' as a result of the reestablishment of parliamentary democracy can also be misleading. In fact, some of the crucial structures of welfare, such as the national health service, were created in the Francoist period, although they did not involve universality, and therefore did not constitute full citizenship. The welfare policies of democratic governments from 1977 onwards have partly consisted in universalizing those existing structures and partly in creating new ones (mainly social services). In the area of industrial relations, employers and workers were reaching wage agreements outside the official structures almost twenty years before the unions were legalized. Civil society began to organize either openly from 1964 onwards (in civic and professional and religious associations) or in a clandestine form (workers' unions and political parties) from the 1950s.

Two specific questions to consider here are: (1) the extent to which the social dimension of citizenship has been developed before and after 1977; and (2) the participation of civil society in the development of citizenship, also before and after that date.

Whereas in most West European countries the period after the Second World War saw a move ahead in the expansion of social citizenship, during which the populations of those countries experienced a sense of unity while embarking on economic reconstruction, in Spain, the end of the Civil War in 1939 not only brought the end of the civic and political rights of the Spanish population, but also left a divided nation of winners and losers. Instead of a political community, the Francoist regime decided to encourage a nation based on patriotism under an authoritarian rule that did not involve the idea of citizenship. Moreover, the dictatorship actively tried to enforce an artificial cultural unity during its first decade in power, thus exacerbating the antagonism between the regions with strong national identities and the centralist aspirations of the nation-state rulers. However, the inability of the regime to 'articulate national interests' also came from the arbitrary way in which policies were implemented without democratic control. This is especially relevant for social policies, mainly in the sphere of education.

The regime's interest in integrating and controlling the workers, though, was manifest in the Labour Charter, which was promulgated before the war ended (March 1938). In this Charter work was stated as a right and as a social duty; there was also a regulation of employment which among other things involved the prohibition of the employment of married women in workshops and factories; an enunciation of the areas to be covered by social insurance and the lines on which vertical trade unions could organize. However, it was not until July 1945 that a wider declaration of 'rights' and 'duties' appeared under the title of Charter of the Spanish People ('Fuero de los Españoles'). This Charter stated that every Spaniard was a member of a national community as well as a member of institutions such as the Catholic Church, the family, the vertical syndicate, the municipality and the company. Within this corporatist model designed by the regime civil rights were subjected to the fundamental principles of the 'spiritual, national and social unity of Spain' (in that order), and therefore any opposition was considered not only illegal but a threat to national security.

In 1950, after four years' of widespread condemnation of the regime, the General Assembly of the United Nations welcomed Spain back into the international arena. This occurred mainly as a result of geopolitics. However, it did not bring about positive changes with regard to civil and political rights. State control over the population was exercised through public institutions and the media. A declaration of loyalty to the regime would have to be made by anyone, from civil servants to university professors, on assuming official state posts. Censorship continued to be implemented while the state was, directly or indirectly, controlling the mass media. But instead of actively enforcing an ideology the despotic regime encouraged passivity and intellectual silence. The Catholic Church provided the ideological engine of the regime, particularly during its first twenty years. In May 1958 the Law on the Principles of the National Movement (Ley sobre los Principios del Movimiento Nacional) re-emphasized the Catholic Faith 'as inseparable from the national consciousness'. This and other similar statements have been used to defend the argument of 'national-catholicism' in Spain.

In comparing both Charters it can be seen that, while on a rhetorical level and as a principle Spaniards were considered equal before the law in 1945 and 1958, social rights such as the right to work, education and instruction, health and unemployment insurance and minimum state support were included in the 1945 Charter but not in the 1958 Principles of the National Movement. The 1958 Charter also restated the importance of the already mentioned institutions (vertical trade union, family, municipality) as well as the active role of the state in encouraging economic progress, including industrialization and scientific research. However, the emphasis on corporatist elements was weaker. Relations between the public economy and the private economy were defined in this somewhat more liberal manifesto according to the principle of subsidiarity.

The peculiar character of the regime inhibits any application of the model of the Keynesian welfare state to a pre-democratic Spain.[8] The Francoist regime has been characterized as basically authoritarian and corporatist.[9] However, in order to explain a model of social policies during the dictatorship I use the distinction made by S. Ringen between *marginal* and *institutional* welfare states. The first type has 'goals of limited ambition', and uses 'mainly selective and income-tested anti-poverty policies' with no clear re-distributive goals. This type contrasts with the institutional welfare system, which has 'more ambitious goals', 'universal programmes' and clear redistributive policies. Only within the second type are the needs and aspirations of citizens taken into account and is social and political consensus established.[10] One of the interesting aspects of the Spanish marginal welfare approach is its character and timing. Whereas in most modern industrial societies the welfare system has been developing from the 1950s with social consensus,

8. The Keynesian welfare state has adopted, however, different expressions in Europe, according to particular histories of national integration and public–private sector mix. G. Esping-Andersen (1990) has distinguished three types of welfare regimes: conservative, liberal and social-democratic.

9. S. Giner (1985) uses the term 'modern despotism' to characterize the regime, emphasizing its class content.

10. See S. Ringen (1989), Chapter 1.

and retrenchment has taken place in the 1980s, partly as a result of economic recession, in Spain most welfare policies were initiated without consensus (from the late 1950s to the 1970s) and were universalized during the recession of the early 1980s. This original pattern has involved tensions between policies aiming at redistribution and the constraints on public resources arising from the policies adopted by the Government to administer the recession in the first part of the 1980s and to help economic growth and adjustment to the EC in the second half of the 1980s.

The marginal social policies pursued by the Old Regime failed to encourage the idea of citizenship, since civic and political rights were restricted. Aspirations to universal rights came from the heterogeneous opposition, often at the grass-roots level, while the structures of welfare were designed by the regime. The weakened civil society was therefore unable to participate in that design. This peculiar pattern of developing social protection has had, I will argue, a decisive role in the present developments of citizenship and civil society in Spain (both still relatively fragmented).

What kind of social policies did the Francoist regime implement? How remote were they from the principles and the realities of welfare societies, and how much have the policies been universalized since 1977 ?

The original design of services was intended to protect workers alone. For example, in 1942 the Services for insurance against industrial accidents and Compulsory Health Insurance (Seguro Obligatorio de Enfermedad) were created, in which about 25 per cent of the population were included. In 1967, the Health Insurance was transformed into a wider structure called Social Security Health Assistance (Asistencia Sanitaria de la Seguridad Social), which reached about 84 per cent of the population.[11] Other social services, such as education, remained highly élitist, and a universal system was never introduced. Private schools and Catholic Church schools enjoyed full support from the state in the form of finance through state subsidies. Thus an important part of public finance in education went to private education. (In 1964 there were fewer state secondary schools than there were in 1935.)

By the 1950s, there was also a clear need for the provision of insurance against unemployment, which eventually led in 1961 to the setting up of a scheme to provide National Unemployment

---

11. See M. Guillen and J. de Miguel (1990): 474–5.

Insurance. The regime had committed itself to full employment, and it must be said that it achieved a certain amount of success. This was helped by the labour-intensive nature of production and by the regulation of the labour market, which allowed dismissals of workers only in cases of bankruptcy or near-bankruptcy. It was also achieved through more perverse measures, such as the de-activation of female participation in the labour market in the 1940s and the export of labour to Europe in the 1960s. Workers from rural areas were encouraged to migrate to northern Europe, with the result that between 1961 and 1973 a total of 1,753,200 migrated to other European countries (emigration to other areas amounted to more than 200,000).[12]

In the 1977 democratic general elections, principles such as respect for the individual and individual rights, democracy, social and economic policies with a Christian humanist ethic, and the protection of social justice and equality, all of which are principles of citizenship in European social democracies, were exhibited in the programmes of the main political parties. All these principles were to be made a part of the Constitution in 1978. This Magna Carta, has marked a turning-point in Spanish history for two reasons: first,by binding successive governments to policies which do not undermine the achievements of citizens' rights; and second, through its consensual character in taking into consideration the aspirations of the different social groups and communities which form the country.

Some of the most relevant aspects of the content of the Constitution concerning citizenship are the following. In Section I, the Constitution gives priority to the civic and political rights of the individual first and then to those of organized groups, ending with a repertoire of social rights. From the right to work to social services all the possible social rights are included. The Constitution includes the principle of equality throughout the text.[13] There are articles (40.1/31.2) which specify that income redistribution should pertain to both people and regions, and the equity principle is introduced in the concept of public expenditure. However, although all levels

---

12. Although the return flow from North Europe became significant from 1964 onwards, by 1974 there were still about 700,000 Spanish workers in central and northern Europe (Spanish Emigration Institute in OECD, *Economic Surveys, Spain* 1981).

13. The references to these rights in the third Chapter are clearly influenced by the European Social Charter of 1961, the International Pact of Economic, Social and Cultural Rights of 1966 and the Consumer's Magna Carta of 1973. See O. de Juan Asenjo (1984): 106–32.

of government are obliged to pursue policies which will provide such services, they are not required to ensure results.

As a final comment on the social rights content of the Constitution it can be said that whereas the overall picture of the direction of change is consistent with the principles of the mixed economy and the welfare society, the magnitude of change is less clear. While, on the one hand, the institutional guarantees to endorse the rights are objectives and not principles, on the other, there is no timetable for introducing institutional measures to transform these objectives into reality. The Constitution leaves open, though, one recourse to Spanish citizens. When they feel their rights have been neglected they can make a formal complaint to the Ombudsman, whose role has become highly significant in contemporary Spain.

The principles of social citizenship underlying the Constitution have been translating into the world of facts as follows: (a) Health care was universalized in 1986 with the constitution of a fully-fledged National Health System, which in 1989 covered 99 per cent of the population. (b) Public education is free at all levels with the exception of universities, where a small fee is paid. Schooling has been made compulsory from 6 to 16 years. The number of students in higher education increased dramatically: in 1989 schooling among people between 20 and 24 years old was 28.49 per cent. However, the number of teachers is considered as one of the lowest in the OECD area, and professional training courses have been heavily criticized for having a high drop-out rate and for failing to provide the skills required by enterprises.(c) Maternity leave for all women has been extended from 14 to 16 weeks and a more explicit statement has been added to the 1964 civil law in which equality at work for men and women is promoted.[14] Also family planning has been made possible. One interesting change has been that since 1981 parental authority is shared by mother and father, carrying the obligation for protection and education. However, family allowances are very small, although there is tax deduction for each child; but clearly women have less control over the income from this indirect form of allowance. (d) Pensions have also been universalized. In 1985 a new Law changed the qualifying conditions and income basis for calculating an extension to the minimum contribution period to 15 years, and real benefits have grown faster than average earnings, especially for those who retired before 1974.

14. In S. del Campo (1990): 335–45.

The public pension system has been considered generous by the OECD in comparison to those of its other member countries.[15]

If a consideration of the areas of health, education, and pensions gives a bright picture of social citizenship in democratic Spain, there is, nevertheless, a dark side too. Between 1974 and 1985 a total of 2.1 million jobs were lost. The contrast with the economies of other European countries shows that in Spain structural factors have been more determinant than cyclical factors. High employment in agriculture during the previous decade has been one of the important causes of the rise in unemployment; over the last decade agricultural employment declined by about 1,000,000 persons, or about 40 per cent of the increase in total unemployment over the same period. Industrial restructuring, demographic factors (the baby boom) and the return of migrants from northern Europe complete the series of crucial variables contributing to the dramatic rise in unemployment.

The OECD has stated that 'the development of the underground economy has been favoured by structural factors (a sizeable tourist sector, important seasonal agricultural work and a large number of unincorporated small companies and self-employed people), and a change in social attitudes. Thus, a rapidly growing number of individuals who cannot easily find jobs tend to accept lower pay, less attractive working conditions and reduced job stability in the underground economy while registering as unemployed.' In addition many people who work do not declare themselves as employed and are, therefore, excluded from the statistics. This causes a further distortion in the unemployment figures.[16]

With the restructuring of the labour market old social inequalities have re-emerged alongside the appearance of new ones. Thus, although the participation of women in the labour market increased from 23 per cent in 1970 to 30 per cent in 1985, in 1986 female unemployment was 20 per cent higher than male unemployment. Also the youth unemployment rate is more than double the average in OECD Europe. Since the mid-1970s the unemployment rate of those with secondary education (32 per cent) experienced the fastest rise. Unemployment is lower in the higher educational category (15 per cent). Moreover, the proportion of long-term unemployed has

15. See OECD, *Economic Survey of Spain* (1988–1989).
16. See OECD, *Economic Surveys* (1984); OECD (1986).

increased considerably, especially in depressed areas and among the poorly-qualified. The level of long-term unemployment would have been even higher if a substantial number of those older than 45 years of age had not dropped out of the labour force; this is particularly true of women. Thus, there are two kinds of worker in the labour market: one protected by union negotiations and the other lacking labour rights. There is a further unequal distribution of employment opportunities along territorial lines. Thus, while important advances have been made in the social dimension of citizenship with the re-establishment of democracy and the universalization of social services, there remains one major drawback in the shape of the rise of unemployment, which is reinforcing old inequalities and generating new ones.

The Constitution and Civil Society

There are different interpretations of the extent to which civil society was present and relevant in the restoration of democracy in 1978. However, those who have studied the period with an open mind seem to agree that, no matter how weak and dilapidated civil society had been under the Francoist regime, it reappeared long before 1978.[17] The difference is one of emphasis, depending on the significance attributed to the underground political culture (of both working-class grass-roots and bourgeois élites) and its role in the design of democratic Spain.

Those who support the view of democratic transition from below point out the existence of organized groups, especially in the large urban centres from the late 1950s. The activities of workers' organizations, Christian Democrats, neighbourhood associations and university students increased considerably during the 1970s. While, on the one hand, the numerical significance of stable organizations was small, on the other, their capacity for co-ordinating collective action was notably high, especially in the labour movement (after the 1958 Law of Collective Bargaining). It has been argued that the diversity of civic and political organizations in different areas of the country (Catalonia, north Spain, Madrid, Andalusia) can be seen as a prelude to the peaceful

17. See Carr and Fusi (1981); Balfour (1989); Foweraker (1989).

and consensual politics of the democratic restoration.[18]

Following the 1964 Law of Associations, these spread throughout the country, representing economic and social interests. The market economy and the increasing internationalization of the Spanish economy favoured the development of 'sociedades anónimas' (limited companies) in production and commerce, while civic associations also proliferated in the urban areas of the largest industrial centres. Thus civil society continued to exist, albeit in a very weakened form and with almost no impact on the structures of wealth redistribution or as an engine of political participation.

Another line of argument has stressed that, although there was an increase in the organization of dissent and demonstrations of civil disobedience during the 1970s, the political culture of Spanish society in general was lacking in strength. With some exceptions, politically active minorities were concentrated in the larger cities, while large sectors of the population were 'depoliticized'. While there was a strong consciousness of social inequalities existing in the country, only a small proportion considered that what had to be done in Spain was a strictly political issue or showed themselves to be very interested in politics.

One explanation for the relatively small political commitment of the Spanish population is that economic growth and the improvement of the well-being of large sections of the population during the 1960s and 1970s favoured individual welfare and social mobility, which became private achievements outside the participation in formal organizations. Thus, increasing life chances were disassociated from political participation for the majority of the population, who wanted democracy, but in the face of possible changes stressed order and peace as the most important values to maintain. Perhaps this development can explain why, while the majority thought it necessary to have more civic and political freedom, only half were in favour of legalizing political parties. However, the geography of political aspirations was divided between those regions which most favoured political parties and those which were more reluctant. Among the first were the two larger cities, Barcelona and Madrid, in addition to regions such as the Basque country and Navarre, the Canary Islands, Galicia and

---

18. For example as S. Giner *et al.* (1990) have pointed out, in 1971 the Catalan Assembly (*Assemblea de Catalunya*) was able to organize the opposition (from moderate Christians to Communists) in Catalonia.

Asturias – that is, the urban and industrial centres and those regions with a strong national identity.[19]

There thus exists enough evidence to support the idea that an expression of civil society existed before 1977 and that it played a part in the reconstruction of democracy. So the new civil society only became visible with the official political transition, long after it had first come into being. However, what it is particularly important here is the kind of civil society that existed and the way in which it was to participate in the design of people's rights. Before 1977, social 'welfare' developed from the structures of the Franco regime and to a very small extent from the 'anti-state' civil society, since there was no substantive dialogue between the majority of citizens and state agencies. In contrast, the struggle for civil and political rights consistently came from civil society, and in some instances its claims were accepted by the regime. During the years of economic growth the opposition forces had to direct their energies towards gaining basic rights without been able to develop and structure their organizations. As a consequence of this, as in the case of political participation, most citizens had not developed habits of membership in organizations within civil society or been familiar with practices of co-ordinating organized interests.

There is one crucial element differentiating the 1978 Constitution from previous declarations of principles and objectives: this is the presence of civil society in its design. The sociological and political significance of the Magna Carta lies in the fact that it is the result of a mixture of consensus and transaction between the representative political forces elected in 1977. Consensus existed in the values and principles, whereas transactions or negotiations had to be made to endorse the content of those principles. This is why there are articles which aim to satisfy all the parties involved.

However, it is relevant to the present discussion that civil society in Spain, no matter how weak it was, could still leave its mark on the Constitution. As well as the seven representatives of the largest five parties and the six parties present in the Commission, suggestions from workers' unions, employers' associations, consumers and professional associations were also incorporated. Even some of the interests of the historical peripheral communities of Catalonia and the Basque Country, where a close relation can be observed between their national identity and the vigour of their civil

19. See the study conducted by FOESSA (1975).

societies, were incorporated before the process of decentralization had began. Considering the Constitution as a turning-point in the development of civil society two important questions are: first, to what extent has civil society developed in the last twelve years?; and, second, to what extent has it constructed institutional links or lines of communication with the state? A general view of organizations such as trade unions, employers and civic and political organizations provides some guidelines.

Although employers and workers backed up the Moncloa Pacts (1977), they were not called on to discuss them. However, their role in the making of democratic Spain has not passed unnoticed. If on the one hand from 1977 to 1980 industrial relations were operating in a relative institutional vacuum (since the Workers' Charter was not introduced until 1981), between 1979 and 1983 several important measures contributed to shaping the institutional framework for collective bargaining. Four rounds of negotiations contributed in those years to the drawing up of the 'rules of the game' in industrial relations. Thus discussions covered a wide range of issues, from setting up the themes to include in collective bargaining to working out structures of participation in economic policies.

From an organizational perspective both the employers' representative body (the CEOE) and the unions (mainly the UGT) were favoured by this high level of negotiations, which allowed them to achieve a high profile. On the other hand, the largest union in 1977, the CC.OO (which claimed to have 1,820,000 members in 1977), only signed the 1981 and 1983 agreements. The 1981 agreement has been considered especially relevant, as it took place only three and a half months after the attempted military coup. The workers' representatives agreed to set wages at a level just below inflation, while working out a policy of 'solidarity' towards those without jobs. The Government entered into the agreement and undertook to create new jobs – a promise on which it did not deliver. Also, it was agreed to 'acknowledge the right of the most representative trade union and employers' organisations to participate in supervising the management of a number of public and semi-public institutions'.[20] This idea which remained on paper at the central level, has been put into practice at a regional level in the Basque Country, Catalonia, Andalusia and Madrid, with

20. ILO (1986): 64.

varying degrees of success.

With these impressionistic remarks I intend to stress the fact that industrial relations and workers' participation were taking an institutional shape in a context of political uncertainty and economic recession. Some external observers have emphasized the civic and political responsibility demonstrated by the actors involved, which was reflected in decrease in the number of working days lost in the early 1980s. However, workers' unions' relations with the Government deteriorated from 1986 onwards, partly because the latter did not deliver on its promise to extend social protection to the unemployed. So it came about that the high cost paid by the workers for economic restructuring still left the unions with the image of being representatives of workers in employment only. The general strike that took place in December 1988 was seen as marking a change in the unions' strategy for compromise.[21] On the other hand, although trade unions have played an important part in the expansion of social citizenship in the course of representing the interests of workers, the level of unionization remains one of the lowest in Western Europe (11 per cent in 1989).

While party and union membership has shrunk, membership of voluntary associations has expanded. Also, political and civic associations have experienced a process of growth and diversification. The number of registered 'political associations' reached 871 by 1991; although very few of them are represented in the different layers of Government as political parties, the practice of fragmentation is revealing. The number of civic associations has also increased throughout the country (almost double in 1990 in relation to 1982). All this indicates that civil society is expanding; but what is less clear is the interconnection between civil society and state agencies, and the operational value of many of such organizations.

A further consideration is the process of decentralization in Spain, which has involved the creation of 17 Autonomous Communities of regional scope through which social services are administered. The original goal of making citizens' participation more feasible through these administrations needs to be reconsidered. Thus political decentralization, instead of involving decentralization of management, has often implied a duplication of offices and an inflation of the number of bureaucratic posts. This

---

21. See S. Aguilar (1991).

has resulted in an enlargement of public space at the cost of civil society.[22]

Some Conclusions

The Spanish example of the development of social welfare and the constitution of citizens rights shows how important it is to be flexible in our analysis of patterns of citizenship. As I have tried to demonstrate, the introduction of social welfare in Spain took place before civic and political rights existed. This pattern, similar to that of the old Communist regimes, in which a dilapidated civil society could not participate in the design of social rights until the reestablishment of democratic institutions, has had distinctive consequences for the present relations between the state and citizens. Despite the recent interrelation between workers' organizations and state institutions, the instruments for co-operation between civil society and the state remain opaque and relatively weak. Thus civil society is too fragmented, in a diversity of organizations which have little impact on the way social policy is developing.

Democratic governments have been unable to translate into the world of facts some of the social rights they defend in the world of principles. Thus the right to work, written into the Spanish Constitution, does not sort well with the highest unemployment rate in Western Europe. On this question, I agree with Dahrendorf that 'to stipulate a right to work instead of trying to abolish unemployment helps no one, and serves to dilute the notion of entitlements as part of the basic status of membership in a community'.[23] Citizenship is basically about providing options, giving entitlements and opening paths to participation in civil society. On these criteria, Spain and other southern European countries have a long way to go to match their northern partners in Western Europe. To what extent a full European citizenship might encourage convergence would be an interesting line of research for the 1990s. However, the present definition of European citizenship does not encourage one to think along these lines, since neither human nor social rights have yet been included in the limited scope

22. For a substantiation of this argument see V. Perez Diaz (1987).
23. See R. Dahrendorf (1991).

of this principle.[24]

At this point it is useful to remember the Hegelian distinction between a member of civil society and a citizen. The first one is a private person, whereas the second is a participant in a political collectivity. In the Spanish context civil society was not destroyed, but citizenship could not be developed for lack of the necessary democratic institutions. A parallel can be found with the European Community, where the development of European citizenship requires more participation of citizens through democratic mechanisms in a political community.

References

Aguilar, S. (1991). *Sindicalisme i canvi social a Espanya, 1976–1988*, Barcelona: Publicacions de la Fundació Jaume Bofill.

Aron, R. (1974). Is Multinational Citizenship Possible? *Social Research*, **41**, 638–56.

Balfour, S. (1989). *Dictatorship, Workers and the City*, Oxford: Clarendon Press.

Carr, R. and Fusi, J. P. (1981). *Spain: Dictatorship to Democracy*, London: Allen & Unwin.

Dahrendorf, R. (1979). *Life Chances*, London: Weidenfeld and Nicolson.

Dahrendorf, R. (1988). *The Modern Social Conflict*, London: Weidenfeld and Nicolson.

Dahrendorf, R. (1991). Some Remarks on the Quality of Citizenship. Paper presented at the Conference on 'Quality of Citizenship', Utrecht, March 20–22.

Del Campo, S. (1990). Spain. In *Family Policy in EEC – Countries* (ed. W. Dumon), Commission of the European Communities.

Esping-Andersen, G. (1990). *The Three Worlds of Welfare Capitalism*, Cambridge: Polity Press.

FOESSA (1975). *Estudios sociológicos sobre la situación social en España*, Madrid.

FOESSA (1986). *Estudio sobre el cambio político en España*, Madrid.

Foweraker, J. (1989). *Making Democracy in Spain*, Cambridge: Cambridge University Press.

---

24. The commitment of the EC to these rights is stated in other chapters of the Maastricht treaty (i.e. the Social Charter).

Garcia, S. (1990). Collective Consumption in Barcelona During the Franco Era. In *Family, Class and Nation in Catalonia* (ed. J. Llobera), London: Critique of Anthropology–Mare Nostrum Editions.

Garcia, S (ed.) (1993). *European Identity and the Search for Legitimacy*, London: RIIA–Pinter Publishers.

Giner, S. (1985). Political Economy Legitimation and the State. In *Uneven Development in Southern Europe* (eds J. Lewis and D. Hudson), London: Methuen.

Giner, S. *et al.* (1990). La sociedad española en la encrucijada. In VV.AA. *España. Sociedad y Política*, Madrid: Espasa Calpe.

Guillen, M. and Miguel, J. de. (1990). La sanidad en España. In VV.AA. *España. Sociedad y Política*, Madrid: Espasa Calpe.

Hammar, T. (1990). *Democracy and the Nation State*, Aldershot: Avebury.

Heater, D. (1990). *Citizenship*, London: Longman.

ILO (1986). *The Trade Union Situation and Industrial Relations in Spain*, Geneva.

Juan Asenjo, O de. (1984). *La Constitución económica Española*, Madrid: Centro de Estudios Constitucionales.

Kant, E. (1989). Idea for a Universal History from a Cosmopolitan Point of View. In *Kant On History* (ed. L. White Beck), London: Macmillan/Library of Liberal Arts.

Mann, M. (1987). Ruling Class Strategies and Citizenship. *Sociology*, **21**, (3).

Maravall, J. (1978). *Dictatorship and Political Dissent*, London: Tavistock.

Marshall, T. H. (1950). *Citizenship and Social Class and Other Essays*, Cambridge: Cambridge University Press.

Montero Garcia, F. (1988). *Los Seguros Sociales en la España del Siglo XX*, Madrid: Ministerio de Trabajo y Seguridad Social.

OECD (1981). *Economic Surveys, Spain.*

OECD (1984). *Economic Surveys, Spain.*

OECD (1986). *Employment Outlook.*

OECD (1986). *Living Conditions in OECD Countries*, Paris.

OECD (1988). *The Future of Social Protection*, Paris.

OECD (1988–1989). *Economic Surveys, Spain.*

Perez Diaz, V. (1987). *El retorno de la sociedad civil*, Madrid: Instituto de Estudios Economicos.

Ringen, S. (1989). *The Possibility of Politics*, Oxford: Clarendon Press.

Chapter 13

Citizens' Europe and the Construction of European Identity

Cris Shore and Annabel Black

European Commission documents frequently stress that political union must not be seen simply as a legalistic exercise but rather as a humanistic enterprise; a 'union among peoples' rather than just formal treaties between states (CEC 1983: 113; Fontaine 1991: 6). Indeed, the European Community (EC) was founded with the explicit aim of forging an 'ever closer union among the peoples of Europe' (CEC 1983: 109). Since the 1970s the concepts of a 'Citizen's Europe' and a 'People's Europe' have gradually, if sometimes falteringly, emerged as key to the whole vision of European union. Central to these concepts is the belief in the need for a Europe close to its well-informed citizens, the latter acting as prime movers for change, actively demanding their rights and advancing the vision. The promotion of this belief has been the subject of countless fine words set down in reports, resolutions and directives introducing ambitious programmes aiming to raise consciousness and to promote awareness, movement and freedom. With ratification of the Treaty of Maastricht – which came into force on 1 November 1993 – for the first time in history the twin notions of 'European Union' and 'Citizen of the Union' became enshrined as legal concepts. Indeed, Union citizenship has become mandatory for nationals of the Member States. Whatever rights and duties may be conferred by Union citizenship, the right to choose whether to claim it or not is not open to those qualifying for it.

Two ironies emerge from the new situation. First, the decision to make Union citizenship mandatory was taken without reference to the citizen at all, thus contradicting an important theme of the Treaty itself – that decisions should be taken as closely as possible to the citizen. Second, as Allott (1992) notes, 'all the talk about creating, in the minds of the citizens, a sense of loyalty and attachment to the EC is not worth much now, given that the new total structure will be as obscure as the Holy Roman Empire. One may be called upon to die for the EC in war, but will not be able to say quite what one is dying for.' We shall be exploring some of the questions and implications arising from these observations. If the vision of a united Europe is seen by some of its architects to rest upon this 'European idea' being shared by its well-informed citizens, all harbouring a sense of 'Europeanness', how is this sense being lived by the architects themselves, and to what extent is it being communicated to citizens in the Member States?

This chapter addresses these questions by looking at institutional attempts to forge a European unity and identity by promoting the ideas of European citizenship and a 'People's Europe'. It also examines the hypothesis that a sense of community and 'Europeanness' can be brought about by, and through the activities of, the Commission itself and its growing body of *fonctionnaires*. It is sometimes argued that these people represent a new international élite of intellectuals and bureaucrats. But if this is so, what kind of culture do they represent? Are they emissaries of a new pan-European identity which will transcend nationalism, or is theirs simply the bureaucratic culture of an international civil service, increasingly detached and alienated from the peoples in whose name it claims to serve?

To date, most studies of the social and cultural aspects of European integration and of the attempts by the European Union (EU) to pursue its goal of 'ever closer' integration have focused on EU policies, legislation and institutional questions. Little attention has been paid to the institutions of 'European culture', and still less to the 'culture' of those European institutions themselves. In our view these areas of investigation are inseparable from an understanding of the meaning of concepts such as European union and European identity, particularly in the light of theories of political integration. Begining with a brief review of these theories, we then turn to discuss what it means to talk about European citizenship by examining the legal and socio-cultural dimensions of the concept, and by tracing the Commission's campaigns to rally popular consciousness around the concept of a 'People's Europe'. Finally, we ask just what kind of European unity has been achieved to date?

European Integration: The Role of Elites

As textbooks frequently note, many attempts have been made throughout history to unify Europe, from the Romans and Charlemagne's Holy Roman Empire, to Napoleon and Hitler's Third Reich. Yet far from uniting Europe, the result has been, as Anthony Sampson (1971: 26) says, 'not unity but a fragmentation verging on near-total self-destruction'. It was the experience of that destruction after the Second World War which provided the impetus for the latest push towards unity – this time based on co-operation and consent rather than invasion and coercion. Visions of a united Europe thus have a long legacy and considerable ideological potency, particularly among European intellectuals and Political elites. But Europe is also home to another, perhaps more powerful concept; the nation-state and its allied notions of nationalism and state sovereignty. As Gordon Smith points out (1983: 244), 'the effect of these two opposed ideas has been to set up lasting tension which the two "world" wars of this century only partially dispelled'.

As we argue below, nation-states and nationalism are relevant to European integration for three reasons. First, because they are seen as key obstacles to European union; second, because both Europe and the nation-state are, to use Anderson's (1983) phrase, 'imagined communities', and it is important to explore how, from an anthropological perspective, such imaginings are constructed and articulated; and third, because the formation of European nation-states provides useful parallels, perhaps even a model, for understanding some of the processes involved in European political integration and state-formation. This raises a further question, addressed at the end: how far are national sovereignty and European union compatible or mutually exclusive?

Among the pressures toward increasing European union, the economic are by far the most important. As Smith has argued (1983: 244), 'the need for wider markets, the harnessing of investment potential, the desirable mobility of labour and capital – all of these made the boundaries and restrictions of the nation-state an increasing hindrance to the fulfilment of economic possibilities'. Following this logic some writers argue – at least from an economic perspective – that the nation-state is 'historically obsolete' (Wallace 1990; A. D. Smith 1990). Yet paradoxically, many would argue that nation-states continue to be powerful political and social forces and a major barrier to European integration. The economic argument about the inevitability of European integration echoes a theme developed in Gellner's (1983) theory of nationalism; namely, that the formation of nation-states in Europe occurred as a necessary adjunct to the process of industrialization and the needs of nineteenth-century capitalism. It could thus be argued, particularly since the completion of the internal market, that conditions are ripe for the creation of a supranational state. A corresponding weakening of the nation-state in Western Europe, partly through economic rationalization and the statutory elimination of barriers to free trade and partly through the transfer of political powers to Brussels, is arguably a necessary step for European union. At one level at least, therefore, the rationale behind European union could be seen as 'rationality' itself – understood in a strictly capitalist sense. This point seems to have eluded some of the EC's more nationalistic opponents. For example, Mrs Thatcher's single-minded advocacy for the European single market ironically helped to unleash the very integrationist forces she opposed. As Buchan noted (1991: 186), 'businessmen, unbothered as a breed about sovereignty in Britain and elsewhere, began to see no reason why a single market should not be crowned with a single currency'.

The ineluctable process of European economic integration is ultimately bound to lead to the emergence of some form of common political, legal and administrative authority with jurisdiction over the previously independent nation-states – though the extent of that authority and the precise nature of the European Union's federalist goal have yet to be defined. The European Commission under Jacques Delors, however, has provided a fairly clear vision of Europe's federal destiny – and has done much to manôeuvre things its way. A review of the so-called 'theories of European integration' developed by political scientists highlights this. Smith (1983) highlights three alternative solutions to securing political integration by political means. The first and most direct way is through federalism. This involves creating one central political authority with a territorial dispersion of power and a binding commitment on the part of the Member States to irrevocable union. The key feature of this federalist solution is that it gives decisive power to the centre and it lays down clearly and explicitly a vision of some final political form – for example, a United States of Europe.

The alternative to this, labelled the 'neo-functional' solution, entails a form of integration that proceeds gradually by the harmonizing of specific governmental structures and policies. In principle, this approach never ventures a final or total union, but simply outlines steps toward an incremental process of economic and legal aggregation, leaving the political structure of the nation-state intact. However, while this may avoid any major head-on confrontation with national authorities, the effect of a steady harmonization of laws cannot but fail to have a knock-on political effect. The next step is to bring pressure to bear on member states to make key public policies collectively. The result might be a series of minor conflicts and compromises, but as one piece of legislation falls into place there is an inescapable pressure on other areas to do likewise. For example, membership of the European exchange-rate mechanism leads to pressure for full monetary union and to the creation of a common currency: it is then only a matter of time before pressure emerges for a European Central bank. In terms of political strategy, 'neo-functionalism' might also be called 'federalism by stealth', as it basically aims to achieve the same thing as federalism, but without ever giving national political authorities grounds for a confrontation by never conceding that there is any *final* political form. This was very much the strategy pursued by Jean Monnet (Taylor 1983; George 1985).

The third approach to political integration is one that Haas (1958) defined as the process whereby political actors in several distinct national settings are persuaded to shift their loyalties, expectations and political activities towards a new centre, whose institutions possess or demand jurisdiction over pre-existing national states. This is the more ambitious approach, one that moves the emphasis from a political union understood in terms of a set of institutional arrangements towards the people of Europe themselves – which is where it becomes an issue of particular interest to anthropologists. According to this theory, union will come about through a gradual change in the behaviour, perception and outlook of the peoples of Europe as they come to identify increasingly with the new central authority.

A key question is how are these changes in consciousness and allegiance to be brought about, and what is it that could 'make people identify with Europe?' (Wistrich 1989: 77). The 'neo-functionalist' answer was that such identification would emerge as an inevitable consequence of institutional and economic change.

The cumulative impact of EC laws would lead to a chain reaction or 'spill-over effect' whereby harmonization in one sector would precipitate convergence in another. Aiding this is another process involving the progressive cementing or 'enmeshing' of the activities of parallel institutions (for example banks, businesses and government agencies), so that the necessary process of co-operation leads steadily toward permanent relationships. With the progressive erosion of national sovereignty the Member State governments would find it increasingly difficult to veto community decisions. Hence Community institutions and Community legislation will eventually supersede their national counterparts.

Another key factor is the creation of supranational cadres. As Smith (1983: 248) observes, 'no significant degree of integration could take place without the provision for personnel to administer the integrated sectors. And once these officials are appointed they will tend to acquire a loyalty to the organization rather than to the states of their origin.' Certainly there appears to be evidence of what informants called a tendency to 'go native' on the part of many of those officials appointed by their national governments to serve on the Commission. But most informants explained this as simply an institutional loyalty that one would expect to find in any organization. As one Commission employee put it, 'most of us owe allegiance to the Commission because it's our employer'. However, others perceived it as something more than this; not quite a 'European identity', but certainly a solidarity and growing Euro-consciousness among EU staff.

The formation of the nation-state in Europe provides an interesting model for comparison. An essential ingredient in this process was the creation of a new class of leaders and intellectuals; a vanguard inspired by an ideology of nationalism which enabled them to transcend parochial loyalties and rivalries. The rise of an élite cadre – equipped with a new and distinctly 'national' self-consciousness and with a vested interest in promoting the idea of nationhood which enabled them to perceive themselves as 'Frenchmen' rather than Parisians, or Germans rather than Bavarians and Prussians – thus became pivotal to the process of nation-state formation. Sartre, responding to Marx and Engels' critique of Christianity as the 'opium of the masses', commented wryly that 'Marxism is the opium of the intellectuals'. Historically, however, the more potent opiate would appear to have been nationalism (see Llobera, Chapter 4, and Bowman, Chapter 7, this volume).

The question has been raised by EU supporters and integration theorists of whether or not a supranational European-consciousness capable of transcending the ties of nationhood might be emerging among those bureaucrats who work in the institutions of the Community. Our evidence, outlined below, suggests that this may be happening. However, that consciousness, such as it is, is indelibly tinged by a bureaucratic mentality – which is perhaps inevitable, given that most EU officials owe their livelihoods to élitist bureaucratic structures. This has reinforced certain negative public stereotypes of EU officials. As one official described it, 'the popular image of us is one of meddling bureaucrats eating smoked salmon', or simply 'grey-suited businessmen stepping out of sombre, chauffeur-driven cars'. Furthermore, this emergent sense of 'Europeanness' is a consciousness shared by few people in the Member States themselves. These factors, combined with what most officials recognize as the European Union's failure to promote a positive image of itself, explain why some architects of European integration have turned their attention increasingly to the idea of citizenship.

European Citizenship – The Legal Dimension

Provision for Union citizenship is condensed into seven articles of the Maastricht Treaty (CEC 1992). In Article B, one of the Union objectives is 'to strengthen the protection of the rights and interests of the nationals of its Member States through the introduction of a citizenship of the Union'. Although the precise status of 'the Union' is undefined, it is significant that citizenship is introduced as one of its basic objectives.

The other six articles covering citizenship are in the section which amends the Treaty of Rome. They are articles 8–8e; and although the rights conferred might appear modest, problems could arise when it comes to their implementation. These articles provide, in summary:

Under Article 8:

- for establishment of citizenship of the Union;

- that every person holding the nationality of a Member State shall be a citizen of the Union; and

- that citizens of the Union shall enjoy the rights conferred by 'this Treaty' (i.e. the EC Treaty) and shall be subject to the duties imposed thereby.

Member States differ over their nationality laws, and there is no provision or concession made to immigrants who are not already citizens of Member States.

The vague second provision, for the enjoyment of the rights conferred by 'this Treaty', is open to wide interpretation, and it will be interesting to see how the Court of Justice interprets it. As for duties, it is not clear in what directions the provision may be leading. It is possible that in the future, should a common foreign and security policy take shape, there may be pressure to require citizens to support the Union, and thus Member States other than their own, irrespective of other considerations.

Under Article 8a:

- for citizens of the Union to have the right to move and reside freely within the territory of the Member States, subject to various limitations and conditions laid down in the Treaty and by the measures adopted to give it effect; and

- for the Council to adopt provisions facilitating the exercise of these rights, by unanimity and after receiving assent of the Parliament.

The 'limitations and conditions' clause means that although the right to move and reside freely as a citizen of the Union broadens the scope of existing provisions for the free movement of workers in Article 48 of the Treaty of Rome, the right will be subject to the same limitations. One of these is that the right of free movement is subject to limitations on grounds of public policy, public security or public health, as provided in Article 48, paragraph 3. But the Council, with the Parliament's assent, is given power to build upon these rights, so they are not set in concrete. It is also in relation to this article that protocol 17 was introduced. This provides that nothing in the Treaties should affect the application of the article in the Irish Constitution which forbids abortion. A rape victim case in 1992 almost called the whole protocol into question, jeopardizing ratification of the Treaty by Ireland.

Under Article 8b:

- for citizens of the Union to have the right to vote and stand as a candidate in municipal elections and elections to the European Parliament in the Member State in which they reside.

Extensive exercise of these rights could have potential for the development of European consciousness. But it is not yet clear how this measure will be exercised. It depends on implementing rules, which may include derogations. It is a sensitive political issue, especially in France, where it has met with right-wing opposition in wider debate encompassing the issue of immigration. It is also sensitive in Luxembourg, where up to 40 per cent of the potential electorate are Portuguese and Italian residents.

Under Articles 8c and 8d:

- for citizens of the Union to be represented in certain non-Member States by the diplomatic or consular missions of any Member State (8c); and

- for citizens to petition the European Parliament and apply to the Parliamentary Ombudsman (8d).

Both the right to diplomatic representation and the Ombudsman provisions (amplified later in the Treaty in Article 138e) await detailed implementation. Although the former provision will require modifying consular conventions with third countries, something which could provide an interesting test of the Union's international clout, little can yet be said about these provisions.

Under Article 8e:

- for a report by the Commission on the application of the citizenship provisions, by the end of 1993 and every three years thereafter; and

- for the Council, by unanimity and after consulting the Parliament, to add to or strengthen the citizenship rights conferred by the preceding articles, subject to ratification by all Member States.

Although other Treaty articles deal with the rights of individuals and may affect the interpretation of the articles outlined above, no special rights are conferred upon 'citizens'. Thus the new provisions on 'culture' refer to 'European peoples', and those on public health and consumer protection refer to 'human health' and to 'consumers' respectively.

Also of significance is the new chapter on education, vocational training, and youth. Whilst harmonization of laws and regulations is expressly excluded in this area (as in that of culture), stress is placed upon developing the European element in education (particularly through language teaching) and upon implementing a vocational training policy aimed at facilitating adaptation to industrial change and improving social and vocational integration in the labour market. The aim is to heighten the Community's industrial competitiveness and ensure higher levels of employment.

Finally, there is the complex and sensitive question of people's rights as citizens of the nation states making up the Union (and members of the regions therein) versus the powers conferred on the Community as a supranational body. It is reflected in the principle of subsidiarity and the peppering of the text with statements uneasily stressing diversity within unity. For instance, in Article 128(1) – one of the provisions on culture – under which 'the Community shall contribute to the flowering of the culture of the Member States, while respecting their regional diversity and at the same time bringing their common cultural heritage to the fore'. Apart from this being, in the words of one commentator, a nice example of the EC's baroque legislative language, the lay reader is left wondering what these words could mean in practice. More fundamentally, the need to reach a compromise on the different levels of power and authority of the different Community institutions has led to an increase in the complexity of the decision-making procedures. No attempt will be made to explain their contents here; but suffice it to say that there are now no less than six such procedures with, in some cases, more than one applying to the same area of legislation. They are certain to keep the administrators, politicians and lawyers in work for some time to come, but are anything but transparent for the ordinary citizen.

Thus, whilst the introduction of citizenship within the Union Treaty is undoubtedly a landmark with implications for the future, it is still uncertain the extent to which this will influence the thinking and behaviour of the Union's 350 million inhabitants. To examine this question we shall turn to discuss the socio-cultural dimensions of European citizenship and explore the background, development and impact of the Community's attempts to construct a 'People's Europe'.

Creating The 'Citizens' Europe': A Review of EU Cultural Initiatives

The idea of a 'People's Europe' became an avowed political objective in the 1970s. In 1975 a report on European Union was drawn up by the Belgian Prime Minister Leo Tindemans, following a request from the European Council. This emphasized that 'the construction of Europe is not just a form of collaboration between States. It is a rapprochement of people' and that, 'Europe needs to be closer to its citizens' (Fontaine 1991: 6). Following this, the European Council meeting in Fontainebleau in June 1984 set up an *ad hoc* committee chaired by Pietro Adonnino, which subsequently produced two further reports proposing a series of practical measures designed to promote greater freedom of movement and citizens' rights within the Community. Among these were measures to ease 'rules and practices which cause irritation to Community citizens' including facilitating the crossing of intra-Community frontiers, intensifying efforts to promote mutual recognition of professional qualifications and rights of residence, improving information for tourists, and encouraging broadcasts of news, weather and tourist information in languages of other Community States (Adonnino 1985: 9). The second report focused in particular on action geared toward 'strengthening of the Community's image and identity' in order to 'enhance the sense of belonging and identifying with the Community' through cultural exchanges and the creation of new symbols of 'Europeanness' (Adonnino 1985: 29–30). These were, as one informant put it, 'the first steps toward "selling" the Community'. Indeed, the marketing of Europe as a kind of 'brand product' has come to characterize much of the way in which the Commission has sought to tackle its problem of image (cf. Shore 1995). These two reports also set the agenda for what might be described as the 'invention' of the new European order (Shore 1993).

Publication of these reports in 1985 coincided with the appointment of a new Commission under Jacques Delors. That year also saw a significant name-change spearheaded by Carlo Ripa di Meana, the new Commissioner of DG 10 – the Directorate responsible for 'culture' – to 'Audio-visual, Information, Communication and Culture'. The inclusion of 'Information' had important consequences for the development of the idea of a 'People's Europe'. In particular, it led to a tendency to link the citizen's Europe project rather narrowly to information campaigns rather than with environment, consumer affairs or competition policy and the internal market – where responsibility for this area had previously been vested. This had little to do with any explicit strategy or theory about the centrality of information policy for the achievement of a citizen's Europe. Instead, it arose, as one informant put it, from the logic of internal 'empire-building and power struggles' and the successful appropriation by a junior Commissioner of new areas of jurisdiction. After 1985, therefore, emphasis was placed on the cultural and symbolic dimensions of citizenship, including education, training and 'consciousness-raising' campaigns involving the creation of a new repertoire of self-consciously constructed 'Euro-symbols'. For anthropologists (or even nationalist leaders) it might seem obvious to stress these areas, but for the Commission this represented something of an innovation in its approach to laying the foundations for European unification.

Among the various new symbols and initiatives that resulted from the Adonnino reports were the European passport and the standardized European driving licence, a European anthem (taken from the prelude to the 'Ode to Joy' from Beethoven's Ninth Symphony), and a European flag (taken from the Council of Europe's twelve-star logo). In addition, the Commission proposed a number of what it called 'consciousness-raising' measures reckoned to be of specifically 'symbolic value' (CEC 1988: 5). These included the 'European Road Safety Year', 'European Fight Against Cancer Year' and 'European Cinema Year'; the harmonization of car number-plates and the incorporation of the European logo; sponsorship of a European Youth Orchestra and a 'Europe of

Tomorrow' young scriptwriters competition; town-twinning; European sports events (the European Community Games, the European Cycle Race and the European Yacht Race, to name but a few); and the European City of Culture project. The Adonnino Committee even drew up plans for a Euro-lottery, the results of which would be 'televised throughout the Community' and 'expressed eventually in ECU' (Adonnino 1985: 22).

Reflecting on these and other initiatives, the Commission concluded in 1988 that 'a sense of European identity has begun to take shape' (CEC 1988: 3). Yet another official report published in the following year observed that cultural measures are still needed 'to make people more aware of their European identity' (CEC 1989: 139). As one EC information booklet justifying these measures proclaimed:

> Everyone nowadays recognises the sky-blue banner with 12 gold stars symbolising European unification, which we see more and more often flying alongside national flags in front of public buildings. Is there anyone who can fail to be moved on hearing the Ode to Joy . . .? What Community national does not enjoy following the "European Community" sign in airport arrival halls, and passing through simply by showing the uniform passport adopted in 1985? (Fontaine 1991: 7)

These declarations contradict Commission officials' repeated insistence that 'European integration must be a natural process' and not something 'imposed' from above. However, there was little agreement about the degree of instrumentality acceptable for constructing the desired 'People's Europe'. For some it was important that 'the Commission shouldn't be seen as "Big Brother" laying down cultural dictates'; but others had a sense of mission in the project and in their own role. As one informant, closely involved in these symbolic enterprises commented, 'we tried to create a double sense of belonging. The aim was to construct a supranationality . . . to show that united we are strong: one for twelve and twelve for one'.

Within this context, Felipe Gonzales' proposal, at the 1990 inter-governmental conference, to introduce the notion of 'European citizenship' in the new European treaty represented a logical extension of this project. But how successful these initiatives are likely to be in raising European consciousness among the public at large it is perhaps too early to tell – and a detailed investigation of this issue is beyond the scope of this chapter. Our interest, for the present discussion, is the consciousness of EU officials and their ideas about the relationship between citizenship and European consciousness.

'New Europeans': Life at the Heart of the Union

'To say I feel a cultural identity with Europe would be to put it too strongly ... Obviously you develop some kind of institutional loyalty, but wouldn't that happen if you worked for Shell? ... Personally, I feel most European when I'm with other Europeans in Japan.'

'When negotiating, you go in to bat for Europe ... Many people believe, as do I, in the importance of this institution ... but I'm not sure this solidarity is the same thing as identity ... Europeanism doesn't exist; there are no cultural roots for it to exist. The only time I feel European is when I'm in the USA.'

These two views expressed by people working within the Commission on their personal feelings about the development of a European cultural identity provide insights into why one's first impressions of the culture of Europe from within the institutions, can be so contradictory. Although on some levels it appears that a common European consciousness is developing amongst those working in the institutions it is difficult to see how this relates to the population in general. The core area of all the activity deserves description in itself, as the centre of Brussels, for all that it might have become the heart of Europe, has been carved up by traffic lanes and office blocks and can seem a soulless place. True, the twelve-star Euro-totem is ubiquitous, it decorates shop windows, coffee cups, car number-plates, advertising hoardings – and of course takes its place amongst the many flags which indicate the buildings housing the institutions of the EU. There are also the various Euro-shops – emporia where you can kit yourself out with every item of Euro-paraphernalia imaginable. These emblems do generate a sense of place, albeit in a slightly heavy-handed way. But the most potent reminder of where you are is still the star-shaped but now condemned Berlaymont building. Riddled with asbestos, it currently stands empty, awaiting future decision and action (funds permitting). It continues to function as an impressive landmark and useful orientation point; a serious consideration, as it lies in the middle of a confusing maze of building sites intersected by office-lined highways. It is ironic that the building also retains symbolic power – pressure groups campaigning from regions both in and outside the Union still gather around the facade to deliver protests or pleas for support, unaware that the building is now empty.

However, in spite of the forbidding surroundings there is a definite atmosphere to the area, and a shared sense that some kind of culture is being developed. The pavements bristle with bureaucrats clutching briefs, sometimes engaged in street-corner meetings, sometimes sprinting to – one presumes – the next committee or working group. At lunchtime the clusters of small restaurants in the area overflow with groups of people conducting working lunches and the odd senior statesman hiding behind a newspaper. Outside working hours, a large proportion of social activity for people working in the Parliament and Commission involves mixing with colleagues, and the conversation is almost exclusively focused on European Union matters, often involving detailed exchanges employing terms and language baffling to any uninitiated outsider. Thus, even from these few superficial observations it seems valid to envisage the emergence of a specific Euro-culture, certainly in Brussels, where so much of the work done for the Community takes place. But a culture appropriate for the generation of a more general consciousness of Euro-Citizenship?

It seems not. Rather, it appears that an important area of failure, acknowledged within the Commission, lies in the very lack of development of a sense of popular identification, and of any real feeling of belonging amongst its inhabitants. A number of obstacles contribute to this lack of popular identification with the EC. The first lies quite simply in the complexity of the institutions and in the procedures which have been developed to enable their interaction. A common theme in Commission and Parliament statements on this topic is the need to guarantee citizens fair, transparent and efficient administration as well as access to information (cf. EP 1992: 7). Yet the main obstacle to fulfilling these obviously commendable aims lies within the institutions themselves and in the need to try and strike a balance between a wide variety of different interests and power domains. To date, attempts at simplification and solving the 'democratic deficit' have only resulted in the invention of ever more complex procedures.

In talking to Commission officials, it is this which is often raised as one of the major problems for the future. In the words of one informant:

> EC procedures need to be simplified and streamlined. At present clarity has been sacrificed for compromise . . . The democratic deficit hasn't been solved and as long as there is no government structure that touches the man in the street the EC goal will never be achieved. As soon as we implement a clear structure of government the better. Indeed we will be in trouble if we don't. It was lack of government structure that led to the collapse of the Austro-Hungarian Empire.

A closely related problem, as EU officials perceive it, is distance and lack of communication, both at a political and cultural level. Despite talk of transparent government, many decisions made in Brussels filter back to those affected by these decisions, if at all, only by indirect channels, mostly via reports in the press. Lack of communication is also a problem within and between the institutions, with many confused and overlapping areas of responsibility.

Important here is the question of allegiance to nation-states, and the relationship between citizenship and loyalty at the two levels of the nation and the Union. The Commission and the Parliament are often unequivocal on this matter, arguing that 'the notion that European law is directly binding on individuals, together with the principle that Community law takes precedence over national law, is one of the pillars of the system' (Fontaine 1991: 10). And from the Parliament:

> There are two reasons for believing that the concept of citizenship must increasingly be linked to the establishment of a supranational European political system. The first is the obvious crisis affecting the nation-state, which is unable to meet all the needs of the society which it represents. The second is the Community experience, which has seen the establishment of a genuine European society on the basis of extremely significant economic and social achievements. (EP 1991: 9)

Yet many see the problem as more complex, not least because most EC citizens feel closer to their own national parliaments than to Strasburg (and better able to understand how they actually operate) and believe that their national politicians are more responsive to popular will. Also, at the national level, ideally and often in practice, people are in contact with the debates and issues surrounding decisions which affect their lives, even if they disagree with the outcomes. But when decisions made in Brussels affect people's working and personal lives they do often seem to have 'been made from above' in an undemocratic and authoritarian manner.

However, there are instances where the opposite holds true. One is the case where regions and ethnic groups within nations are either engaged in a struggle to assert their identity and independence in opposition to a nation-state and/or feel that their interests are being ill-represented at that level. Here the presence of a larger, more inclusive tier of authority and power can exert a powerful attraction. Commission personnel frequently stress this link, volunteering the idea of a future 'community of regions', and citing the examples of the Welsh, Scottish, Basque and Catalan communities. To the sceptic this could conjure up a vision of a future community of local grievances, with the added risk that a renewed stress on regional identity and the erosion of national consensus might lead to greater intolerance. Asserting old identities might lead to the exclusion of new outsiders. This is discussed in greater detail below.

The distance factor also operates on the more subtle level of collective identification with the Community. What individual nation-states of Europe hold in common is the existence of symbols, rituals, collective representations and political myths. These are born of shared history and experiences which are intimately connected with a sense of 'belonging', and which act as foci for the regeneration of collective identity, or the means through which this is manipulated by political groups seeking to legitimize their authority. As Anthony Smith – who argues against the likelihood of a pan-national consciousness or culture transcending national divisions – states, 'national identifications possess distinct advantages over the idea of unified European identity. They are vivid, accessible, well established, long popularised, and still widely believed, in broad outline at least. In each of these respects "Europe" is deficient both as idea and as process' (A. D. Smith 1992: 62). There is no European analogue of Bastille or Armistice Day and for all that there might be attempts to foster identity at this level (for instance one idea is to promote a Euro-wide day of celebration of the birthday of Jean Monnet), it is difficult to imagine much popular enthusiasm for this. It is interesting that in the field of education – a core breeding ground for the promotion of such a feeling of common identity – the stress remains very much upon maintaining national heterogeneity.

A third problem concerns the *raison d' être* of the Community. The quest for unification has involved grafting political and social measures onto a union originally created for pragmatic, economic purposes. This has led to two sets of problems. First, the continued strength of the Union and its attraction for its members undoubtedly lies in its remaining economically successful. Increasingly this is seen as performing competitively against the US and Japan. Few would go quite so far as to subscribe to Michael Tosner's cynical summary of the situation that 'the wealth, the trading power and the yet untapped potential of the Community are essentially what make the whole thing work. For all their differences, the countries are united in one over-riding ambition: that rich though they are, there is plenty of opportunity for growing richer still. This is sometimes known as the European ideal' (1988: 10). But there is the problem of matching economic ambition and competitiveness with the wish for humanitarian social policies and the aim to promote social cohesion through aid to the poorer, less developed regions. It is one thing to join an economic club, but quite another to develop a body of political consensus with commonly identified political interests. A key area where this will be tested is the implementation of a common foreign and defence policy.

A final area which deserves consideration is language. Like most bureaucracies, the institutions of the European Union have spawned a series of terms to label its aims, policies and projects. However, as the language used often reflects conflicts between the institutions themselves and contradictions within even the shared aims and interests, it often appears to slide into ambiguity and sophistry. Apart from the well-known problem with 'federalism' (to some this implies centralization of administrative power, to others its opposite), EU jargon (or 'Eurospeak') is loaded with terms which shift their meaning; the tags 'social cohesion' and 'competitiveness', for instance, have a dizzying range of referents. Some terms such as 'comitology', 'unicity' or 'aquis communautaire' simply have no meaning outside the context of Eurospeak, others precious little even within it; 'horizontalism' for example. Meanwhile there exists a whole range of apparently quite innocent terms, including 'harmonization', 'co-operation', 'co-decision' and 'common political basis' which act as cover for many a minefield of dispute. Here again the whole vision of the citizen's right to transparent government tends to be belied in practice.

Although the EC and its institutions might appear remote to many of Europe's inhabitants and its symbols lacking in force, it seems inevitable that shifts in popular consciousness will follow once the effects of the Union Treaty become felt. A new sense of pan-European identity may well emerge spontaneously – but what might form the political and symbolic bases for such a new pattern of identification?

What Sort of European Unity?

If the unity and identity so far created is not that which we read about in official reports and EU information booklets,what, then, is the state of the Union? As noted, the key to a citizens' Europe lies in the erosion of barriers – legal and material barriers first and foremost, and only then symbolic barriers. In practice, this means eliminating intra-European national border controls and customs and immigration checks. But if existing borders and boundaries are to be broken down, new ones will inevitably be created. The question of how and where these new boundaries will be drawn has perhaps already been answered by recent developments in European immigration policy. As the barriers come down within the Union the walls separating 'Europe' from the dark continents of non-Europe seem to grow higher and more impenetrable, all of which adds further weight to the charge that the EU is creating a 'Fortress Europe' (Pieterse 1991).

Two questions follow from this. The first stems from the fact that identity is invariably a dualistic concept: for every 'Us' there must be a corresponding 'Them'. Who, therefore, will become Europe's significant 'other'? If identity entails inclusion, who must *de facto* be excluded and classified as the outsider? This problem becomes most acute with respect to drawing the EU's eastern border and dealing with requests for membership by the former Soviet Republics and East European states. As Schlesinger (1989: 4) notes, what is meant by the expression 'European identity' is 'largely taken for granted, not least because it permits some awkward questions to be sidestepped'. Yet in order to foster a sense of 'European identity' the Commission and Parliament must promote the values and virtues of that 'common cultural heritage' which they say all Europeans share (however unaware they may be). This puts them in an invidious position of trying to develop a sense of Europeanness that is proud, patriotic and distinctive, but avoids exclusiveness and jingoism. The dilemma is reflected in the writings of advocates of European federalism. For example, among the features of the 'common cultural heritage' said to have indelibly shaped European values, Wistrich (1991: 79) lists Greek thought, Roman law, Christianity, the Renaissance, the Age of Reason, the Industrial Revolution, Imperialism and Social Democracy. But what this list of historical currents amounts to, or what makes them exclusively European, is rarely addressed. However, the superiority of European culture and its great patrimony of ideas is clearly implied. The result is a highly selective definition of Europe that is politically biased and potentially racist, where 'European culture' is equated with 'Western Civilization' (as opposed to 'African barbarism' or 'Oriental despotism', perhaps) whose distinguishing landmarks are Plato, NATO, science and the rule of law (cf. Pieterse 1991).

Secondly, the idea that 'citizenship means diversity' is rendered meaningless because the emphasis behind the campaign to promote awareness of 'European identity' or shared ancestry has to be based on what is held in common, not on cultural dissimilarity. The position of the apostrophe in 'people's Europe' (as opposed to 'peoples' Europe') emphasizes unity at the expense of multi-culturalism. The Commission would counter this by emphasizing its policy of promoting local identities and European regions. However, this raises other questions about the potentially conflictual relationship between the nation-state and the European Union. As some officials admitted, emphasizing an enhanced political role for the regions as part of the policy for promoting European cohesion also conveniently allows the Commission to bypass national governments. This therefore becomes a tactic for subverting the authority of the nation-state – a policy not inconsistent with the neo-functionalist theory of integration outlined earlier. There was a marked reluctance to question the compatibility or otherwise of these different levels of identity and authority. One Commission official illustrated the model by drawing a series of concentric circles, each representing a different level of identity and authority (local, regional, national, European), like so many Russian dolls. Within this simplistic and functionalist model of political organization that seemed to sum up the bureaucratic vision of identity-construction in the new Europe, the implicit assumption is that each hierarchical tier of identity will nest harmoniously inside the next, and that the nation-state would thus be consigned to a marginal role.

Conclusion: An Agenda for Future Research on the EU

In exploring some of the possible bases for the development of a popular identification with the European Union and the forms this might take, the main point to emerge is the need to be wary of presuming that there will be a comfortable passage towards a pan-European culture. The Commission still appears a long way from translating Jean Monnet's vision of 'a union among people' into lived reality. Meanwhile, the theories outlining the possible paths to European integration discussed earlier do not appear to have been borne out at all straightforwardly in practice.

Of the themes we have discussed, five require further research: First, while there is evidence of an embryonic culture and consciousness emerging among European civil servants, it remains nonetheless a bureaucratic culture, remote and inaccessible to most Europeans outside these circles. The reasons for this distance lie in the complexity of the institutions and the fact that their procedures, processes and aims (the daily diet of debate and conversation amongst the *fonctionnaires*) remain impenetrable to lay people. Without radical change, this problem can only become worse should the Community take on more decision-making powers.

Second, although employees of the Community perceive the EC's failure to capture the hearts and minds of its members as a problem, attempts to tackle this have so far been misconceived. Whilst the various consciousness-raising campaigns have led to the production of a new repertoire of symbols, these have yet to prove to be functioning as anything more than devices lending limited verisimilitude to the notion of a common culture. However, the programmes operating at the level of the exchange of culture and ideas, particularly in the field of education, may prove to provide some basis for a greater pool of shared experience and identity in the future. Maybe the *fonctionnaires* are correct in their vision that 'the hope for true integration lies with the young'.

The third theme concerns the contradictions involved with grafting a political and cultural unity on to an economic union. This is reflected in the tensions that exist between the institutions themselves, particularly between the Council and the Commission, and in the confusion over which interests are to be protected or sacrificed in the name of closer union. Rhetoric about 'unity within diversity' can hardly hope to solve the substantive problems involved; whilst a championing of regional interests over those of nation-states might simply encourage further division.

A fourth theme concerns the apparent conflict between European union and the interests of the nation-state. So far advocates of federalism have played down or dismissed as nonsense the argument that unification entails greater centralization and a corresponding loss of national sovereignty. Yet this is clearly implied in the theories of integration discussed earlier, and it is tacitly recognized by most of the EU officials we questioned. On present reckoning, and without substantive changes in popular consciousness or a resolution of the EU's democratic deficit, one can foresee major conflicts arising from this tension, not least because it will be exploited wholeheartedly by disgruntled nationalist politicians. Furthermore, anti-European sentiment is likely to grow should the Union fail to deliver economically, since its legitimacy, to date, has rested largely on its capacity to generate wealth and prosperity for its Member States.

It is possible that changes in popular political consciousness might flow, quite independently of any Commission-backed consciousness-raising campaigns, from the processes entailed in bringing about economic unity. Thus, a fifth theme involves the political implications of the internal market and the removal of internal frontiers. This raises two questions. First, as noted earlier, if internal boundaries are to be dismantled where are the new ones to be erected? Here there is the obvious danger of adding fuel to current xenophobic movements which champion national exclusiveness. To extol the virtues of our common European cultural heritage might seem a fine thing, provided this isn't converted into a new form of Euro-racism, or White Continentalism (cf. Alibhai 1989). The second question is: how will the EU treat immigrants already settled in Europe? As mentioned, European citizenship makes no concessions to immigrants who are not already citizens of Member States, and neither the weakening of the nation-state nor the development of a new regionalism have yet produced a vision of Europe that could accommodate ethnic minorities. The EU has so far given the question of integrating immigrant communities a low priority.

Remarking on the growing Euro-nationalism among some European politicians, one commentator (*The Economist* 1991: 20) quotes Hans Dietrich Genscher's (Germany's ex-foreign minister) assertion that 'for every European problem there should be a European solution'. The writer comments that a charitable view of Euro-nationalism is that it is the embryo of a European identity that could in time make a United States of Europe workable, but warns that like nationalism it carries the risk that 'Europe' might be invoked to keep out everything from American culture to Japanese computers, Ukrainian corn and Arab immigrants. Indeed, Euro-nationalism should not be allowed to slide into Euro-protectionism or Euro-racism. A dark, but maybe appropriate note to end upon.

References

Adonnino, P. (1985). A People s Europe: Reports from the Ad Hoc Committee, Luxembourg, *Bulletin of the EC*, Supplement No. 7.

Alibhai, Y. (1989) Community Whitewash, *Guardian* (23 January).

Allott, P. (1992). How to Cross the EC Pain Barrier, *The Wall Street Journal*, 5 March.

Anderson, B. (1983). *Imagined Communities*, London: Verso.

Buchan, D. (1991). The Constraints of the European Community. *Political Quarterly*, **62**, (2).

CEC (Commission of the European Communities) (1983). *Treaties Establishing the European Communities* (abridged edn), Luxembourg: Office for Official Publications of the European Communities.

CEC (1988). A People's Europe: Communication from the Commission to the European Parliament, COM (88) 331/final, Luxembourg, *Bulletin of the EC*, Supplement No.2.

CEC (1989). *23rd General Report on the Activities of the EC*, Luxembourg: Office for Official Publications of the European Communities.

CEC (1992). *Treaty on European Union Signed at Maastricht on 7*

February, Luxembourg: Office of Official Publications for the European Communities.

The Economist (1991). Europe s Ugly Nationalism, 28 September.

EP (European Parliament) (1991). *Report of the Committee on Institutional Affairs on Union Citizenship*, DOC EN/RR/118476, PE 153.099/fin., 6 November.

EP (1992). *Draft Report of the Committee on Culture, Youth, Education and the Media on Education and Training Policy in the run-up to 1993*, DOC EN/PR/122197, PE 148.197/A, 5 February.

Fontaine, P. (1991). *A Citizen's Europe*, Luxembourg: Office of Official Publications of the European Communities.

Gellner, E. (1983). *Nations and Nationalism*, Oxford: Blackwell.

George, S. (1985). *Politics and policy in the European Community*. Oxford: Clarendon Press.

Haas, E. (1958). *The Uniting of Europe*, Oxford University Press.

Pieterse, J. N. (1991), Fictions of Europe. *Race and Class*, **32**, (3), 3–10.

Sampson, A. (1971). *The New Europeans*, London: Hodder and Stoughton.

Schlesinger, P. (1989). Imagining the New Europe. *New European*, **2**, (3).

Shore, C. (1993). Inventing the 'People's Europe': Critical Perspectives on European Community Cultural Policy. *Man*, **28**, (4), 779–800.

Shore, C. (1995). Usurpers or Pioneers? EC Bureaucrats and the Question of European Consciousness, in A. P. Cohen and N. Rapport (eds). *Questions of Consciousness*, London: Routledge (forthcoming).

Smith, A. D. (1990). Towards a Global Culture? *Theory, Culture and Society*, **7**, (2) and (30), 171–92.

Smith, A. D. (1992). National Identity and the Idea of European Unity. *International Affairs*, **68**, (1), 55–76.

Smith, G. (1983). *Politics in Western Europe: A Comparative Analysis*, Aldershot: Gower.

Taylor, P. (1983). *The Limits of European Integration*, Croom Helm.

Tosner, M. (1988). *Bluff Your Way in the EEC*, London: Ravette Books.

Wallace, W. (1990). *The Transformation of Western Europe*, London: Pinter.

Wistrich, E. (1989). *After 1992: The United States of Europe*, London, New York: Routledge.

Index